MEXICO

A HIKERS GUIDE
TO MEXICO'S
NATURAL HISTORY

JIM CONRAD

THE
MOUNTAINEERS

This book is dedicated to Kevin Healey
of Balaclava, Australia, good friend and master
cartographer of tropical American lands; he died while
working on his Venezuela map in 1994.

Published by
The Mountaineers
1011 SW Klickitat Way
Seattle, Washington 98134

Published simultaneously in Canada by Douglas & McIntyre, Ltd., 1615 Venables Street, Vancouver, B.C. V5L 2H1

Published simultaneously in Great Britain by Cordee, 3a DeMontfort Street, Leicester, England, LE1 7HD

Manufactured in the United States of America

Edited by Kris Fulsaas
Maps by Jody MacDonald
All photographs by the author unless otherwise noted
Book and cover design by The Mountaineers Books
Typesetting by The Mountaineers Books
Book layout by Nick Gregoric
Cover photographs: *Overlay: Opuntia engelmannii,* or pricklypear cactus © Jim Conrad; *Insets:* Scarlet Macaw © Greg Dimijian; Hiker in lush stream bed in western Chiapas © Sigrid Liede; Snowstorm of monarch butterflies © Greg Dimijian; El Castillo, Mayan temple at Chichén Iztá © Jim Conrad

Illustration of Mayan stela (pages 7, 29, 67, 85, 107, 141, 154, 180) from *Mayapan Yucatan Mexico,* reprinted courtesy of Carnegie Institute of Washington

Library of Congress Cataloging-in-Publication Data
Conrad, Jim.
Mexico : a hiker's guide to Mexico's natural history / Jim Conrad
p. cm.
Includes bibliographical references and index.
ISBN 0-89886-424-0 (paper)
1. Hiking–Mexico–Guidebooks. 2. Mexico–Guidebooks. 3. Natural history–Mexico. I. Title.
GV199.44.M6C66 1994
796.5'1'0972–dc20 94-45479CIP

♻ Printed on recycled paper

CONTENTS

```
                              KEY

──────────   Paved Road              🦋   Butterfly Reserve

...........   Dirt Road              ⛪   Church/Altar

- - - - - -   Path/Trail             🏛   Ruin

~~~~~~~~~~   Stream                  ⚖   Falls

▪▪▪▪▪▪▪▪▪▪   Hike                         Pasture

  ⊙          Larger Town or City     ★   Tourist Area, Special Feature

  ○          Town                         Cornfield

  ⋏          Trees/Forest            ⋎   Marsh

  ⌒⌒         Mountains                    Lake

             Geothermal Well         ■   House or Other Building
```

PREFACE

Except for my aversion to drugs, you could say that I am one of those "old hippies" you see from time to time, who, despite graying hair and creaking joints, still speaks believingly of flower-power and love.

I am worried about what is happening in our world. This is not what we visualized back in the sixties. My writing this book, then, is one thing I am doing to try to help things. I believe that when people get to know one another, and that when we humans sensitize ourselves to other living things and learn to care about them, we improve ourselves....

In Zacatecas once I met a California woman who said that a few weeks in Mexico had accomplished for her what $5,000 of Marin County therapy had not. I understood completely. I cannot imagine how less self-confident, less interesting, and more dried up and desperate I would feel right now if during the last thirty years I had not escaped many times into Mexican forests, deserts, and mountains, and if I had not learned to see at least a few things from the Mexican point of view.

This book informs you that the Western Sierra Madre range is mostly volcanic, while the Eastern chain is mostly uplifted sedimentary limestone. This book also passes along my advice to eat *frijoles y huevos a la mejicana* in mom-and-pop *comedores*. However, this book carries no step-by-step guide to realizing the kind of spiritual metamorphosing to which I am alluding.

Somehow, pretty much on your own, it is up to you to discover within yourself and then nurture that magical spark that enables certain individuals to blossom in uncommon ways where the sun is bright, the air fragrant, and the people friendly and forgiving.

ACKNOWLEDGMENTS

Thanks to Jack Joyce, International Travel Map Productions of Vancouver, Canada, for helping with map needs; to Dr. Joe Winstead, Western Kentucky University, Bowling Green, Kentucky, for refreshing my memory on what I had forgotten from his ecology class; to Patricia Buck Wolf of New Haven, Connecticut, for sharing her masses of information about the Yucatán; to Jeff Hersk of Nashville, Tennessee, for contributing the book's snorkeling section; and to Dr. Sigrid Liede, Universität Ulm, Germany, for the summertime use of her computer, and that delicious Schwäbischer *Zwiebelkuchen*.

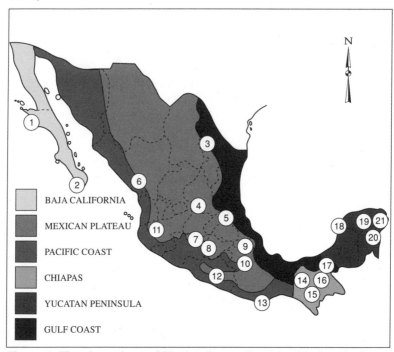

Figure 1 *The six regions of Mexico (as outlined in this book); the numbers represent the hikes described in Chapters 3 through 8.*

Figure 2 *Mexico's thirty-one states*

CHAPTER 1

THE JOY OF TRAVELING THROUGH MEXICO

IS THIS BOOK FOR YOU?

This book is intended for nature-minded day hikers heading for the Mexican backcountry. Much more than with many such guides, the main emphasis here is on understanding what is to be seen, not in cataloging numerous trails.

Mexico is a vast country, and one of the most geographically diverse countries in the world. Therefore, clearly, the twenty-one day-hike destinations included here are merely *samples* of Mexico's day-hike possibilities; by no means is this the final word on what a day hiker can do in Mexico.

In a sense, this a how-to book—how to make yourself into a day-hike–defining, Mexican-landscape–appreciating expert. Once you have completed a few of the hikes included here, you should be able to find and successfully conduct your own hikes anyplace in Mexico. Nearly always, among these twenty-one *samples*, at least one other hike will lie not too far away, or be in a very similar setting; thus these samples serve as an example of how such a hike can be done. There is a certain art to locating eligible trails, and judging their hikability, that you can learn from this how-to book.

Day hikes are not just anemic, attenuated backpacking trips. Day hikes have their own feeling, their own reason for being, their own unique manner of pleasing. . . . Day hikes are their own thing, and day hikers have their own identities.

Unlike backpackers, day hikers see little reason to go onto the land just to huff and puff all the time. Day hikers cherish being able to walk and calmly chat, and exchange ideas and observations with friends. They want to take their time, muse on the meaning of the lay of the land, sit on a rock as they snack on a sandwich while a nearby lizard sunbathes. Then maybe they will

spend a couple of hours identifying trees, flowers, and rocks, and talking with whomever happens along. And finally, maybe early in the afternoon, how nice it would be to go back to the motel or campground in time for tea. . . . Day hikers are a sociable, reflective lot.

But, back to the question: Is day hiking for *you?*

Right now, the average reader probably is saying to himself or herself, "Sure, I would love to hike where I might see monkeys or crocodiles, where exotic birds such as motmots and trogons abound, and where other hikers met on the trail may be speaking Nahuatl or Tzotzil. But is this something that really can be done by someone like me? More importantly, is it *safe?*"

Physically, certainly you can do it. Most of the hikes in this book require little physical exertion, and their trailheads are accessible by cars and buses.

But is day hiking in Mexico *safe?*

Certain problems can affect backcountry hikers in Mexico—diseases, robbery, peasant uprisings. . . . Certainly these topics are daunting. However, here is the truth: If you stay reasonably informed and use reasonably good judgment, it is very unlikely that you will have problems. You will just have fun. During my own thirty years of day hiking in backcountry Mexico, I have never had any trouble of any kind. For me, Mexico's trails have always been nothing but a joy.

This is not to say that a Mexican day hike is equivalent to a stroll through Disneyland. Plant spines penetrate shoe soles, scorpions shelter beneath bushes, rocks become slippery, cattle stampede, and, yes, there's an occasional bandit or uprising. Even during the preparation of this book I was robbed of nearly everything by two fellows with a *pistolo,* but that was because I was unwisely camping overnight in the wilderness, not taking a day hike.

But I am not encouraging readers to camp overnight in the wilderness. I *am* encouraging day hikes, using common sense, and staying well informed.

ATTITUDES FOR THE BACKCOUNTRY

The more Spanish you speak, the less chance you will have for problems, and the more chance you will have for an enjoyable experience. At least learn to say *Buenas dias* for "Good morning" and *Buenas tardes* for "Good afternoon." Simply making an effort to greet native hikers in their own language opens all kinds of doors.

Make a special effort to project a friendly attitude toward fellow hikers. Especially in the backcountry, some Mexicans are a bit nervous around us *gringos.* Several times I have spent such lengthy periods of time among Mexicans that to some extent I actually began seeing the world through their eyes. Always, when I met my first white North American after these stays, those *gringos* looked so large, spoke so loudly, and moved around in such aggressive ways that even I was a bit intimidated by them. Mexicans have a completely different perspective on what human relations are supposed to be like. A pleasant smile is one thing that both cultures feel good about.

Two personality traits surpass all others as being appropriate—maybe requisite—for hiking backcountry Mexico: a sense of humor, and patience.

A prune-faced non–Spanish-speaker might be able to successfully hike most or all of the hikes described in this book, but on any Mexican trail I would never want to accompany someone who could not make a joke of stepping into a pile of mule manure, or who did not have time to chat or gesture with a toothless old Indian needing to complain about crows eating his corn.

On a more practical level, especially if you are scouting for do-it-yourself day hikes, absolutely avoid assuming that Mexican concepts of society and land ownership and usage are the same as your own. Before embarking on any unknown trails, even if it is just for a few hundred feet, become knowledgeable about and sensitized to the Mexican way of viewing the land.

Very different from North America but similar to most of Europe, Mexican farmers—poor people called *campesinos*—typically live in small villages scattered in the countryside; they seldom live on family plots next to the parcel of land they farm. *Campesinos* typically rise early and walk to their cornfields (*milpas*), machetes slung over their shoulders. During the hottest part of the day, the farmer will either walk back home or take a long *siesta* beneath a shade tree. Often a *campesino*'s *milpa* lies several miles from home. This is one reason Mexico's backcountry is crisscrossed with a superabundance of trails. In country too dry for farming, trails have been made by shepherds and hunters. In short, in Mexico you can nearly always find a trail going wherever you wish. . . .

Who owns the land these trails cross? Especially in Indian territory, many or most trails have been used by the local people for centuries; land ownership patterns have developed around the trails, and everyone has always considered the trails to be public thoroughfares. In much of northern Mexico, however, the desert and grassland are often owned by large landowners, and it can be hard to know whether a trail is "public" or not. If the land is very dry, rocky, and useless for grazing, a trail is probably OK to travel; if enough herbage is present for occasional grazing, you had best ask, or stay off. Never cross fences. Great effort has been made to assure that none of the trails in this book traverse property where non-natives would not be welcome.

A word about *ejidos* (pronounced eh-HEE–doughs): *Ejidos*, very important in the history of Mexican land reform, are official, bureaucratically organized farming communities abundantly scattered throughout Mexico. *Ejido* members are assigned parcels of land that only they can farm, though the land remains the property of the *ejido* cooperative. Collectively, *ejido* members can do things that individual poor *campesinos* can only dream of—borrow money to buy large tractors, fertilizers, and pesticides, for instance.

Though in Mexico's northern irrigated territory some *ejido* members have become prosperous, in most of Mexico *ejido* communities look like nothing other than very poor farming villages. Even villages of Indians speaking only their own Native American languages are often organized as *ejidos*. If you take hikes not described in this book, keep *ejidos* in mind because one just never knows what rules a community's *ejido* officials will have formulated concerning *ejido* land being visited by outsiders. In practice, well-established trails in *ejido* territory are nearly always considered open to the general public.

Just keep the situation in mind, and remember that asking permission to pass by a field never hurts, but not asking permission conceivably could.

If you enter Mexico from the north you may be surprised how modern and industrialized the country seems: good roads, polite and effective officials, regular stores stocked with many consumer goods, and north-of-the-border prices. . . . Do not assume that all of Mexico is the same. In general, the farther south you travel, at least in the interior, the more undeveloped things become. By the time you enter the southernmost state of Chiapas, you will suspect that there is more difference between Chiapas and Mexico's northern states than between those northern states and the United States.

Thus keep in mind that Mexico is not just one homogenous culture; it is a high-contrast mosaic of cultures. The traveler cannot survive with a single "Mexican strategy." Be informed about the place you are passing through, and be flexible. Reacting to Mexicans as people, not Mexicans, is a good first step.

As recently as the late 1970s, I felt particularly comfortable strapping on a backpack, wandering deep into Mexico's Indian territory on unmapped trails, especially in Chiapas and Michoacán, buying food from *campesinos* as I needed it, and just drifting along week after week. This was an exquisite experience. However, when I started running into isolated fields of marijuana, and sometimes entered villages where nearly everyone seemed more or less engaged in the drug trade, I gave up my wanderings. Nowadays no one should wander too far off well-established routes. It hurts to say that, but it is true.

In a very few places, particularly in the overpopulated uplands, and especially in the southern state of Chiapas, *campesinos* are in great conflict among themselves about who owns the land; there is simply not enough productive land to go around. Occasionally groups of armed men invade property claimed by others, and begin farming it. Even *ejido* communities have been known to invade land claimed by other *ejidos*, which in the Mexican mind is nearly sacrilege. Naturally the tension in these areas is tremendous.

If you hear about an "invasion" taking place in an area, or if in a certain area you suddenly find yourself being greeted by scowls instead of the usual very open and friendly manner, then leave the place. In this book, the only hike in an area where land-ownership battles are currently taking place is the Yerba Buena hike in Chiapas. However, because this is a very short hike right next to an important road, the government officially invites hikers to enter the area, and outsiders have experienced no trouble in the past, the hike is included here.

Admittedly, some of this sounds a bit grim. Of course, I am erring on the side of caution, wanting to be perfectly honest about all conceivable problems that can arise.

PASSPORTS, CURRENCY, AND OTHER PRACTICAL CONCERNS

United States citizens do not need passports or visas to travel in the interior of Mexico, but they do need tourist cards, which are issued free at most border crossings. Proof of citizenship is required, such as a birth certificate or a copy of a birth certificate certified by the agency issuing it. Voter registration cards and armed forces ID papers also are accepted. Canadians also need proof of citizenship for a tourist card; a birth certificate issued within Canada will do if no passport is available. Naturalized Canadians must carry a passport inside Mexico. Other nationalities must obtain proper documents from their nearest Mexican consulate.

Though it is not required, in the backcountry it is certainly best to travel with a passport. When passing through military checkpoints, which occasionally appear in areas where trouble is brewing, and when soldiers are occasionally met on patrol in unlikely places, one is hardly ever asked for the tourist card. No matter what the law is, soldiers want to see passports. If you explain that all that is needed is a tourist card, they probably will agree and be content with seeing that.

However, especially if you return to the United States with a backpack, dusty clothes, and a few scratches, your greatest documentation problem may well be with U.S. customs, not Mexican. Possibly you will be able to cross back into the United States showing nothing but a broad smile, but if there is anything suspicious about you at all, you may be reminded that U.S. Customs recognizes only birth certificates and passports.

At most border crossings, right around the entry point on the U.S. side, money-changing offices and booths buy dollars for pesos. Typically the exchange rate in these places is as good as or more favorable than in Mexican banks.

Travelers checks are a good idea in any foreign country. One advantage to carrying regular U.S. currency in Mexico is that when it is changed in banks for pesos, usually you must wait in fewer lines, and have fewer officials sign for the transaction. When banks are not open, usually someone can be found who will exchange dollars for pesos; owners of hardware stores seem to be especially congenial to the idea.

Before leaving home, it is a good idea to find someone with a fax number whom you could fax in case an emergency arises. Mexico has made a major effort to see that most fair-size towns have at least one publicly available fax (called *fax* in Spanish). Larger bus stations are usually equipped with public faxes and some small-town telephone offices have them.

Calling from regular public phones in Mexico's backcountry can be very frustrating. Try to organize calls from major hotels or public phone offices in towns. If you are in an area where functioning phones bear the words LADATEL, surely the most elegant way to call is to use a "debit card," which can be bought at a pharmacy, from one of the corner kiosks selling magazines, sodas, and cigarettes, or from a Gigante supermarket. Usually they can be bought in airports and major bus stations, too. Debit cards come in a variety of denominations. Just find a LADATEL phone that accepts cards (not all do), and use the card until your money is exhausted. To find out how much the call's first minute costs, dial the country code (91 for inside Mexico, 95 for the United States and Canada, and 98 for other countries) and the amount should appear on the phone's digital display window.

Accommodations in Mexico range from among the very best to among the very worst. In general, if you wish a hotel room that is as clean, luxurious, and well served as its northern counterpart—and there are many—be prepared to pay northern prices, or higher. On the other hand, Mexico does not have the North's strict codes, so if you want to pay less and receive less in return, that is quite possible, and in many medium-size to small towns, this is the only option. In such places it is a good idea to carry earplugs for sleeping, and maybe even blinders for those occasional rooms without blinds but with a bright billboard right outside the window.

If you fall in love with a place like Playa del Carmen or Puerto Escondido and you have run low on dough, do not forget the option of renting a hammock, living off tortillas and bananas, and surviving on two or three dollars a day.

TRANSPORTATION

Since other guidebooks, such as *Let's Go Mexico* and *Mexico & Central American Handbook*, devote ample space to both driving and riding trains in Mexico, this book focuses on busing. Mexico is a bus-oriented country, so it makes good sense for independent travelers to consider "traveling like Mexicans."

Mexico's busing infrastructure is unequalled in car-oriented North America and Europe. The Greyhound terminal in New York's Grand Central Station is runty and cramped compared to, say, the second-class terminal in Villahermosa, Tabasco. Just about every Mexican destination that can be visited in cars also is served by buses. Even roads that respectable cars would avoid usually carry at least one bus a day. Moreover, riding Mexican buses can be a colorful, merry experience.

What a pleasure to lean from the bus window and buy greasy *tacos*, bean-filled *gorditas*, succulent oranges and bananas, and cold, fizzy *refrescos*! How liberating on a hot day to sail across the desert or along the coast with windows open and hot wind pouring in, not having to worry about the car's radiator overheating or buying a tank of dirty gas.

While spirited mariachi music jars the dashboard, maybe the bus driver's gaudy Virgin of Guadalupe hovers next to the windshield, which is ornamented with embroidered curtains and elaborate dangles. Fellow passengers blab and joke with one another, and when a *señora*'s massive, ill-stored bundle tumbles from the luggage rack, everyone laughs and tries to help squeeze it back, just the way it was, and it will fall again. Lots of men unabashedly read trashy novelettes about macho cowboys and sexy bar-room *señoritas*. On Mexican buses a northerner's existential anxieties and inhibitions dissolve like chili powder and salt on the juicy face of an orange.

In car-oriented societies, sometimes the whole bus-riding scene is thought of with less than charity. In contrast, Mexicans justly have a high regard for their bus service and everything associated with it; bus drivers often project a sense of authority and expertise that northerners expect only from jumbo-jet pilots. This sense of professionalism diffuses down to ticket-takers, baggage handlers, et cetera, and this means good service for bus riders. In general, Mexican buses run on time; during a quarter century of traveling on Mexican buses, I have never lost a single belonging.

Mexican bus tickets do not cost much, either. In 1993 the price of a ticket from Monterrey to Ciudad Valles—a distance of 278 miles and therefore greater than the stretch between New York City and Washington, D.C.—was $13.87 US, first class.

Of course, the main reason Mexican buses go unused by foreigners is the language problem. Happily, a fluency in Spanish is not really necessary if the general principles of Mexican bus-riding are understood, which are thoroughly covered in the next section.

Driving in Mexico also is possible; moreover, it is not nearly as hair-raising as it used to be. *Autopistas*—well-maintained, expensive, four-lane toll roads—now connect major northern border towns with cities deep in the interior, and run between a few major southern Mexico cities as well. On old two-laners, open, unmarked manholes in the middle of streets, and policemen demanding *mordidas* to forget trumped-up charges, are not nearly as prevalent as they used to be. In many cities, road signs even show how to get from one side of town to the other.

Parts of Mexico are served by trains. Train riding in Mexico can be colorful and pleasant, but too frequently trains run mind-bogglingly late, and anyone not quick enough to grab a seat early may have to stand many hours next to a horrendously stinking toilet. Mexican trains should be experienced at least once, but their scheduling and level of service is too unpredictable for regular traveling.

How Mexican Bus-Riding Works

Here are some miscellaneous bus-riding facts:

- First-class bus tickets usually do not cost much more than second-class ones. However, first-classers typically do not stop in as many places as second-classers, so first-class buses arrive at their destinations considerably quicker.
- Numbered seats are assigned in most first-class buses, so on them there is little chance passengers will have to stand up; second-class buses can become incredibly stuffed. Of course, second-class buses are more colorful and adventurous than their fancier cousins.
- Often a town's first- and second-class terminals are in different places. If seats are filled for a destination at one terminal, usually it is possible to buy a ticket at the other.
- Some towns have no terminals at all; buses leave at designated spots along streets, or each bus line operates from its own terminal.
- In smaller towns sometimes the departure mentioned on the company's schedule board refers to a bus that is just passing through—it is coming *de paso*—so the ticket agent cannot sell a ticket until the bus arrives and the driver says whether seats are available. If all seats are occupied, the passenger has to wait for a later bus. If that bus also is coming *de paso*, the problem may repeat itself. This seldom happens, though, except on weekends and during *fiestas*.

Here are the steps in buying a ticket and then riding a Mexican bus:

1. Choose the bus line. Several companies may operate from a single terminal, so check to see which offers the best connections. Some companies consider themselves super-first-class (they advertise on-board drinks) and charge much more than regular first-class companies, even though the latter may offer equal or better service. Super-first-classers often serve on-board drinks, but their air conditioners frequently do not work, and windows are sealed shut.

2. Buy the ticket. Tell the ticket agent how many tickets are needed, at what time, and to where. "*Dos boletos para Xalapa a las 1800*" is a good way to say it—"Two tickets for Xalapa, at 6:00 P.M." Passengers on first-class buses might be asked to choose a seat number; No. 16 or thereabouts usually is a good location. If the agent writes a number on the ticket's back, it is either the bus number, which is also painted next to the bus door, or the station's bay number, where the bus will be parked. The seat number, if present, is written in the square named ASIENTO, which means "seat."

3. Find the bus. Sometimes passengers are not allowed into the bus-leaving area until the departure is announced. Because English speakers may not understand the distorted Spanish on loudspeakers, it is appropriate to ask fellow passengers for help in listening; this is when the Mexicans' habitual friendliness and helpfulness really is appreciated. If no one can be recruited for listening service, at least 10 minutes before departure go looking for the bus or appropriate bay. Maybe four-fifths of the time the city indicated in the destination window over the bus's windshield is the true destination. If the bus still has not appeared 5 minutes before departure time, ask for help. If a ticket-checker at the door refuses to let you into the departure area, that is good, because it means that the checker is paying attention to what buses are arriving and leaving, and your bus simply has not arrived yet.

4. Store the baggage. Most Mexican luggage racks are more roomy than North American and European racks. Nonetheless, most drivers want backpack-size luggage stored below. When passengers begin boarding, anyone with baggage to be stored below should stand beside the baggage bay of the bus (usually on the boarding side) until a handler comes. Tell the handler your destination; probably he will provide a claim stub. If the bus is a second-classer with no assigned seat number, have a friend enter early to claim seats. Otherwise, be prepared to stand.

5. Find the appropriate seat. Inside the bus, seat numbers are usually designated in little windows on the baggage racks' sides; one might say VENT 22 PAS 21. In Spanish the word *ventana* means "window" and the word *pasillo* means "aisle," so VENT 22 is the seat next to the window, while the aisle seat is No. 21. If no number appears on the ticket, then sit (or possibly stand, in second-class) anyplace.

BACKCOUNTRY BASICS

This guidebook assumes that its readers have at least minimal backcountry experience. If you do not, and seeing Mexico's backcountry is your first venture into the wilderness, please consult an introductory hiking guide such as *Wilderness Basics* (Seattle: The Mountaineers, 1993). Whether you are a seasoned veteran of the wilderness or a novice, be sure to bring along the Ten Essentials:

- map
- compass
- flashlight with extra bulb and batteries
- sunglasses
- extra clothing
- extra food and water
- pocket knife
- candle or fire starter
- first aid kit
- waterproof matches

Also keep in mind basic wilderness ethics and hygiene when visiting any backcountry area or camping in remote villages:

- Keep any fires small; build only in existing fire rings and only where safe and legally permitted. Consider using a backpacking stove even where wood fires are permitted. Use only dead and down wood from outside the camp area.
- Leave flowers, rocks, and other natural features undisturbed.
- Store food out of reach of animals.
- Boil drinking water from a natural source for 20 minutes.
- Use established backcountry toilets when available. Bury feces and dispose of waste water at least 200 feet from all water sources. Do not bury toilet paper; pack it out.

Maps

Good maps are essential for the independent traveler. In Mexico City maps are sometimes available at the Mexican Government Tourist Secretariat (Avenido Masaryk 172, 11587 México, D.F.), but one just never knows if the right people will be in, if the right maps will be on sale, or if the office will be closed for a special holiday. Similarly unpredictably available are free pamphlets or *folletos* issued by the Secretaría de Turismo and the individual states. Profiling one Mexican state at a time, these are found at larger hotels, restaurants, and tourist information booths, and are worth asking for. Sometimes they are available in English, and often feature worthwhile destinations overlooked by usual guidebooks.

I consider the most accessible and generally excellent maps of Mexico to be those published by International Travel Map Productions (P.O. Box 2290, Vancouver, BC V6B 3W5 Canada; telephone 604-687-3320; fax 604-687-5925). ITMP produces 1:1,000,000 maps of Southern Mexico, the Yucatán, and Baja. At this scale, even one-lane dirt tracks show up. These maps have contour lines; locate marshes, sandy areas, salt basins, temporary streams, and such; and highlight in red print everything from interesting caves to whale-watching areas.

In this book, precise compass directions are often given, so take a compass. For example, in a later chapter it is written, "Here turn left, to South 190°, and continue directly up the steep slope." Especially when it is doubtful whether the correct route is being followed, finding that the supposed left turn truly bears "South 190°" can be very comforting.

CLOTHING AND GEAR

The happiest travelers are those carrying small loads. When clothes can be washed and hung to dry each night in hotels and campgrounds, there is simply little need to carry more than two or three shirts or blouses, an extra pair of trousers or an extra skirt, a pair of shorts, and a similarly scant stock of all other items.

On the other hand, even Mexico is not hot or even warm every place, all the time. In August, following afternoon thunderstorms in high-elevation Mexico City, it can be downright nippy; during northern winters when cold fronts barrel down across northern Mexico and the Caribbean, anyone in a hammock slung in a *palapa* (an open-air thatch-roofed shelter) at Playa del Carmen or in a thin-walled hotel in San Luis Potosí will be eternally grateful for thermal underwear and/or a good sleeping bag.

Even for those who plan to camp in villages when possible rather than stay in other lodgings, minimal camping gear is needed. You likely will not need a tent, because *palapas* offer shelter when it is necessary. In some areas, *cabañas* (cabins) provide beds but not bedding, so all you need is your sleeping bag. *Palapa* and *cabaña* sleepers often wish for mosquito nets. Rented rooms often have hammock hooks, and you can either buy or rent a hammock and mosquito net (*mosquitero*). You will probably find that cooking your own food in Mexico is a waste of time; good food can be found almost everywhere, so leave behind your backpacking stove and camping cookware. Buying bottled water is probably less cumbersome than carrying a water filter or a stove for boiling water.

Layers of clothing are more effective at keeping in body heat than individual pieces of heavy apparel. Nothing but vanity keeps a cold person from donning three or four shirts. Light windbreakers that can be rolled into a frankfurter-size packet are useful. Everyone knows that heat escapes from an unhatted head; the same is true for inadequately cloaked waists; one-piece coveralls of the kind car mechanics wear keep the belly-button cozy.

In cold, wet places, 100 percent polypropylene long johns are wonderful because polypropylene retains heat even when wet. Ponchos are good for sweating hikers because air circulates beneath them. In chilly, wet cloud forests, a weird-looking but comfortable hiking ensemble consists of a poncho worn over nothing but polypropylene long johns.

Bandannas make quick-drying washrags and sweatbands; tied around the neck, they protect the nape against sunburn, and they can be worn like bandit masks to filter air on dusty roads. Brimless, stretchy headgear (socktops) are good not only on cold nights but also for pulling over the eyes when riding overnight buses.

Cholla-cactus fruits inspire hikers to appreciate thick-soled shoes.

Blue jeans are seldom appropriate for Mexico. They are hot and heavy and develop disgusting sheens if worn unwashed for long. Light, dust-colored khaki trousers with several pockets are better. Camouflage clothing tends to unnerve police and army folk, so do not wear it in Mexico. Except on trails with spiny plants or where mosquitoes or biting flies are bad, shorts often are preferable to trousers. At least one light, long-sleeved shirt should be carried for protection against sunburn.

If a hat is needed, consider buying a straw hat like those Mexican *campesinos* wear; they are well constructed, organic, and cheap.

Of course, hiking shoes should provide good arch support and have soles that do not slip on slick rocks. In especially hot, humid, level places, canvas gym shoes may do; they are well ventilated and dry out fast. On the other hand, they offer less ankle support and protection against sole-penetrating cactus spines than regular hiking shoes. Nearly anyplace in Mexico, well-crafted, inexpensive leather sandals can be bought that are even cooler and faster-drying than gym shoes. However, these are poor protection against cactus spines and hookworms.

FOOD AND WATER

Other travel guides do a good job describing restaurants in Mexico. In this book, the focus is on eating in tiny mom-and-pop places. Of course, a prime concern is how to eat without getting sick.

Some would consider Mexico's outback culinary scene as more fun, cheaper, and—perhaps surprisingly—*safer* than eating in urban tourist spots. That is because in regular restaurants, customers cannot monitor what goes on in kitchens. However, at a *comedor* consisting of an open-front stall and a *señora* with a gas burner, the patron sees whether the pot of chicken stew or black beans is kept piping hot (and therefore sterile), and how dishes are handled. If more than the usual number of flies are buzzing around and the *señora* scratches unholy places, just keep walking.

Nearly always the *señora* in such places permits guests to step behind the counter to wash hands. Sometimes eating utensils can be adroitly and furtively sterilized in steamy coffee. Otherwise, folding tortillas and scooping up bite-sized portions the native way may be the most hygienic manner of transferring food to mouth.

Do not eat unprocessed food that is not piping hot, or else has a shell, husk, or peel that can be removed with clean hands. A bottle of alcohol comes in handy for sterilizing hands when food must be touched—also it can sanitize fingers at flossing time.

Mexican *kioskos* and *mini-supermercados* (and probably even the *mega-mini-supermercado* recently spotted in Puebla) usually carry little more than crackers, *refrescos* (beer and soda), and cookies. However, in medium-sized *supermercados* usually something can be found to maintain a hiker's energy and protein level. For example, most *supermercados* usually carry *leche ultrapasteurizada en cajas*—"ultrapasteurized" milk sold in liter cartons, capable of being stored at room temperature for months.

Tostadas taste like corn chips (they are made of toasted corn), but are hard and tortilla-shaped, and sold cheaply in plastic bags; *tostadas* are whole-grain, thoroughly traditional, and delicious, especially when smeared with bean paste and graced with a few shakes of Tabasco sauce. *Animalitos*, or animal crackers, for some reason are widely available throughout Mexico. They are a sweet, lightweight, very inexpensive snack that can be carried several days before going bad. Oatmeal often is available because Mexicans pulverize it for a sweet drink. Typically clerks know oatmeal, *ojuelas de avena*, only by its brand name, which is Tres Minutos.

Never pass up a chance to visit a good Mexican *mercado*—one of those places with lots of stalls filled with fresh fruit and vegetables, often near the town's center. Some *mercados* are open-air but often they occupy huge, warehouselike buildings that inside look, smell, and sound like nothing north of the Rio Grande. It is especially fun to sample fruits and nuts, breads and pastries that may be particular just to a tiny area of the country.

For example, the multiplicity of bananas Mexicans have is astounding. Most Mexicans disdain the typical banana of North American supermarkets. For snacks they prefer the tiny, extra-sweet ones, or maybe the purple ones with a slightly sourish tang. Though Mexicans use huge, pithy *plátanos* only for cooking, some North Americans eat them raw. Even the stubby, angular bananas that Mexicans roast in the coals of their cooking fires are worth tasting raw.

Sometimes wild fruits gathered in the forest make it into *mercados*. The two kings of wild forest fruit are chicozapote, from the tree producing natural chicle (chewing gum base), and mamey. Both possess exotic, musky-sweet flavors unmatched by any temperate-zone fruit. Papayas usually are available, but do not travel well. And then there are pineapple, guava, passion fruit (*granadilla*), cherimoya (*anona*), pomegranate (*granada*), the inch-long, potato-shaped, acidy/musky, weirdly nice fruit called hog plum (*jobo*). . . . Especially in Indian territory, there is just no telling what will turn up in a good *mercado*.

Be extremely careful with water. Even in clean, well-maintained hotels, water issuing from taps may be bad. Many well-educated Mexicans with access to city water buy all their drinking water. In stores, the plastic, cylindrical bottles of *agua purificada* are OK, but the gallon-size, square-bottomed, plastic containers are notorious for being "unofficially recycled"—even those with "tamper-proof seals."

Because the hikes in this book are day hikes of short duration and distance, purifying water on the trail should not be necessary; bottled water is the thing for day hikers. If you should find yourself in a situation where you must purify your own water, boil it for 20 minutes or use a water filter or iodine tablets.

STAYING HEALTHY

Here is a truly important gem of health-related wisdom: Anyone traveling for long without eating and sleeping properly, and without drinking enough pure water, will gradually, imperceptibly, and inexorably begin losing resistance to *all* communicable diseases. One problem after another will begin cropping up. Common sense goes a long way in the Mexican outback.

Diarrhea

Traveler's diarrhea (Montezuma's revenge) results from eating food contaminated with bacteria. Taking two Pepto-Bismol tablets with meals, at bedtime, and during risky periods seems to prevent some cases. Recovery can often be sped up by taking two Pepto-Bismol tablets each half hour for 4 hours—eight doses—along with Imodium in the recommended amounts.

Cholera

Cholera is returning to Mexico. This disease is basically a horrendous case of diarrhea, often leading to dehydration and consequent disruption of the body's balance of electrolytes. By taking the eating precautions mentioned in the preceding section and being particularly sure to avoid seafood, cholera should not be much of a problem. Anyone developing severe, long-term diarrhea when proper medical attention is unavailable should drink a rehydration solution consisting of *four level teaspoons of sugar and ¼ teaspoon of salt for each liter or quart of liquid.*

Malaria

Malaria also is making a comeback in southern Mexico; both the malaria-carrying mosquito and the one-celled parasite causing malaria have become resistant to chemicals traditionally used to combat them. Travelers planning on visiting malarious areas should talk with their doctor; sometimes pills must be taken a couple of weeks in advance of the trip. Malaria's characteristic symptom is fever alternating with chills.

The malaria mosquito is active mostly at dusk. Visitors to small towns in southern Mexico may be wise to carry mosquito nets that can be strung over their beds (*mosquiteros*). The net should be large enough to cover the feet, and wide enough to curl up in without the rump touching the wall. North Americans can hear up-to-date news about malaria by phoning the Centers for Disease Control in Atlanta, Georgia, at (404) 332-4559. In England, the Malaria Reference Laboratory at 071 636 7921 offers a tape on malaria in Central America.

Probably the most effective, generally available insect repellents are those containing diethyltoluamide, or "Deet." One problem with Deet is that it is absorbed through the skin, and allergic reactions have been reported; also it tends to melt plastic items like eyeglass frames and expensive tents. Travelers who enjoy sitting outside at dusk or sleeping in rooms with open, unscreened windows may want to carry mosquito coils—spiraling, incenselike items that smolder slowly, issuing fumes that drive away mosquitoes. Long-sleeved shirts and full-length pants afford some protection against blood-suckers. Light-colored clothing attracts mosquitoes less than dark-colored. Perfume, after-shave lotion, and scented soaps attract them.

Ticks

Trails passing through areas heavily populated with deer or cattle often are infested with ticks. Beside using repellent, it helps to stick trouser legs inside socks. Remember that tall grass in moist areas may be infested with chiggers, which burrow into the skin and cause red bumps that itch like crazy. Scratched chigger bumps in hot, humid areas can quickly become infected.

Bees

Especially in southern Mexico, beekeeping is big business; many forest trails leading into clearings shelter numerous hives inhabited by bees programmed by nature to attack sweet-toothed visitors. Single wasps and bees buzzing around the tip of a nose or one's sweet soda should be left alone; swatting only triggers defensive behavior, which may include stinging.

Tarantulas

Tarantulas are big, fuzzy softies. They would not hurt a person for the world—unless the person poked or tried to handle them, in which case the arachnid might be coaxed into a non-venomous bite. Tarantula hairs can irritate the skin. Just leave tarantulas alone.

Scorpions

Scorpions are all over the place in Mexico. Mexican country folk regard them with the same degree of awe northerners have for wasps. Unless a special sensitivity is involved, scorpion stings hurt badly for a few minutes, but after an hour or two they can be forgotten.

Worms

Anyone wearing sandals or going barefoot in villages can get hookworms—intestinal parasites. Roundworms and pinworms can be contracted by eating food contaminated with worm eggs. If one's anus itches or if something in the feces looks like grains of rice or earthworms, a good deworming is called for. Large worm populations can drain a person's energy, and big roundworms (they grow to more than a foot long) can perforate intestinal walls. One way to handle worms is to walk into a Mexican pharmacy and ask for something for "*mis gusanos intestinales*," "my intestinal worms." Usually but not always this inexpensive shotgun approach works. It is better to visit a doctor, who will send a feces sample to the lab. Sometimes after a deworming, when food energy suddenly is shifted from the worms back to the human body and brain, it is as if someone turns on the lights.

Snakes

People keeping hands and feet out of places they cannot see will have no problems with the *barba amarilla*, or fer-de-lance, southern Mexico's main venomous snake. Poisonous snakes inject venom only about half the time they bite. According to current theory, anyone bitten far from help should *not* tie a tourniquet between the wound and heart, and probably would do more harm cutting around the bite than leaving it untreated. One school of thought urges treating snakebite victims for shock: have them lie flat, make sure their breathing passages stay open, keep them warm, and try to keep everyone's excitement level low. Do not use alcohol or food. The bite of a venomous snake hurts like hell, so a powerful painkiller might be appreciated.

Rabies

Being bitten by backcountry dogs can lead to rabies; few *campesinos* inoculate their dogs. If you are bitten, see if it is possible to have the dog tied up so that later it can be examined, then contact a local doctor or clinic. Hopefully, rabies cases will be unknown in the area. If rabies is common, then patient, doctor, and dog-owner will have to make some serious decisions. Just do what the doctor says.

Cacti and Thorns

Mexico's thorn forests, deserts, and humid lowland forests are well

Hikers in Mexico probably stand a greater chance of being seriously scratched or punctured than being seriously bitten or stung.

equipped with spines and thorns. Anyone spending much time in natural areas stands a greater chance of being punctured and scraped by plants than being stung or bitten by dangerous animals. Especially in hot, humid environments, punctures and scrapes can easily become infected. Trousers instead of shorts, shoes with tough soles on them, and an abiding alertness are prime defenses. Especially in cactus country, tweezers come in handy for extracting stickers.

Heat Exhaustion and Heat Stroke

Do not get too hot. Anyone who is hot, feeling faint, or nauseous may be suffering heat exhaustion. More critical symptoms consist of rapid, irregular heartbeat, being pale, and having skin that is cool and clammy when it should be hot. If these warning symptoms do not immediately result in a rest and cooling-off period, a heat stroke may result, possibly causing brain damage or death. Cool off heat-stroke victims (fan them, sponge them, splatter cold water on them) and massage their arms and legs.

PERSONAL SECURITY ON THE OPEN ROAD

Because Mexicans are among the most friendly, generous, hospitable people on earth, robbery is an awkward subject. However, all travelers need to develop strategies for protecting themselves against it, no matter what country is involved.

Disperse money in different places. During one robbery in which I was a victim, money and checks in three places were found, but several $50 bills in a money belt never were, and that meant the difference between hitching to the border or taking a train.

Of course fanny packs and waist pouches are useless during violent robberies. In fact, they tend to give a false sense of security, and announce to the world that something being carried is worth protecting. They are good for securing valuables that otherwise would be kept in open pockets. Chest pouches are good for documents and folded money, except when it is hot; then they become visible inside light shirts, and soak up sweat.

When choosing clothing for a trip, keep security demands in mind. Think in terms of pockets with zippers or well-anchored buttons. Remember that things fall out of shallow pockets; go for nice deep ones.

The best idea is to just avoid carrying valuables not truly needed. Many travelers carry camera equipment that is far too sophisticated and expensive for the general snapshots being taken. Unless superior photography is a major goal and special lenses and high-tech camera bodies really are needed, plenty of snapshot-worthy 35mm models can be purchased rather cheaply.

Especially in Michoacán and the surrounding uplands of southern Mexico, considerable marijuana is cultivated. It can be dangerous to wander into isolated regions where local growers prefer to remain undiscovered. Probably any well-trod trail less than a half-hour walk from the nearest road is safe. In any place, if unctuous young men smelling of aftershave and wearing gold rings ask if you are interested in marijuana, politely answer in the negative and get away fast.

Do not even think about handling illegal drugs in Mexico. More than a few Mexican police and military personnel take special joy in shaking down *gringos*—especially young ones with backpacks—looking for drugs. Several times, scroungy-looking men who tried to sell me drugs turned out to be plain-clothes Mexican policemen. And officials on the U.S. side are just as sneaky; it is amazing how many drug-sniffing dogs there are nowadays.

Finally, after all this talk about robbery and drugs, do not get paranoid. The vast majority of Mexicans are humble, honest, hard-working, religious, and sincere in a way that cynical northerners can hardly imagine. If you do encounter a serious problem, your best bet is probably to contact the nearest consulate for your country.

FOR THE NATURALIST

Paraphernalia

Superior photography simply requires bulky, heavy equipment. For good depth of field and non-fuzzy pictures, when light is insufficient for shooting at 1/250 of a second or faster, a tripod is indispensable. In forests, flashes increase depth of field without requiring slower shutter speeds or stabilization with a tripod; however, the flash's removal of natural shadows and subtle tones usually results in artificial-looking pictures. Flashes produce the most pleasing results when used not for entirely lighting subjects, but for partially filling in jet-black shadows. Kodachrome film, accentuating the red end of the color spectrum, is appropriate for pictures of Indians in costume and *mercados* stocked with ripe fruit; Ektachrome, emphasizing the blue band, is truer to the colors of green forests and blue oceans.

Binoculars can be both powerful and light; the popular 9x25 Nikon Travelite weighs only eleven ounces. However, because the field of such binoculars is so narrow, practice is needed before using them effectively; employing binoculars with a narrow field is like shooting from the hip. Nothing is more frustrating than failing to spot with binoculars a bird that is in plain view, but too far away.

Hand lenses—special magnifying glasses with two small lenses mounted above one another and usually swiveling into a handle—are as important as binoculars. Powers of 7x to 10x are fine; more powerful ones have too-shallow depths of field. Hand lenses reveal crystal faces in rocks and minerals, the complex anatomy of tiny flowers, bug mouthparts, ants milking aphids, star-shaped hairs on the undersurface of leaves. . . .

Pocketknives peel *mercado* fruit, dissect flowers, and stick into roasted corn's pithy cob, becoming a handle, when fingers are too dirty to use for grasping. A sketchbook comes in handy when a plant or an animal is not included in field guides being carried; draw the organism's main obvious identification features, then later in a good library try the identification again. Ballpoint pens fare badly in hot, humid environs; carry some pencils.

A plant press is not suggested as something to carry along. Heavy-duty plant collecting requires permits from the Mexican government. Even a few leaves stored between the pages of a book must be declared when returning to the United States, and they had better not be from a rare or endangered species, be from citrus species, or have dirt or any kind of parasite or mold on them. Do not think about bringing back living specimens. Even someone assuming a little organic material can be sneaked past U.S. Customs (a risky assumption) should be concerned that exotic Mexican soil organisms, insects, et cetera, might wreak havoc on U.S. ecosystems.

Names Are Magical

Here is the magical process in which *names* are so important: First, identify a particular plant or animal. Then look up the name.

Along all of Mexico's coasts it is possible to spot a large, black bird with

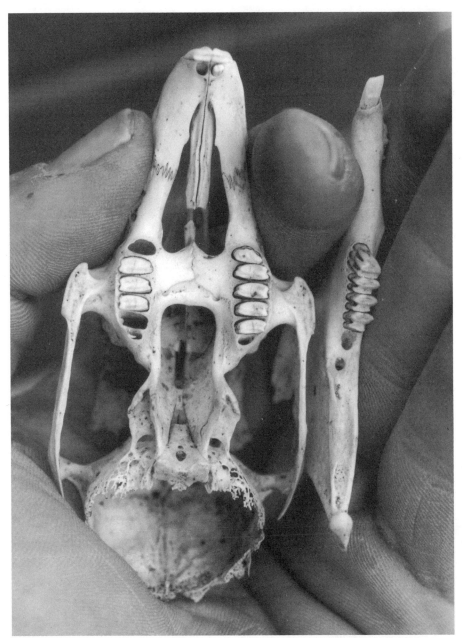

Using dental formulas in a field guide to mammals, it was discovered that this skull is that of a blacktail jackrabbit.

a deeply forked tail, narrow, bent wings, and a red throat-pouch sailing along the water's edge. A quick check in the bird book reveals that this is unmistakably a male magnificent frigatebird, *Fregata magnificens*. The first step is completed when the name is written into the notebook.

The second step takes place back home. From the bookshelf beside the bed, Volume 1 of *The Audubon Society Master Guide to Birding* is retrieved, and "magnificent frigatebird" is looked up. Here it is found that frigatebirds often chase and steal food from other birds, and that in flight they can take food from the water's surface without alighting. The bird's red throat area is a featherless, red-skinned pouch that can be puffed up like a balloon, to help males show off before females; females have white breasts and no red throat pouch. The species is distributed from Florida south through the Americas to southern Brazil. This second step is never finished, for always the name "magnificent frigatebird" will constitute a key for accessing any new information source that comes along.

Of course, nothing is ever simple. One problem with names like "magnificent frigatebird" is that they usually change from region to region and language to language. In Germany a magnificent frigatebird is a *Prachtfregattvogel!* This predicament is addressed by scientific names. Even German bird watchers agree that a *Fregata magnificens* is a *Fregata magnificens*. In the name *Fregata magnificens*, the word *Fregata* is the genus name and is always capitalized; the word *magnificens* is the species name, and is not capitalized, even when it is a proper name.

This book supplies the scientific names of each of the 600-plus species of Mexican plants and animals mentioned herein (see appendix A), and common names have been used consistently throughout. Even when the common name being used means nothing to the reader, it is important for anyone wanting more information. Chapter 7, for instance, states that the tree called *chiquinív* grows on a certain slope. Looking up *chiquinív* in appendix A reveals that *Quercus acatanangensis* is being talked about. A quick glance in a field guide to trees discloses that all *Quercus* species are oaks. Further burrowing into a good technical library will turn up what science knows about *Q. acatanangensis*. Scientific names are powerful tools for those willing to use them.

However, even scientific names are not foolproof. As taxonomists learn more and more about the organisms they study, they regroup them— "lumpers" throw them into bigger groups and "splitters" do the opposite. Thus anyone using Standley's comprehensive but badly out of date *Trees and Shrubs of Mexico* may identify one of the many cacti seen during the Xoconostle hike in Chapter 4 as a species of *Echinofossulocactus*, only to find out that other books do not even mention *Echinofossulocactus*. Nowadays that genus is lumped into *Echinocactus*.

There is no elegant way to solve this problem. Just keep in mind that the problem exists, especially when dealing with older literature, and try to work around it. This problem is a genuine plague, even to professional biologists. But it is not nearly as bad as dealing with common names.

SNORKELING AND DIVING

Probably the best snorkeling in Mexico is off Cozumel Island, on the Yucatán Peninsula's eastern shore. Out west, congenial water temperature and excellent visibility make the reefs around Isla del Carmen and Isla

Coronado just offshore from Loreto, in the Gulf of California, favorite destinations. Sometimes, because there are fewer tourists, snorkeling in less spectacular spots can be the most fun.

To find a good reef while walking, driving, or biking along the coast, look for telltale dark spots in the turquoise water. A reef's landward side is generally shallow and flat for several hundred yards before dropping off to greater depths. In many places the reef may be spotty, with small coral outcroppings surrounded by otherwise lifeless sand. However, even these small areas make interesting study.

Basic equipment for casual coral watching includes a mask, a snorkel, and a pair of fins. While these can be rented, it is recommended to purchase them in advance; a leaking mask or ill-fitting fins can ruin a dive. Also, it is good to become familiar with equipment before having to depend on it.

The mask is the single most personal component of the system, and pains must be taken to find one that fits. In the store, fit the mask against your face, letting the strap dangle. Pressing lightly on the glass's center, the mask's pressure should be felt evenly distributed around your face. If it touches, for example, on your forehead and upper lip before the sides, try another size. For the final fit test, inhale through your nose while pressing slightly on the mask's front. Then, while holding your breath, remove your hand and bend your head down. If the mask fits, it will stay on your face. If it falls, look for another mask.

Cheap snorkels probably work just as well as fancy ones, so for those on a budget this is the place to scrimp. Before buying a snorkel, fasten it onto the mask to be sure the whole assembly fits comfortably upon your face.

Fins are either "full-foot" or "adjustable-strap." Full-foot models are somewhat lighter and less expensive but, since they are bought for specific sizes, often they cannot be shared with other divers. Though they are fairly comfortable worn by themselves, you may need to wear ordinary socks with them to prevent chafing. Adjustable-strap fins tend to be larger and heavier than full-foot ones, plus they are more expensive, and require the purchase of a bootie to wear underneath. However, they are appropriate for anyone who might later get into scuba, or for those who want to share their fins with others. Snorkeling can successfully be done in tennis shoes, though this severely reduces kicking power, restricting snorkelers to very shallow water without strong currents. A basic snorkeling kit will probably cost at least $100—easily twice that much for those who do not shop around.

Lots of snorkeling and diving tricks can be mastered in a swimming pool. For instance, smearing a few drops of spit on the inside of a mask's window can prevent fogging. More importantly, the technique of exhaling sharply to expel water when it enters the snorkel (as it will in choppy water) can be mastered. Statistics show that no safety practice is more important than this: Do not mix drinking with diving.

While most Mexican dive shops offer dive certification courses, it is better to train before making the trip. For one thing, certification requires several hours of reading and classroom study, and who wants to waste precious

hours in Mexico under electric lights?

Travelers planning on joining organized dive tours should have their local dive shop recommend a dive operator who does not quickly herd clients through crowded dives. Expect to pay $60 US to $75 US for a two-tank dive, and slightly less if no gear is rented. Carefully inspect rented equipment before using it. On dives, usually the dive master takes the lead, with the rest of the group trailing behind. Boat pilots generally do a good job watching bubbles, so when clients come up the boat is usually not far away.

Advanced divers carrying their own air compressors and using an inflatable boat can explore reefs to their hearts' content. Keep an eye on the "home beach" to avoid being carried too far away. Divers in waters frequented by boats are wise to put out dive flags. Recently four divers were encountered who for *two months* had camped on a beach called Playa Maya, just south of Chankanab Lagoon National Park on the west coast of Cozumel Island. For little more than the cost of their food and compressor gas, they had become intimate with a gorgeous undersea world just a stone's throw from their tent flaps.

A NOTE ABOUT SAFETY

Safety is an important concern in all outdoor activities. No guidebook can alert you to every hazard or anticipate the limitations of every reader. Therefore, the descriptions of roads, trails, routes, and natural features in this book are not representations that a particular place or excursion will be safe for your party. When you follow any of the routes described in this book, you assume responsibility for your own safety. Under normal conditions, such excursions require the usual attention to traffic, road and trail conditions, weather, terrain, the capabilities of your party, and other factors.

Current political conditions also may add to the risks of travel in Mexico in ways that this book cannot predict. Keeping informed on current conditions and exercising common sense are the keys to a safe, enjoyable outing.

The Mountaineers

CHAPTER 2

MEXICO'S NATURAL ENVIRONMENT

CLIMATE

Because a unit volume of cool air holds less moisture than the same volume of warm air, moisture in the equator's hot, rising, cooling air condenses into cloud-fog, and eventually into rain. That is why so many forests at the equator are lush and wet.

The equator's hot air cannot ascend and cool forever, so high in the sky part of it embarks toward the North Pole and part streams southward. In the vicinity of the Tropic of Cancer in the Northern Hemisphere, and in the vicinity of the Tropic of Capricorn in the Southern Hemisphere, part of the pole-streaming air descends. Because this plunging air has been dried out during its equatorial ascent, the regions of earth it now descends upon—land in the vicinity of the Tropics of Cancer and Capricorn—tends to be arid. Thus the great deserts of the earth lie in the vicinity of either the Tropic of Cancer or the Tropic of Capricorn. The Tropic of Cancer crosses the heart of Mexico, so Mexico's vast, general dryness should come as no surprise.

Notice on the map in Figure 4 that the California Current flows off Mexico's Pacific Coast. This current is a river of cold water streaming down from offshore Alaska, so westward-blowing winds that pass over it and onto the Mexican coast bring coolish air onto the beaches of such popular Pacific Coast resorts as Mazatlán, Puerto Vallarta, and Acapulco; no such cool current graces the Gulf Coast, where Tampico and Veracruz stay muggy most of the time.

When these cool breezes off the California Current hit hot land, naturally the air heats up fast. The air's relative humidity plummets and, from such dry air, rainfall seldom develops. Thus much of Mexico's Pacific lowlands are arid, particularly Baja.

Figure 3 Mexico's most conspicuous physiographic features

During the northern summer, Mexico's landscape heats up and the air becomes unstable. From June or July to October or November, afternoon thunderstorms bring a rainy season to Mexico. The rains are usually short and violent, and come in the afternoon, after a sunny morning with fast-rising temperatures. During the rest of the year most of Mexico sees a dry season. Nowadays, with the earth's climate possibly becoming more erratic due to the carbon dioxide–caused greenhouse effect, the advents and durations of Mexico's wet and dry seasons seem less predictable than before, but they still comprise very distinct seasons.

In the northern winter, cold air masses from Canada and the United States, called *nortes*, penetrate far into northern Mexico, as well as across the Yucatán Peninsula. During this time, northern Mexico sometimes experiences two, three, or more weeks of continuously overcast, drizzly, bone-chilling, very un-Mexican weather, and this can constitute a "second rainy season," one consisting more of drizzle than cloudbursts. Some plants in the north bloom twice a year, during each rainy season.

Occasionally water currents in the Pacific alter, creating the phenomenon known in English as El Niño. When El Niño is visiting during the winter, Baja and the northern third of Mexico can experience one impulse of rain after another, converting vast deserts into lakes. Along the Gulf Coast and in the

Yucatán, violent hurricanes are possible from August through October. Tropical storms off the Pacific sometimes pummel the Isthmus of Tehuantepec and the Pacific Coast.

Central Mexico consists of an elevated interior valley framed by the Western Sierra Madre mountains in the west and the Eastern Sierra Madre in the east. Air on the Mexican Plateau, finding itself inside something of a bowl, often stagnates. This is bad news for people stuck in Mexico City when, day after day, the only change in the pocket of air enveloping the city is higher and higher levels of exhaust fumes.

Though the greater part of Mexico lies south of the Tropic of Cancer, and thus is "tropical," most of Mexico's landmass stands so high in elevation that its weather is anything but tropical. Guadalajara lies at about 5,140 feet, Puebla at 7,093, and Mexico City at 7,350. In general, northern Mexico is arid, southern Mexico is rainier. In an average year, northwestern Mexico, including Baja, can expect about 270 sunny days; in contrast, in Chiapas in the far south, the sun shines through only for about 60 days.

GEOLOGY

Off southern Mexico's Pacific Coast, from just north of Manzanillo all the way south to the Guatemalan frontier, there exists a vast underwater valley. Off Tapachula, Chiapas, this Middle America Trench reaches 21,857 feet deep—deeper than Alaska's Mount McKinley is high. Off the Pacific Coast of Baja lies a similar slash named the Cedros Trench. Not long ago no one had a clue as to why these trenches existed. Now we know; they are artifacts of continental drift, a feature of the science known as plate tectonics.

Geophysicists say that a little over 300 million years ago, during the Pennsylvanian Period of the Paleozoic Era, the earth's landmasses were gathered into one supercontinent now referred to as Pangaea. Early reptiles roamed

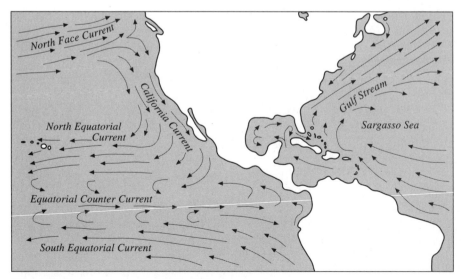

Figure 4 Ocean currents around Mexico

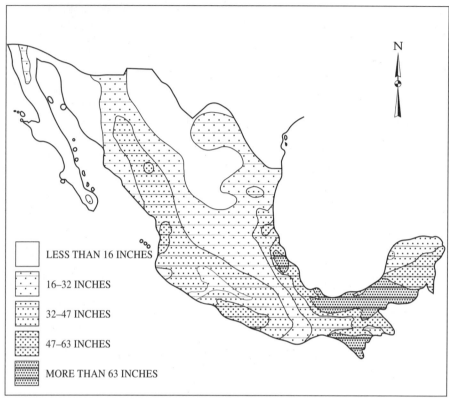

LESS THAN 16 INCHES

16–32 INCHES

32–47 INCHES

47–63 INCHES

MORE THAN 63 INCHES

Figure 5 Average annual precipitation in Mexico

the land then, but dinosaurs and mammals hadn't yet evolved.

By 130 million years ago, during the Cretaceous Period of the Mesozoic Era, Pangaea had split into two fractured landmasses; the northern one, on which the future North America, including Mexico, and Eurasia rode, we call Laurasia; the southern one, on which the future South America, Africa, Antarctica, and Australia clung together, we call Gondwana. Now dinosaurs ruled the earth and birds and flowering plants had evolved. Mammals existed, too, but they were just mousy, insignificant things.

As millennia passed, North America split from Eurasia, and Africa drifted apart from South America. India, earlier split from Antarctica, shot across the Indian Ocean and crunched 1,250 miles into Asia, bulldozing up a heap now referred to as the Himalayas.

Today the earth's rocky crust is fractured into about twenty vast slabs or plates floating atop a relatively thin, partly molten zone of the earth's interior. The plates still move. The ocean floor in the vicinity of an advancing plate is mashed down like gelatin around a fingertip pressed onto its surface. The trenchlike depressions in front of advancing plates are called subduction zones. Friction from the grinding plates produces unimaginable heat. Rocks comprising both the old seafloor and the continental plate scraping over it melt, and magma is formed. Just behind the advancing plate and deep

Era	Period	Epoch	Began millions of years ago	What happened then in Mexico
CENOZOIC	Quaternary	Recent		During four Pleistocene ice ages North America's temperate and boreal life zones shift south into Mexico.
		Pleistocene	3	Extinction of large mammals.
	Tertiary	Pliocene		Flowering plants and mammals evolve into
		Miocene	22	many species; insects and flowers co-evolve.
		Oligocene		
		Eocene		
		Paleocene	65	
MESOZOIC	Cretaceous		135	First flowering plants; dinosaurs disappear; mammals proliferate; Pangea splits.
	Jurassic		200	Dinosaurs, marine and flying reptiles dominate. Gymnosperms create forests.
	Triassic		240	First mammals and dinosaurs; earth predominantly arid.
PALEOZOIC	Permian		280	Decline of amphibians, first mammal-like reptiles.
	Pennsylvanian		325	First reptiles appear; vast coal-swamps; Pangea intact.
	Mississippian		370	Amphibians appear on land.
	Devonian		415	First land vertebrates, many fish, land plants.
	Silurian		445	First land life, coral reefs; first jawed fishes.
	Ordovician		515	First vertebrates; many clams; marine communities develop.
	Cambrian		590	Tribolites rule oceans; first primitive life with skeletons; many mollusks, crustaceans.
	Precambrian		± 4,700	Life appears.

Figure 6 Geological Time Scale

below the earth's crust, pressure builds up, the land rises like skin above a boil, and if the pressure keeps up, volcanoes erupt, disgorging enormous quantities of lava, ash, dust and gases.

Thus the Middle America Trench off southern Mexico's Pacific Coast, and the Cedros Trench off Baja, are subduction zones formed in front of the North American Plate as it plows over and mashes down the Pacific seafloor. The Western Sierra Madre are largely once-molten material disgorged by volcanoes formed to release energy built up by friction of the North American Plate scraping atop the Pacific floor.

Is eastern Mexico's coastline marching into the Gulf of Mexico? No, because the Gulf of Mexico itself lies deep within the realm of the westward-advancing North American Plate; the Gulf is like a saucer of water on a westward-scooting dinner tray.

Tectonic plates do not always march head-on onto ocean floors. Baja California and an extreme southwestern sliver of the United States, in the state of California, ride a minor block at the moment being ripped sideways off the North American Plate. Land west of the fault system formed where the two plates slide past one another eases past the mainland at two to three inches a year. Someday Baja and southern California will become an island. In about 10 million years, island-borne Los Angeles should draw even with San Francisco; in 50 million years, Baja's southern tip will lie offshore Oregon and Washington, and Los Angeles will say hello to Anchorage, Alaska.

Geological Zones

Figure 7 reflects both the age and the nature of rock outcroppings across Mexico's landscape. The geological eras are the Precambrian, the Mesozoic, and the Cenozoic; the rock types are igneous, sedimentary, and metamorphic.

Igneous rocks are those derived from volcanic activity. Basalt, obsidian, pumice, scoria, and ash are all igneous material ejected from erupting volcanoes, and are referred to as "extrusive" because they have been extruded. Often magma wells up inside the earth but instead of being ejected remains where it is, cooling in place. Rocks formed from such unejected magma, like granite and gabbro, are "intrusive" igneous rocks.

Sedimentary rocks are formed from material that has settled someplace. Sandstone is a sedimentary rock made of cemented-together sand grains; limestone is formed from calcium-rich mud and often includes seashells. Nearly all fossils occur in sedimentary rocks.

Metamorphic rocks are rocks that, under tremendous pressure and/or heat, have recrystallized into new rock types. Metamorphic rock can be formed where tectonic plates grind together or molten magma touches sedimentary rocks. The rock called marble is metamorphosed limestone; quartzite is metamorphosed sandstone.

Notice that the area occupied by the Western Sierra Madre is mantled with "igneous extrusive" material, while the area occupied by the Eastern Sierra Madre is predominantly Cretaceous. In the Eastern Sierra Madre, most Cretaceous outcrops are sedimentary limestone. This fundamental difference

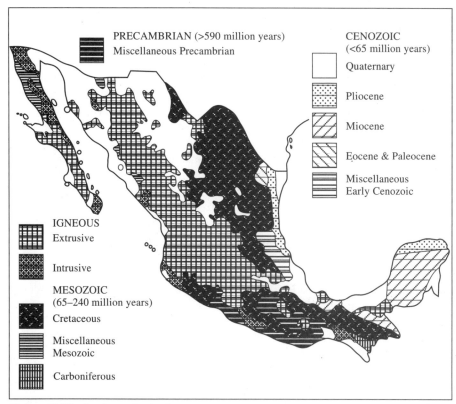

PRECAMBRIAN (>590 million years)
Miscellaneous Precambrian

CENOZOIC
(<65 million years)

Quaternary

Pliocene

Miocene

Eocene & Paleocene

Miscellaneous
Early Cenozoic

IGNEOUS
Extrusive

Intrusive

MESOZOIC
(65–240 million years)
Cretaceous

Miscellaneous
Mesozoic

Carboniferous

Figure 7 Mexico's geological zones

in geology between these two Sierra Madre ranges accounts for their different landforms and biological communities.

On the Los Azufres Park hike in Chapter 5, The Mexican Plateau, a road cut slices through very deep deposits of volcanic ash; it is possible to walk up to grayish road-cut walls and scrape away compacted but not cemented ash with a fingernail.

The extrusive igneous rocks and ash mapped here have been ejected over a very long period of time, all through the Mesozoic, clear into recent times. Mexico's most recent volcanic eruptions have been Paricutín in Michoacán (1943–1952), Chichonal, sometimes called Chichón, in Chiapas (1983), and Colima in Colima (1991). The small areas of intrusive igneous rocks shown on the map are primarily ancient granites from above which overlying rocks have eroded.

The fact tht the Cretaceous-age outcroppings (135 million to 65 million years old) occupying the Eastern Sierra Madre region are mostly limestone reflects the fact that during the Cretaceous Period this part of Mexico was submerged beneath a warm, shallow sea. Later the sea's lime-rich marl was uplifted as limestone, and eventually showcased as the majestic, white cliffs seen on Highway 70 during the drive from Río Verde to San Luis Potosí (see the Xoconostle hike in Chapter 4, The Gulf Coast.)

Not all of the east coast uplands are sedimentary. From certain vantage points on the Mamulique Pass hike in Chapter 4, peaks can be observed toward the northeast that are obviously volcanic. These are very ancient volcanic "necks"—the remaining cores or "skeletons" of old volcanoes from around which most of the surrounding rock has been eroded. In southern Veracruz, in the vicinity of San Andrés Tuxtla, Highway 180 passes through rugged volcanic mountains, the Tuxtlas, seemingly unconnected to other mountain ranges.

Those interested in delving into the geological history of eastern Mexico and the Gulf region can find additional information in *Tectonics* in an article by Pindell and Dewey (see Bibliography).

If all igneous and Cretaceous rocks are mentally removed from Figure 7, mostly what is left is outcropping Cenozoic-Era material deposited within the last 65 million years—fairly recently in geological time. Cenozoic material often is so young that it has not had time to consolidate into rock; frequently it is sand, dust, ash, gravel, or just plain, unconsolidated dirt. Figure 7's extensive white areas denote Quaternary deposits set down within the last 3 million years (almost today in geological time!). Primarily this is outwash from surrounding mountains deposited during Ice-Age flooding.

What may be one of the most significant geological events in the history of life on earth occurred in the area covered by this map. About 65 million years ago, at the time-boundary between the Cretaceous and the Tertiary, something happened that caused most of the species of plants and animals on earth to become extinct. Much evidence suggests that the event was an object from outer space hitting the earth in the Gulf of Mexico just northwest of Mérida, Yucatán. In late 1993 the submerged crater was determined to be about 185 miles across. At the time of the impact, a warm sea still covered the Yucatán Peninsula, so during the Celestún National Park hike in Chapter 8, The Yucatán Peninsula, anyone gazing toward the northwest imagining the chaos in that very spot 65 million years ago should visualize themselves in a dinghy—a dinghy soon to meet a tsunami capable of unimaginable destruction.

Desert Landscapes

Central Mexico's Plateau has been "uplifted." When an area is uplifted it immediately begins eroding. If for many millions of years the region neither is uplifted more nor subsides, it will eventually erode to a level plain.

Young landscapes, immediately after uplift, have streams coursing across broad, flat uplands. A desert landscape in its youthful stage has steep stream slopes. In a recently uplifted desert, one may be walking across flat land and suddenly meet a vertical drop-off into an arroyo.

In the middle stage of an arid landscape's erosion cycle much of the original flat surface between streams still exists, but now steep-walled arroyos have become steep-walled canyons. Visitors to the Monarch Butterfly Ecological Reserve and Los Azufres Park (in Chapter 5, The Mexican Plateau) traveling Highway 6 between Atlacomulco in the state of México, and Maravatio, Michoacán, will see a classic arid highland in its middle stage of erosion. In some places along Highway 6 it is possible to pull off the road and drive right to a canyon's edge, sit there in the car, and spit into an abyss!

In the last stage of the arid erosion cycle, level canyon floors coalesce to form broad, level plains mantled with sands, gravels, and general dirt left from millennia of upland erosion. In these landscapes, for one reason or another, hills or mountains are sometimes left standing in the plains. As might be expected, they have steep sides and flat tops; these flat tops are actually relics of the ancient plain existing before the uplifting. The flat-topped hills are *mesas*; if the top is fairly rounded, with only a limited flat area, but still with very steep sides, it's a butte.

Mature arid landscapes occur along the extreme northeastern side of the Mexican Plateau, just west of Ciudad Acuña, across from Del Rio, Texas.

Of course the most stunning desert setting is one populated with sand dunes. What an experience it is to sit atop a sea of dunes at dawn or dusk when stark dune-shadows form ever-changing arabesques. Among the dunes at dawn, sand grains can be heard tumbling down slopes where beetles scamper. There are dunes galore along Highway 45 in the vicinity of Samalayuca, Chihuahua, south of El Paso, Texas, and on Highways 2 and 8 crossing the Desierto de Altar in northwestern Sonora, near the Arizona border.

Paradoxically, arid landscapes, like moist ones, are mostly shaped by water erosion. However, in the desert, streambeds may lie dry for months, but then a hard rain will produce such violent, impetuous flow that during a few hours boulders are shifted around and the stream's course is possibly altered. In Mexico and the western United States, intermittently flowing desert streambeds are usually called *arroyos*. Arroyos, unlike streams in moist areas, have no floodplains.

Arroyos often carry floodwaters into extensive bowl-like depressions called *bolsons*. In rainy areas water eventually fills such basins, forming lakes. In *bolsons*, however, temporary lakes may form but then extreme heat and dryness evaporate the water, leaving flat plains. The periodically flooded level plain inside a *bolson* is called a playa. Playa soils often are encrusted with glistening, white salts precipitated from evaporated water. Broad, level, salt-covered plains are called alkali flats. Small, salty lakes in *bolson* environments are called salinas. One area with all these features comprises western Coahuila, eastern Chihuahua and northeastern Durango. In southeastern Chihuahua, just east of Ciudad Jiménez, there is the Bolsón de Mapimí.

Where arroyos debouch from mountains onto level valley floors, often they form broad fans. In desert areas, mountain slopes themselves often have an upper, steep mountain front composed of exposed rock, and a lower, less steep slope composed of sand, gravel, rocks, and other loose material. The loose material below the mountain front is called the *bajada*; the sharp break in slope where the *bajada* meets the mountain front is called the nick. Classic *bajadas* consist of coalescing fans. A general term for rock debris at the base of a cliff is talus.

Limestone Geology

Limestone bedrock produces a distinctive landscape referred to as karst topography. Mexico's Yucatán Peninsula is basically an enormous slab of limestone with classic karst topography developed on it. The motor behind karst topography is this chemical reaction: limestone (calcium carbonate) plus carbonic acid yields calcium bicarbonate (in solution).

The carbonic acid is very dilute stuff found naturally in all rainwater. The above formula says that limestone rock goes into solution, or dissolves, leaving cracks and holes. In the karst landscape these cracks and holes are fissures in the rock, caves, and sinkholes.

Limestone in rainy areas dissolves away so fast, geologically speaking, that all-limestone hills are seldom encountered. Limestone hills that do occur usually are capped by sandstone or some other rain-resistant material. In such hills, rainwater passes down through the limestone's cracks and fissures, dissolving as it goes, often honeycombing the limestone with caves. Hikers on the Juxtlahuaca Cave trip in Chapter 6, The Pacific Coast, can judge for themselves whether this process was responsible for creating that cave.

If a drop of water hangs long enough in a wet cave, the drop's water evaporates a molecule at a time, causing its dissolved limestone molecules of calcium carbonate to concentrate. Eventually the molecules recombine, forming new rock. A general term applied to many forms of calcium carbonate accumulation on cave ceilings, walls, and floors is cave travertine. Forms of cave travertine to look for include *dripstone* (stalactites, stalagmites, columns, and pillars), *flowstone*, created by water flowing in sheets over boulders, and *rimstone,* found where water overflows basins, forming slender rims. Nice examples of rimstone can be seen just below the bridge on the entrance trail at the ruin of Palenque, in Chapter 7, Chiapas. This rimstone on the earth's surface was produced by the same travertine-depositing process occurring in caves.

Sinkholes such as the one in the cornfield on the Agua Azul National Park hike, also in Chapter 7, are produced when caves collapse. In the Yucatán, big sinkholes are called *cenotes*. The Yucatán's ancient Maya considered the netherworld as existing below the waters, and their water supply usually came from *cenotes*, so sinkholes with water standing in them were regarded with reverence. At the important Maya ruin of Chichén Itzá, the Sacred Cenote, or Well of Sacrifice, received all sorts of sacrificial offerings, including jade and gold treasures, and people. At Punta Laguna in Quintana Roo, hikers may be lucky enough to see a functional Yucatec altar set up next to a *cenote* near the reserve's entrance.

On a good map of the Yucatán Peninsula, try to find decent rivers flowing in the interior, north of Highway 186. Some streams may be located, but they start and end without connecting with one another or reaching the ocean. In karst areas, underground drainage usually takes the place of regular surface rivers. Water migrates along narrow, interconnecting fissures in the limestone or, on a grander scale, it may form real subterranean rivers.

At Celestún, the beach slopes gradually into the sea. Wildlife-rich lagoons occur just inland.

Coastal Geology

Hikers at Celestún National Park, Chapter 8, The Yucatán Peninsula, see a Mexican coast that is mild and murky, with narrow sand beaches and a curious series of inland lagoons. Across the Yucatán Peninsula at Playa del Carmen (also in Chapter 8) and Cozumel, snorkelers find coral reefs, which are not present at Celestún; but Playa del Carmen does not have Celestún-type lagoons. On the Playa Ventanilla hike on the Pacific Coast (see Chapter 6), completely unlike both Celestún and Playa del Carmen, waves too large and powerful to fool with thunder onto steep-sloped sand beaches. In short, the world's coastlines are different, and Mexico has its share of examples.

When wind blows up a confused mixture of waves, it is called a sea. When broad-based waves travel from beneath the windstorm that spawned them, sometimes for thousands of miles, they are called swells. Waves rolling ashore and breaking into a thunder of foam and flow constitute a surf. If waves are choppy with steep sides, they are of local origin; if they roll ashore at slow, regal intervals and break boomingly onto the beach, they have come a long way. Big, blue combers 18 seconds apart on Mexico's Pacific Coast may have originated 6,000 miles away!

The simplest coastal erosional cycle is that which takes place on coastlines with no bays or inlets, one where the shore slopes gradually into the sea, continuing underwater as a gentle offshore slope—as at Celestún, Chapter 8, The Yucatán Peninsula.

Under such conditions, large waves break up long before they reach shore.

When a wave runs into shallow water, its crest is pushed upward and forward and it drags below, and more or less "trips" forward, tumbling into a surf. Offshore, where the underwater bases of big waves first hit shallow water, sand and mud get stirred up and redeposited into submarine embankments paralleling the coastline. With the help of storms, this embankment grows into an offshore bar or series of bars sometimes rising above the water's surface. Eventually these bars coalesce into a very long and slender island with its own sandy beach; behind the bar, what once was ocean now is a lagoon.

But it does not stop here. Mother Nature now wants to fill the lagoon with silt. During this second stage, the bar migrates toward land as the long lagoon silts up. Before the lagoon is completely filled, it holds a series of small, shallow tidal marshes or ponds—as at Celestún, in Chapter 8, The Yucatán Peninsula. The cycle ends when the lagoons fill in, becoming just more "inland," and the coastline looks rather as it did before the cycle began.

A different cycle takes place on coasts with inland ridges extending seaward and producing fingers of land or headlands alternating with narrow bays. Some ridge peaks occur as offshore islands in a line marching seaward; hikers on the Playa Ventanilla hike in Chapter 6, The Pacific Coast, will see exactly this. During this kind of coastline's youthful stage of erosion, waves carve sea cliffs on the seaward side of headlands and islands. Spits form across narrow bays, eventually connecting the sea cliffs, causing former bays to become lagoons. These lagoons silt up, forming marshes. All islands are eroded away and a coastline that once was extremely irregular becomes a continuous, fairly straight beach, disrupted here and there by occasional deltas of alluvium projecting into the sea, deposited by streams issuing from between ridges running inland.

In nature, coastlines seldom develop from young through mature stages, step-by-step. In the context of geological time, sea level changes rather frequently—low during ice ages, and high when the ice melts. Also, local geology has much to say about how erosional cycles proceed. A ridge with very hard rock, for instance, erodes very slowly, thus projecting farther into the sea as the cycle develops.

Volcanic Landscapes

Mexico is fairly active in terms of recent volcanic activity. However, most of its volcanic features are ancient, resulting from activity during the Mesozoic Era.

Magma is molten rock below the earth's surface that, if erupted by a volcano, becomes lava. The surface of a lava flow may be nearly flat, or it can be so rough that walking across it is almost impossible, as seen where Highway 15 between Guadalajara and Tepic crosses Volcán Ceboruco's moonscape-like lava field.

When eons pass and rock material around ancient volcanoes erodes away, volcanic skeletons of more resistant magmatic material can be left standing, as seen from Highway 85 in Nuevo León. Slender volcanic necks show where magma once froze in the ancient volcano's lava tube; dike ridges often radiate from the necks.

Amateur Geology in Mexico

Much of Mexico's history is colored by the fact that its highland mines have produced a bounty of lead, copper, cassiterite (the main tin ore), cinnabar (the mercury ore), sulphur, gold, and silver. Among the Mexican minerals that tourists buy today are garnet, topaz, amethyst, agate, and opal. Today in Taxco, in the Western Sierra Madre about 50 air-miles southwest of Mexico City, more than 200 shops specialize in selling silver.

In Mexico's vast arid expanses of unvegetated bare rock and soil, there are fossils, geodes, large crystals, concretions, and rocks composed of beautiful minerals. In the landscape itself, fault lines jag across mountain faces and interestingly deformed layers of different-colored rock strata lie atop one another.

In regions of igneous and metamorphic rocks, rock hounds can have a field day. Around hissing fumarole holes seen during the Los Azufres Park hike in Chapter 5, The Mexican Plateau, sometimes yellow encrustations of native sulphur are seen. Close examination of the pink porphyry encountered during the Mexiquillo Falls hike, also in Chapter 5, reveals a kind of frozen rock mush of various minerals. Beneath the hand lens there is feldspar, tiny, green phenocrysts of olivine, very small crystals of black biotite, and lots more.

In non-volcanic areas extreme desert conditions are often responsible for interesting mineralogy. Travelers traversing Durango's Bolsón de Mapimí might stumble across impressive samples of selenite and calcite—both minerals resulting from evaporation of the Bolsón's mineral-rich water. Selenite is a sometimes-beautiful, coarsely crystalline, often colorless and transparent variety of gypsum. White calcite crystals that are interestingly rhombohedrally shaped sometimes can be found an inch large or even bigger.

As an orchid is not much different from a ragweed to someone completely ignorant of and insensitive to botany, no one can get a kick from spotting tiny, green olivine phenocrysts if they do not know what they are and why they are there. And just as finding a native lady-slipper orchid in its natural setting tells a great deal to anyone knowing basic ecology, anyone with mineralogical savvy seeing the size of the olivine phenocrysts and the color of the feldspar in Mexiquillo's porphyry will be able to visualize the geological processes responsible for that region's exotic-looking landscape. Making sense of a fractured landscape of rocks and minerals conveys a real intellectual buzz!

As with botany, anyone can gather books together and teach themselves the basics of field mineralogy (see Bibliography). Such guides explain the basics of collecting rocks and minerals, and include brief surveys of crystallography so that mineral crystals can be identified by their geometric configuration.

Here is something important: Most people know not to pluck orchids or dig up cacti, but sometimes even informed individuals unthinkingly loot crystals, fossils, and the like from the landscape. All elements of the Mexican landscape belong to the Mexican people, and should be left where they are unless special permission is received to remove them. Many Mexican caves have been ravaged by greedy, unthinking collectors.

Years ago I balanced my rock-collecting urges with my concern for the landscape during a backpacking trip across Chihuahua's mineral-spectacular Copper Canyon. Instead of loading the backpack with heavy rocks, I collected vials of sand along the Río Urique. Back home, beneath a microscope, the sand grains revealed themselves as a spectacular collection of crystals and multi-hued minerals. There were even minuscule gold nuggets! Sand developed near outcrops of igneous and metamorphic rocks is much more interesting than that from ocean beaches.

Do not forget fossils and fossil-identifying field guides. Of course fossils are artifacts of sedimentary rocks, so looking for them in areas of igneous and metamorphic outcrop is fairly useless. However, the Mesozoic limestones of the Eastern Sierra Madre and Chiapas, and the much more recent Miocene and Pliocene limestones of the Yucatán bear looking at.

VEGETATION ZONES

Dissecting landscapes into vegetation zones is one time-honored way that naturalists "get a handle" on any land's biotic diversity. It makes sense to emphasize plants in a book like this because as we travel across the landscape it is the plants we see. Here are the steps to using vegetation zones "to get a handle" on Mexico's biodiversity:

1. Visiting a particular vegetation zone, develop a clear mental picture of what that zone is like, and strongly associate that mental image with the zone's name.

2. While traveling, always notice where the zone occurs in relation to other zones, and to temperature, elevation, and precipitation gradients. Eventually you will be able to predict the presence of specific vegetation zones on a map, and plants and animals will "make sense" in terms of their being where they are.

3. Upon reading or hearing anything interesting about nature, "file" that information in the appropriate vegetation-zone mental pigeonhole. Put what is learned from a TV program about acorn woodpeckers into the oak–pine zone pigeonhole, and then the next time that zone is visited, remember to look for acorn woodpeckers. Notebooks help. If you do not have an appropriate mental pigeonhole for a fabulous piece of information, then you know where one of your next trip destinations needs to be. . . .

How many plant communities does Mexico have? Dennis Breedlove, the dean of Chiapas botany, designates nineteen distinct vegetation zones for Chiapas. For the state of Veracruz, Mexican master-botanist Arturo Gómez-Pompa defines twenty. This book, just concerning itself with the main zones hikers are likely to notice, looks at eleven.

The botanical world uses some very specialized terminology when talking about vegetation zones. In Chiapas, for example, Breedlove speaks of "Lower Montane Rain Forests," "Semi-Evergreen Seasonal Forests," and "Lowland Riparian Forests." Biologists need such scholarly designations to be precise about what they are saying.

However, in this book, for the sake of not getting too bogged down, evocative but non-standardized labels are employed. Here simple thorn forests and savannas are talked about, and foot-long names are avoided.

The main problem with all vegetation-zone maps, including Figure 8 in this book, is that they give the impression that on one side of the line you are in one zone, then the moment you cross the line, you are in another. That is seldom the case. Typically one zone subtly intergrades with another. At least three kinds of intergrading are seen in Mexico.

One type occurs when islands of the vegetation zone being approached begin appearing inside the zone being left. As the new vegetation type is approached, its islands increase in size and frequency until finally they coalesce. Soon the former vegetation type exists only as islands within the new zone. Finally, islands of the former type completely disappear.

A second kind of intergrading, which may coincide with the first, is through the gradual displacement of species. For example, traveling from grassland into mesquite, long before pure mesquite forest is recognizable, widely spaced mesquite trees begin appearing where earlier there was just grass. As the mesquite zone is approached, mesquites begin growing closer together. Eventually it becomes hard to walk through the mesquite's densely entangled, scratchy branches. Such a pure stand would certainly qualify as a textbook example of the mesquite zone, but just where did the zone begin? A "classic" stand of mesquite looks and feels utterly different from the "classic" grassland, but usually no precise boundary separates them.

A third kind of intergrading occurs where fingers of other vegetation zones penetrate larger zones, as where canyons, arroyos, and streams pass across the desert. Along an arroyo through the desert, shrubs and small trees take advantage of the extra measure of water, creating vibrant ribbons of green snaking across the desert's grayness.

In Mexico, west of the Western Sierra Madre, desert usually evolves into thorn forest; east of the Western Sierra Madre, desert usually evolves into grassland.

Desert

Mexico's deserts are not wastelands. They are complex ecosystems supporting rainbows of exquisitely adapted plants and animals. In Baja's northern desert, the arboreal salamander copes with long dry periods by unsalamanderly climbing of trees and moving into mouse nests. North America's common groundsel is a soft-leafed wildflower that loves moist, cool spots, but on this book's deserty Xoconostle hike in Chapter 4, The Gulf Coast, a species of groundsel is encountered with massive, rigid, usually leafless stems and a bulging base that stores water. In the desert, Mother Nature's penchant for pragmatism and innovation surprises and delights.

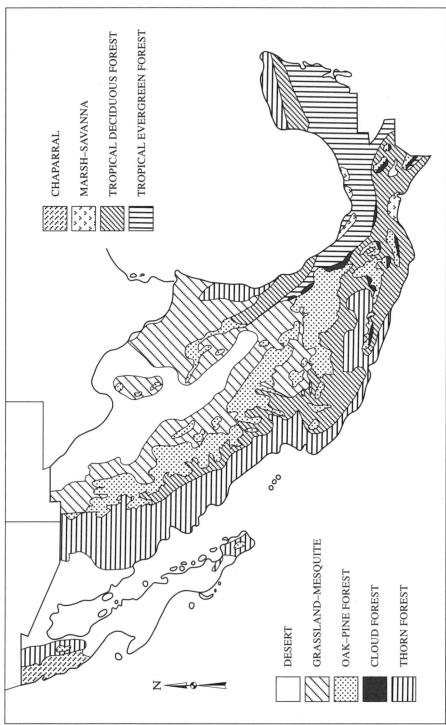

Figure 8 Mexico's major vegetation zones

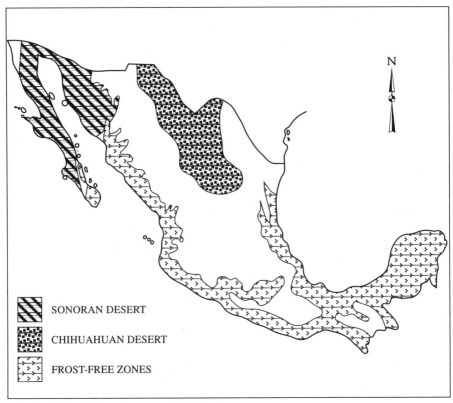

N

SONORAN DESERT

CHIHUAHUAN DESERT

FROST-FREE ZONES

Figure 9 Mexico's deserts and frost-free zones

Figure 9 shows that Mexico's two main deserts, the Sonoran and Chihua-huan, both lie in the north. In most cases the Sonoran is the hotter and drier of the two, yet also the one with the greatest variety of plants and animals. The Sonoran pleases with its wild diversity, the Chihuahuan with soul-pleas-ing, horizon-to-horizon, otherworldly immensity.

Traveling across the barren, dusty expanses of the high-elevation valley floor in Central Mexico, seeing nothing but a few magueys and maybe a runty, scraggly peppertree or two, anyone can be forgiven for believing themselves to be in a desert—even though the vegetation map in Figure 8 designates most of that area as mostly lying within the oak–pine forest zone. . . .

Do not confuse abused, neglected, barren wasteland with real desert. Before the Spanish arrived, most of the unvegetated, dusty expanses now typical of the Mexican Plateau's valley floor were indeed mantled with oak–pine forests. But these forests have been destroyed and replaced with mea-ger agriculture, weediness, and barrenness. This is not desert, but erosion and ecological destruction.

Why not draw the vegetation map showing what is really present instead of what was or can be? That would require too large a map with too much detail. Besides, even around Mexico City on certain steep slopes, remnants

In Chiapas a black sheep helps perpetuate an ecological "desert" by nibbling herbage so close to the ground that few other herbivores can survive.

of oak–pine forest still can be spotted; the land definitely *wants* to be mantled with oak–pine.

Mexico's remaining vegetation zones are more accurately portrayed on the map in Figure 8. However, even for these, plant-zone intergradation, the occurrence of islands of zones too small to appear on the map, and humanity's disruptive influences must always be kept in mind.

The diverse Sonoran Desert manifests at least seven distinct vegetation types. Because Mexico's part of the Sonoran occurs entirely on the Baja Peninsula and in the Pacific Coast region, that desert's zones are analyzed in those chapters, 3 and 6 respectively. Within the Chihuahuan Desert, vegetation ranges from grassland to dense, almost pure stands of creosote bush or mesquite. Since Mexico's Chihuahuan Desert occurs entirely on the Mexican Plateau, its vegetation is considered in greater detail in Chapter 5.

GRASSLAND-MESQUITE

One might expect grasslands to constitute one zone and stands of mesquite another, but in most of Mexico, grass and mesquite mingle so intimately that considering them apart would be unnatural. About one-fifth of Mexico once supported grassland–mesquite; what is left is very quickly being converted to irrigated farms, ranches, and, sadly, wasteland. Starting with very dry desert and moving toward areas of greater rainfall, grassland–mesquite fits into the sequence of vegetation types as follows:

Desert➤ **Grassland–Mesquite**➤ [Tropical Deciduous Forest]➤ Oak–Pine Forest

Tropical deciduous forest is bracketed because it does not always occur between grassland–mesquite and oak–pine forest; it occurs only toward the south, where increasing rainfall permits its development.

Of course the "stars" of grassland–mesquite are mesquite and various species of grass. Mesquite, a shrub or small tree in the bean family, is so rugged and adaptable that it prospers from western Louisiana, southern Kansas, and southern Utah and Nevada south through all arid areas of Mexico, through Central America, clear to Chile in South America! Usually it stands between six and ten feet high, and bears two short spines at the base of each leaf.

Anyone seeing a mesquite seedling surviving on what appears to be intolerably hot, dry soil just has to ask: How can this seedling survive long enough for its roots to reach a water supply, which must be very far below the ground? One answer is that mesquite seedlings hardly grow at all above ground until their roots do reach sufficient water. Mesquite roots can penetrate sixty feet below the soil's surface.

Mesquite is an important food and cover plant for wildlife; Native Americans ground the fruit pods into a coarse flour called *pinole*, used for making a heavy kind of cake. Gum exuding from the trunks was eaten as candy and used as a pottery-mending cement and also a black dye. Its wood is superb firewood. For anyone interested in the heady experience of knowing a world of things about one plant, this is a good species to learn about because it is abundant and fascinating. B. B. Simpson's *Mesquite: Its Biology in Two Desert Ecosystems* (Stroudsburg, Penn.: Dowden, Hutchinson and Ross, 1977) tells all you want to know (see Bibliography). In northwestern Mexico, in Sonora and Chihuahua, mesquite often grows with ironwood, foothill paloverde, and brittlebush.

The main native grass in the grassland–mesquite zone is one called grama grass. Unlike most grasses, this one is easy to identify in its flowering and fruiting stages because its inflorescence, or array of flowers, looks like a cute little false eyelash! In Chihuahua, Durango, and Zacatecas, blue grama once dominated vast treeless and shrubless "short-grass plains." Today this land has been so overgrazed and altered that bushes and small trees have invaded, drastically changing the landscape's original appearance.

Besides grama grass, common grasses in northeastern Mexico include purple three-awn grass, Texas tridens, and hairy tridens, the latter being an

Mesquite is easy to identify from its snapbean-shaped pods and leaves that resemble two feathers joined at the base.

indicator species for overgrazed land. In transition zones where grassland merges with scrubby oak, besides grama grass there are species of three-awn grass, lovegrass, muhlygrass, and bluestem. Once the great lowland (*Bajío*) of Guanajuato, Jalisco, and Michoacán was probably luxuriantly mantled with bunchgrasses—grasses that grow in dense clumps. However, the soil of this great plain, like that of the North American prairie, was incredibly rich, and has long since fallen into cultivation.

Easterners crossing into Mexico from southern Texas enjoy a good look at grassland–mesquite along Highway 85 between Nuevo Laredo and Monterrey, and along Highway 101 between Matamoros and Ciudad Victoria. In northern Nuevo León, mesquite often shares dominance with shrubby species of acacia such as the hairy-leafed Wright acacia and a borage-family member called *anacahuita*. During the northern winter, *anacahuita* puts on a real show with two-inch-wide white, funnel-shaped, five-lobed, starlike flowers at the tips of its branches; its leaf undersurfaces are simple, oval, and white with felt.

Farther south, sweet acacia, probably the most common acacia, and lead-tree sometimes dominate. Among these shrubs often appear various species of prickly-pear cactus and a small (not over ten feet), sparsely branched yucca.

On low limestone ridges, Mexican buckeye sometimes appears; unrelated to North American buckeyes, it is actually a member of the soapberry family.

Oak–Pine Forest

At one time about a quarter of Mexico was covered with oak–pine forests. But oaks and pines are useful trees, and where they grow rain comes fairly regularly, and rain enables agriculture, so today most of Mexico's former oak–pine forests have disappeared.

On the dry Mexican Plateau, if we start in the central valley and travel

The Aztec pine, restricted to higher elevations, bears small cones and long needles in clusters of three.

any direction into the uplands, or if we climb a mountain in arid northeastern Mexico, oak–pine forest relates to its neighboring vegetation like this:

Grassland–Mesquite→   **Oak–Pine Forest→**   Boreal Forest

Lupines, with digitately compound leaves, are common wildflowers in high elevation pine forests.

Starting in the hot, dry Pacific-slope lowlands and ascending the Western Sierra Madre, except in the very dry parts of the region's northern expanses, one passes through this sequence of vegetation zones:

Thorn Forest→ Tropical Deciduous Forest→ **Oak–Pine Forest**→ Boreal Forest

Lower mountains may be too low for boreal forest to appear. Following the same elevation change on the moister Gulf side, this time climbing into the Eastern Sierra Madre, we usually get this sequence:

Tropical Deciduous Forest→ **Oak–Pine Forest**→ Cloud Forest→ Boreal Forest

In northern Mexico, oak–pine forests appear at 4,000 to 5,000 feet; in the south, they usually do not appear below 6,500 feet.

Anyone wishing to know the names of plants dominating each vegetation zone can find oak–pine forests awfully frustrating. Standley's outdated *Trees and Shrubs of Mexico* (Chicago: Field Museum of Natural History, Botanical Series, Vol. III, 1930) lists 112 oak species for Mexico; plodding through his oak keys is worse than picking cactus glochids from fingers. Except near the U.S. border where illustrated field guides for the United States sort out the species rather elegantly, one seldom knows whether the name garnered for a Mexican oak is accurate. Among the most common Mexican species are the Emory oak in northern Mexico and the wrinkle-leaf oak in the south. Identification is not made easier by the fact that oaks often hybridize in nature, producing intermediate forms.

The pines are somewhat easier, and Standley's *Trees and Shrubs* pine key must be one of his best, listing "only" twenty-six species. Probably Mexico's best known and easy-to-recognize pine is the stately Montezuma pine, occurring from Durango and Zacatecas south through Chiapas. It has five long, *drooping* needles per bundle. Unfortunately, several other pines also bear long, drooping needles. The jelecote pine's needles are even longer and droopier—but typically it has three needles per bundle, not five.

It is characteristic for the oak–pine zone's lower-elevation element to be composed of oaks (no pines) intermingled with species from the zone right below it. Higher up, pines appear among the oaks. If the slope continues high enough, eventually pines completely displace oaks. Around Chiapas's San Cristóbal, oaks come in at around 6,500 feet, and pines at around 9,000.

In the oak–pine zone's lower, oak-dominated region, junipers and cypresses are often very conspicuous. In northwestern Mexico, the Arizona cypress abounds; farther south, Bentham's and Lindley's cypress take its place. The two most common junipers are the alligator and drooping junipers, the former with craggy, alligator-skin bark, the latter possessing elegant, drooping branches. The wax alder, with reddish brown branches, neatly toothed leaves, and miniature, woody cones, typically occurs along streams in the oak–pine zone. Also stream-loving, the Mexican alder has opposite, ashlike leaves and flat-topped clusters of tiny, white flowers or dark-blue berries.

Thorny Mexican hawthorns, producing cherry-sized, orange fruits in the fall, often invade clearings in oak–pine forests. During August and September

The alligator juniper, common in northern Mexico's rocky uplands, derives its name from the texture of its bark.

in northern and central Mexico, lucky hikers might spot the lovely, dainty, waxy-white–blossomed lily-family member called Mexican star. Around Mexico City, look for one of Mexico's most beautiful wildflowers, the tiger flower, a member of the iris family. Each tiger flower blossom is composed of three brilliantly red tepals (petal-like items) with dark purple spots and subtended by three smaller, bright yellow, similarly spotted tepals.

Boreal Forest

Boreal forests are similar in structure and ecology to Canada's northernmost forests. They are the highest-elevation forests, the forests at the tree line of the highest mountains. They are not shown on the vegetation map in

Figure 8 because their "islands" are too small to illustrate at this scale. Mexico's most extensive boreal forests occupy high volcanic peaks along the Transverse Volcanic Belt between the 18th and 20th parallels; it is also on a few of the highest peaks of both the Eastern and Western Sierra Madre chains. Here is how boreal forest relates to neighboring vegetation zones:

Oak–Pine Forest➤ **Boreal Forest**➤ Alpine Meadow➤ Lichens on Stone

On the Volcán Malinche hike in Chapter 5, The Mexican Plateau, as the hiker ascends through the oak–pine's uppermost zone where pines finally usurp all oaks, eventually fir and alder appear among the pines; this announces the boreal zone. Still higher, pines and alders drop out, leaving nearly pure stands of fir, and eventually the fir gives way to a new set of pines adapted to very high elevations. These pines are short, stubby, and widely spaced; the ground between them is thickly mantled with bunchgrass. Though the exact altitudinal limits of the boreal forest and its subdivisions vary with slope, latitude, exposure, and local topography, these are the subdivisions within the boreal forest:

7,500–8,500 feet	Pine–Alder–Fir
7,500–9,500 feet	Fir
9,500–11,800 feet	Open Pine–Bunchgrass

Typically the boreal forest's lower-elevation pines are the Montezuma and Mexican white pines. The alder is one called *aile*, with exceedingly coarse, prominent veins on its leaves' lower surfaces. The fir is the sacred fir, sacred because it sprouts new twigs at right angles to the stem, forming cruciform twigs pregnant with meaning to Mexico's faithful, who adorn altars with them. Firs, unlike pines, bear one needle per bundle and, unlike both pines and spruces, hold their cones erect, not drooped. Maybe sacred firs are also sacred because they are such imposing, handsome plants, and the pure air and brilliant sunlight characteristic of their lofty realm can evoke ecclesiastical feelings.

The widely spaced pines occupying the boreal forest's uppermost reaches typically are timberline Montezuma pines—a species different from the regular Montezuma pine. Bunchgrasses, so well developed in the terrain of the Volcán Malinche hike, include two species of muhly, one of which is mountain muhly, also found on high mountains in the western United States. Also there are species of needlegrass, a species of hairgrass, and a fescue species. Besides pine, woody species are represented by stunted Mexican cypresses and an arbutuslike heath-family member with leathery, evergreen leaves and white or pink flowers, called *capulincillo* in central Mexico.

If a mountain rises high enough for bunchgrasses to completely take over from all tree species, alpine meadows are formed. Atop the very highest peaks, even bunchgrasses give way, leaving only mosses and lichens on rocks. Finally, there is perpetual snow. . . .

Cloud Forest

Sometimes high mountain ridges are so frequently enveloped in clouds that cloud forests develop. Oak–pine forests atop mountains not high enough to break into boreal forest frequently take on cloud-forest features. In other words, cloud forests are often high-elevation oak–pine forests with added diversity because of the air's very high humidity. Mainly, gardens of epiphytic plants—bromeliads, begonias, orchids, peperomias, ferns, mosses, et cetera—appear on tree branches. The peak of Cerro Huitepec in San Cristóbal's PRONATURA Reserve (see Chapter 7, Chiapas) tends in the cloud-forest direction, but well-developed cloud forests have many more epiphytes than are there.

One of the great surprises of Mexican botany is that many of the cloud forest's dominant tree species are identical to or very closely related to—of all things—forest trees of the Eastern United States. The story is that the ice ages drove the Eastern United States' biota far south into Mexico. When the last great glacier receded some 12,000 years ago, part of the Eastern-forest organisms migrated back north, keeping pace with the retreating glacier front, but others found their preferred relatively cool, moist habitats by migrating up mountain slopes. Today on certain slopes and ridge tops, especially in upland Chiapas and along the Gulf side of the Eastern Sierra Madre, some of these species still survive in relict populations.

Among the relict trees are sweetgum and blackgum, both characteristic trees of the United States' eastern forest. During 12,000 years of genetic isolation, some species have evolved into special Mexican forms. Mexico's sweetgum, though still considered the same species as Eastern North America's, seems to possess a higher percentage of three-pointed leaves than their northern counterparts, where five-pointed leaves predominate.

Other taxa have evolved into completely new species. The dogwood observed at Yerba Buena Reserve in Chapter 7, Chiapas, for example, is obviously closely related to Eastern North America's flowering dogwood, but the bracts beneath its flower cluster, instead of being large and white, are small and greenish. Cloud-forest understory often is particularly interesting because of the presence of tree ferns—real ferns up to thirty feet high!

Thorn Forest

Mexican thorn forests, as described in this book, are fairly low (head-high to twenty feet, more or less) and composed predominantly of spiny shrubs and small trees, mostly of the bean family. Thorn forests inhabit fairly dry regions. Here is the zone's usual relationship to other vegetation zones: [Grassland–Mesquite]→ **Thorn Forest**→ [Tropical Deciduous Forest/Chaparral]→ Oak–Pine Forest

Grassland–mesquite is in brackets because in some places, especially along the southern Pacific Coast, thorn forest extends to the coast without an intervening grassland–mesquite zone. Tropical deciduous forest and chaparral similarly are bracketed because in some places it is simply too dry for these zones to form. In Mexico, chaparral as we define it occurs only in extreme northwestern Baja.

Mexico's thorn forests are found in three main areas, each constituting long, slender belts along the coast. The largest strand lies within the Pacific Coast region, extending from the Sonoran Desert's southernmost point, south to near Acapulco. Forming a strip about 50 miles wide, sometimes it is interrupted by patches of marsh–savanna or tropical deciduous forest. The second big strip of thorn forest lies along the Gulf Coast from the vicinity of Monterrey to north of Veracruz; the third occurs along the coast of northern Yucatán. Nearly everywhere it intergrades imperceptibly with contiguous zones.

Figure 8's vegetation map shows more thorn forest than other similar maps. That is because when grasslands are overgrazed and tropical deciduous forest is ravaged by firewood gatherers and slash-and-burn farmers, the plants that often invade are common, very tough, spiny members of the bean family—plants similar or identical to those forming genuine thorn forests. Botanists may not consider these weedy, invading species as legitimate citizens of textbook-style thorn forests, but to hikers whose arms and legs get scratched, "thorn forest" is apt enough.

Most bean-family members of the thorn forest bear twice-pinnately compound leaves—leaves of which the main divisions are themselves divided into smallish leaflets, usually imparting to the leaves a vaguely ferny or feathery appearance.

Because so many thorn forests species are look-alike, small trees and bushes belonging to the bean family, identifying the various species becomes a challenge. However, learning the names of the various species is fun, not only because it reveals the zone's surprising biological diversity, but also because it gives a real intellectual and maybe even spiritual buzz to work with so many "variations on the spiny, ferny, beany theme." In fact, it is such fun that in appendix B at the back of this book, I have provided a "key" for "keying out" Mexico's common thorn-forest, bean-family trees and shrubs.

Of all the thorn-forest, feathery-leafed, bean-family trees and bushes mentioned in the key in appendix B, acacias have the largest number of commonly encountered species; some botanists count more than fifty Mexican species! In Mexico the most common acacia is sweet acacia—sweet because of its perfumy flowers. Learn this prolific species first, then later notice how all other acacias differ from it. Much of the year, sweet acacia bears clusters of thick, stubby-looking, dark, two-inch-long pods. Despite its homely appearance and commonness, sweet acacia is of more than just ecological value; tannin can be extracted from its bark and fruits, perfume from its flowers, and ointments and medicine from its flowers and fruits.

Unlike sweet acacia, many acacias are armed with outlandishly huge, broad-based thorns. Often these thorns are hollow and provided with tiny holes that enable ants to stay inside them. This is a beautiful example of mutualism: the acacia provides the ants a place to stay, and anyone brushing against an ant-colonized acacia will discover how ants swarm onto intruders and bite! Among thorn forests' big-thorned acacias are the boat-thorn and hat-thorn acacias along mainland Mexico's western coast, the bullhorn acacia of Mexico's tropics in general, and the flat-thorn acacia of Sinaloa and Nayarit.

Not all the thorn forest's shrubs and small trees are bean-family members. One genus, *Condalia*, of the buckthorn family, has at least three similar species in the thorn forest, the most common being lotebush of northwestern Mexico. *Condalias* are scraggly, up to ten feet tall, with small, simple leaves adorning spinelike stems jutting away from the main branches at right angles. Of course, Mexico's devout *campesinos*, seeing crucifixes wherever right angles occur, call lotebush *crucillo*, or "little cross."

The *guayacán*, of the caltrop family, is one non-bean-family member that looks like a bean tree because it has pinnately compound leaves. However, this spineless species' compound leaves are opposite; bean trees bear alternate leaves. Saponin-rich medicine called lignum vitae is extracted from *guayacán*'s wood.

Among the most spectacular citizens of the thorn forest, at least during the northern winter, are two species of morning glory tree. Of course, morning glories are supposed to be vines, so seeing large white morning glory blossoms on trees is a treat. Cacti also grace certain thorn forests. A tall, saguarolike, conspicuously ribbed, columnar cactus along the Pacific Coast is the comb cactus; its burry fruits can serve as hair combs.

A kind of thorn forest extends up the sweltering, broad Río Balsas valley, wedged between the Southern Sierra Madre and the Mexican Plateau. This area harbors such interesting and fairly unique plants that botanists often consider it a special vegetation zone. The *autopista* between Mexico City and Acapulco dips into it south of Iguala, and so does Highway 134 between Toluca and Zihuatanejo, in the vicinity of Ciudad Altamirano. A tall, columnar cactus called *órgano* is characteristic of this zone. There are also prickly-pear cacti, bullhorn acacias, and fan palms. Just southwest of Ciudad Altamirano, the dense bunchgrass on some hills is a species of bluestem.

Marsh–Savanna

Savannas are grassy areas, sometimes extensive, populated by a few widely spaced trees. Marshes are rather waterlogged places, similarly with few or no trees; in Mexico both savannas and marshes usually appear along the coasts. The two kinds of vegetation are lumped here because often it is hard to tell them apart. No flowchart is provided because these zones may appear without regard to contiguous zones.

Sometimes just a quick glimpse reveals whether marsh or savanna is at hand. Clearly the extensive grassy area with a few widely spaced trees along Highway 180 between Veracruz and San Andrés Tuxtla is a marsh because of the many broad, sluggish waterways running through it. However, along Chiapas's Pacific Coast, extensive grasslands with a few widely spaced trees are tinder-box dry during the dry season, when the locals indulge in an orgy of burning fields and forests (burning favors grasses over woody species), yet often this same ground is flooded for long periods during the wet season. Is this a marsh or a savanna?

The most conspicuous dominant tree of many Mexican savannas is the gourd tree, a member of the bignonia family. Two features make this tree memorable. First, its curious compound leaves look like coarse clover leaves with long, winged petioles and are attached to the stem in such a way that from afar the tree looks like thick-limbed, green-painted, fake-prop trees at a kindergarten play. There is no sense of leaves arising from slender, limber twigs at the end of major branches. Second, gourd tree fruits look like large cannon-balls or grapefruits. One glimpse, and you will never forget the gourd tree.

Another common savanna tree is the pickle tree, a member of the malphigia family. Its opposite, entire, elliptic, evergreen leaves are yellowish below, and its yellow flowers grow in elongate clusters. Its rather sour fruits can be eaten raw, or added to anything needing a weird, tart taste. Its Nahuatl name, *Nantizinzocotl*, means "sour fruit for mothers and old people." Apparently pregnant Nahuatls, instead of craving pickles, covet pickle-tree fruits.

In treeless marshes, most grasses and grasslike plants belong to the same genera found in North American marshes, but they are different species. There are cutgrasses, paspalums, sedges, rushes, cyperuses, beak-rushes, and bulrushes. But Mexico's species are generally larger and coarser than North America's—they are real *macho* species. Curiously, Mexico's cattail is the same as North America's common species. Wild plantains, related to banana trees, with broad, glossy-green, tonguelike leaves surmounted by large, spectacularly red and orange flowers subtended by red and black bracts, also grow here.

Along watercourses it is often possible to spot one of Mexico's most beautiful trees, the Guiana chestnut. This member of the tropical bombax family usually is not taller than ten or fifteen feet, yet its exquisite blossoms grow nearly a foot long—outrageously large for such a small tree. Five white petals curve back revealing a shaving-brushlike cluster of hundreds of stiff, reddish brown stamens. Like its relative the kapok tree, the Guiana chestnut's leaves are palmately compound.

Especially along the coasts, certain marshes and savannas are strikingly populated with palms. Sometimes the palms are widely scattered but other times they form dense stands; frequently they occupy broad, grassy, savannalike areas. Numerous palm species are represented.

Found mostly along southern Mexico's coasts, the cohune palm is the tallest and most showy Mexican palm. With gracefully recurved fronds over twenty feet long, it looks like a gigantic green upside-down feather-duster stuck in the ground. In Chiapas, a slightly different, smaller, but no less pretty species is the corozo palm.

Most palm fronds are divided pinnately—like feathers with barbs arising from the shaft. However, in Mexico a whole group of palms possess fronds with segments arranged like fingers on a hand; they are palmately compound. Often in the wetter soils of savannas and drier soils of marshes, there are extremely dense colonies of a smallish, clump-forming palm with palmately compound fronds, called paurotis. Paurotis leaves are two to three feet in diameter, light yellow-green above and bluish to silver-green below. Though paurotis can grow thirty feet tall, usually it is smaller. Its petioles are bordered with stout, orange-colored teeth. This same species forms extensive thickets in the Florida Everglades.

A third kind of palm frond at first looks fan-palmlike, but really its petiole continues as a sturdy midrib up through the frond and curves to one side, and the frond segments on the outside are more developed than on the inside. This special kind of palm frond is said to be "costate," and some of the best-known palm species have such fronds. In southern Texas and adjoining Tamaulipas, Texas palmettos, growing thirty to fifty feet tall, possess such fronds. So do very common Mexican fan palms and cabbage palmettos, so typical of the U.S. Deep South, with trunks seldom exceeding seven feet.

Mangrove

The word "mangrove" applies both to certain kinds of trees and to the special, incredibly rich ecological community that arises around them. Mangrove swamps, called *manglares* by Mexicans, occur in lagoons and estuaries along the Gulf Coast south of southern Tamaulipas, on the Pacific Coast south of Sonora and Tiburón Island, and on the Baja Peninsula, on the Gulf of California side, south of Santa Rosalía. Because they form such tiny slivers along the coasts, they do not show up on the vegetation map in Figure 8. At Celestún, visitors going to see the flamingos should ask their boatman to point out *manglares*. Mangrove trees appear as a ribbon of small, dark-green trees rooted in shallow water at the water's edge.

Red mangrove, in the mangrove family, is the species that really captures people's imagination. Its numerous forking, above-water, stiltlike stems arch into the water, causing the trees to look as if they were tiptoeing atop the water. Red mangrove seeds germinate while still attached to the tree, each seed issuing a single, stiff, sharp-pointed, downward-projecting root that, when the seed finally falls, stabs into the mud, instantly rooting a mangrove seedling.

A red-mangrove colony's myriad interlocking prop-roots create the ultimate in impenetrable thickets. These provide safe havens for fish and anchoring places for mollusks; also, they do a wonderful job collecting silt. The accumulated silt eventually becomes solid ground. Red mangrove, then, helps extend shorelines seaward. Whenever hurricanes or human developers destroy mangrove swamps, centuries or even millennia of silt-particle-by-silt-particle ecosystem-building are being squandered.

Black mangrove, of the vervain family, also forms impenetrable thickets. However, instead of standing on stilts, it is branched like a regular bush. Its peculiarity is that from below the mud and shallow water its roots form multitudinous brown, slender, fingerlike items called pneumatophores that rise straight up a foot or more above the water, to absorb air.

Dense bushes at the edge of tidal flats, but without stilts or pneumatophores, might be mangroves in the white-mangrove family. Two species are possible; both possess simple, entire, leathery, evergreen leaves, and clusters of smallish, reddish brown, leathery fruits at the end of branches. The way to distinguish the two species is that one, the button mangrove, bears alternate leaves, while the other, white mangrove, has opposite ones.

Mexican fan palms bear costate fronds; the bases of old frond petioles remain on young trunks, crisscrossing one another.

Coastal Strand

Where the shoreline consists of sandy beaches, as at Celestún in Chapter 8, The Yucatán Peninsula, and Playa Ventanilla in Chapter 6, The Pacific Coast, a highly specialized assemblage of plants grows not far from the water's edge. Again, because this vegetation zone is so small, it is not shown in Figure 8.

Plants here must root in sterile, salt-saturated sand and survive the beach's potent sunlight, heat, and stiff breezes. Consequently, leaves of many coastal strand species are tough and leathery, and protected by a glossy, waxy cuticle. At Playa Ventanilla, hikers will see shrubs sculpted by the wind into ground-hugging bonsai.

The first strand of vegetation atop the first landward ridge of sand in a coastal strand may be only five or so yards wide. Among the tough plants able to live here are the beach evening primrose, with large, showy, bright yellow, surprisingly fragile-looking blossoms. Its vegetative parts are mantled with a dense coat of short, gray hairs, which reflects sunlight and deflects wind. The railroad vine is an equally tough morning glory with funnel-shaped, rose-purple blossoms up to four and a half inches across; its large, round, leathery leaves are encased in a waxy cuticle.

Salt marsh grass sprouts from rhizomes, forming large colonies in coastal salt marshes, and it also appears here. It is a coarse, wiry grass with leaf blades less than one-tenth of an inch wide; its inflorescence consists of four spikes on which all flowers grow on the lower side of the rachis. Sea oat is another coastal-strand grass that reproduces by rhizomes; its strongly compressed flowering head consists of numerous nodding spikelets.

Once the first sand ridge is passed, a whole new community of plants appears. One of the most common and easy-to-identify shrubs here is the sea grape. Its leathery, evergreen leaves are *round* and its fruits, when present, really look like clusters of grapes. Being a member of the buckwheat family, its stems, next to each leaf petiole, are encircled by conspicuous "stipular sheaths." Often sea grapes grow with the rose-family member called icaco coco-plum, with alternate, entire, almost-round, leathery, evergreen leaves and plumlike fruit.

One reason round leaves are common in this zone is that round objects expose less surface area per unit of volume than objects of other shapes, and this cuts down on surface evaporation.

Tropical Deciduous Forest

When sufficient rainfall permits tropical deciduous forest to form, its usual position relative to other zones, moving from low-elevation dryness to higher moistness, is:

Thorn Forest *or* Grassland–Mesquite➤   **Tropical Deciduous Forest**➤
Oak–Pine Forest

Making the same dry-to-wet journey, but staying in the tropics *at sea level*, the sequence changes to this:

[Thorn Forest]➤ **Tropical Deciduous Forest**➤ Tropical Rain Forest

Thorn forest is in brackets because sometimes, as on southernmost Mexico's Pacific Coast, sufficient rainfall permits tropical deciduous forest to extend practically to the sea without thorn forest intervening.

Tropical deciduous forest occurs in frostless tropical areas with distinct dry seasons. Some botanists prefer the name "short-tree forest," which alludes to the fact that this forest's trees are not nearly as tall as those in tropical rain forests. A 100-foot tree would be a good-size one in this zone.

Tropical deciduous forests are characteristic for the Mexican Plateau's foothills on both the Pacific and Gulf sides. A nearly continuous, approximately 1,500-mile strand follows the Western Sierra Madre foothills from southern Sonora all the way south past the Guatemalan border. Usually it occurs about 50 miles inland. On the Gulf Coast this zone lies a bit farther inland; the Tetlama hike in Chapter 4, The Gulf Coast, visits it at Tamazunchale. During the summer rainy season, tropical deciduous forest is as hot, humid, rank, and green as can be imagined; even weeds are spectacular. However, during the winter dry season, the many leafless trees, the air's relatively low humidity, and occasional chilly nights cause this zone to feel "Indian-summery" to North Americans; it feels nice.

Because the zone's abundant rainfall favors humans' industry, most of Mexico's tropical deciduous forests have been converted to ranches, orchards, fields of corn, beans, and nopal cactus, and a patchwork of tremendously weedy, brush-and-vine-choked regenerating fields. Today only a few remnants display its "classic canopy structure" consisting of three distinct layers. Usually mature trees occur only in the most inaccessible places.

The tropical deciduous forest zone occurs in such widely separated locations that it is especially hard to designate dominant species for the zone. In the foothills of Sinaloa, about one-third of the way south on the Pacific Coast, in a site tending toward the zone's low, dry limits, typical trees include the trumpet tree, morning-glory tree, one of the kapok tree species producing brown "cotton" and called *guajilote* by the locals, and a gumbo-limbolike tree with reddish brown branches locally called *copal* (*copal* is something else in the rest of Mexico). These are rather scrawny, weedy-looking species only fifteen feet or so high. Nonetheless they are definitely different from the scratchy bean-family members typical of the thorn forest downslope in even drier territory.

Farther upslope in this same area, where more rainfall bestows a lusher aspect, trees grow fifty feet or more, and include such species as an important timber tree of the bean family, the feathery-leafed lysiloma locally called *tepeguaje*, and a tree often planted for its beauty and guava-type fruit, locally called *arrayán*. Even higher up, trees become festooned with bromeliads and other epiphytes, and draped with lianas (woody vines), which are absent in the lower, drier areas.

Some very beautiful trees often survive in even the most devastated parts of the tropical deciduous forest, sometimes protected for their beauty, other times simply because they are rugged, rapidly reproducing, weedlike plants. Among the prettiest, at least during the northern spring, are two species of bignonia-family members. During the dry season when they are leafless or semi-leafless, they put on a show with masses of large, funnel-shaped blossoms. One with rosy-colored flowers is the trumpet tree; another, with yellow blossoms, is called springbells. After flowering, both species produce palmate, kapok-treelike leaves. Another dry-season-naked tree, one with sizable, poppylike, golden blossoms, is the yellowsilk shellseed, of the cochlospermum family. In Latin, *cochlospermum* means "shell-seed"; the "yellowsilk" part of the name derives from the down on the spoonshaped seeds.

In ranch areas formerly occupied by tropical deciduous forest, often a certain small tree is seen growing in straight rows, serving as fence posts for barbed wire; just stick a twig of this species into the ground and it roots, grows, and in early spring adorns itself with myriad pink pea-blossoms. It is the *cocuite*, sometimes called mouse-killer because its leaves, ground with cooked corn, are used for poisoning rats and mice.

Tropical Evergreen Forest and Tropical Rain Forest

Take away the long dry season and consequent leaf loss of many tropical deciduous forest tree species, multiply the tropical deciduous forest's voluptuousness and overwhelming diversity by two, and the result is tropical evergreen forest. Extrapolate the trend even farther and you get the tropical rain forest. In these two zones, the dry season is more limited than in the tropical deciduous forest (perhaps nonexistent), there is little seasonal change in temperature, and most plants bear persistent, evergreen leaves.

The two forest types are being considered together here—though only the tropical evergreen forest is shown in Figure 8—because they are very similar, being composed of essentially the same species. The main difference between them is that tropical rain forest, because of greater rainfall, grows higher. Mature tropical evergreen forest canopies range from "only" about 75 to 150 feet high; the longer the dry season, the lower the trees. At Palenque (see Chapter 7, Chiapas) and Cobá (see Chapter 8, The Yucatán Peninsula), where this book's "most jungly" hikes take place, forest canopies barely reach those heights. Certain tropical rain forest trees rise 225 feet and higher.

If a "jungle" is a hot, dense forest receiving abundant rain, then both of these forest types are jungles. Sometimes one hears the Spanish word *selva* used for forests with two or more canopy layers, while a *bosque* has just one canopy level.

Tropical evergreen forest originally covered great expanses of the Chiapas lowlands, the southern Yucatán Peninsula, and here and there in Veracruz and Tabasco. Now its most extensive tracts are in the most isolated spots of Chiapas, and they are being logged at breakneck speed. In Mexico, full-fledged tropical rain forest occurs only in a few valleys along the Usumacinta River between Chiapas and Guatemala.

Because of the incredible diversity of these forests, there is no point in offering a "representative list of species." However, certain species in these forests are so important and interesting that they just have to be mentioned.

For instance, there is mahogany, with wood of legendary beauty and durability. Mahogany, of the tropical mahogany family, possesses opposite, pinnately compound leaves, causing its branches to look like those of an evergreen ash tree. In the same family as mahogany and nearly as revered for its wood—and thus equally overharvested and abused—is the *cedro*, looking like an ash tree with *alternate*, compound leaves.

Three tropical-fruit trees in this zone are famous. The main star, chico-

A large ceiba tree possesses buttresses that stabilize it in a tropical evergreen forest's soggy, shallow soil.

A strangler fig begins strangling its host tree.

zapote, is the tree whose copious white latex is boiled down to yield chicle, the traditional base for chewing gum. Today North American chewing gums are based on synthetic gums; mainly the finicky Japanese continue to buy chicozapote chicle. Chicozapote fruits—apple-sized, spherical, holding several large seeds, and colored like Irish potatoes—are among the sweetest, most tasty fruits on earth. During the late dry season, often they can be found in *mercados*. Chicozapote trees are so nondescript (simple, evergreen, entire leaves) that the best way to identify them is to look for the diagonal slashes on their straight, gray trunks, where *chicleros* have gathered latex. Chicozapotes are in the sapodilla family.

Perhaps as luscious, and also available in *mercados*, is the fruit of the mamey, likewise a member of the sapodilla family. Mamey fruits are larger than chicozapote fruits, and oblong instead of spherical. They hold just one large seed which, when thrown along the street, looks like an enormous brown cockroach. Mamey leaves are exceedingly handsome, bearing simple, entire, long, dark blades with straight veins arising from the midrib.

The ancient Maya must have treasured these fruits. However, another fruit probably was even more important to them because it could be stored for long periods of time. The ramon, of the fig family, produces half-dollar-size, roundish fruits that when boiled taste something like water chestnuts—not spectacular, but starchy and nutritious. Dried, they can be ground into meal for bread or tortillas. Ramon is such a plain-Jane tree that there is no point to describing it; just have someone in Chiapas or the Yucatán point it out.

The fig family cannot be mentioned without bringing up strangler figs. In the New World, figs are not those sweet, pear-shaped things North Americans usually think of, and American fig leaves are not "fig-leaf-shaped" like European figs. The vast majority of American fig trees bear tiny, spherical fruits that only a parrot would eat, and their leaves are invariably "simple, entire, and evergreen," just like a jillion other tropical trees.

However, American fig trees do possess certain features that make their identification easy. First, where the leaf's petiole attaches to the stem, right next to the bud, there is a faint "stipular ring" encircling the stem—a kind of scar. Second, American fig leaves have secondary veins that are straight and unbranching, herring-bonelike. Finally, many fig leaves, when torn, exude white latex.

Strangler figs begin life when a seed germinates someplace such as the crotch of a tree, producing a vine. As the vine's roots seek the ground, its stem twines around the host tree. Eventually the vine becomes robust, its stem thickens, and other stems appear. The stems coalesce around the host's trunk and the fig's branches overtop the host's branches. Gradually the strangler out-competes its host and the host weakens and dies. The strangler then is left standing in its former host's place, looking as if it had grown up the usual way. Typically on any strangler's trunk, however, one can find ropy hints of its former vininess.

Mexico is home to several strangler fig species. Some produce immense, flaring buttresses at their base—like rocket wings. In the humid forests where stranglers live, these buttresses support the big trees in the soggy soil. On the Cobá hike in Chapter 8, The Yucatán Peninsula, a wonderful strangler with multiple trunks stands along the Macanxoc Group Trail.

One last tree, the cecropia, deserves attention because it is so characteristic of the hot, humid tropics. Also a member of the fig family, cecropias are conspicuous along roadsides because they are somewhat weedy and look so strange. Cecropias are smallish, umbrella-shaped trees with slender, cylindrical trunks. The trunks are segmented like bamboo, and are so pithy that one good swing with a sharp machete cuts right through them. Cecropia leaves are deeply palmately lobed.

Cecropia trunks sometimes contain pea-size holes that, like many acacia thorns, have ants running in and out of them. The same thing is going on here as with the acacias; with mutualistic devotion, ants pay the cecropia rent by

Cecropias, of the fig family, are easy-to-identify "weed trees" characteristic of land that has been disturbed.

biting whatever critter bothers the cecropia.

When I began roaming Mexico during the 1960s, the Selva Lacandona of eastern lowland Chiapas was still one of the largest virgin "jungles" of the world. During the 1970s and 1980s, vast expanses of it disappeared, and it is still disappearing fast. A satellite photo of the region in the October 1989 issue of *National Geographic* magazine shows what has happened, almost overnight. In its place are cattle ranches, weedy cornfields, and refugee camps for displaced Guatemalans. That satellite photo ranks as the saddest picture I have ever seen.

CHAPTER 3

BAJA CALIFORNIA

The Land

Some 5 million years ago, forces associated with plate tectonics (see Chapter 2, Mexico's Natural Environment) nudged Baja California loose from the Mexican mainland. Ever since, Baja has been drifting north toward Alaska at the rate of about 2½ inches per year. In 50 million more years, Cabo San Lucas at Baja's southernmost tip will lie offshore the coast, and northern Baja, with a wedge of extreme southwestern California attached, will be nosing into Anchorage, Alaska.

For a long time, the same powerful earthly forces that send Baja skating toward Alaska have caused this part of the world to be beset with volcanic activity. Chains of ancient volcanoes form a jagged backbone for Baja, from one end to the other (see Figure 3). In the north the main chain is the Sierra de Juárez, reaching 6,496 feet high just east of Valle de Trinidad. Farther south the Sierra San Pedro Mártir chain rises to 10,157 feet at the peak called Picacho del Diablo, near the astronomical observatory in Sierra San Pedro Mártir National Park. In central and southern Baja, the volcanic spine is less spectacular, though in the far south, in the Sierra de la Laguna chain, the peak called Picacho de la Laguna reaches 7,096 feet.

Once, Baja's volcanic ridges were much more lofty and craggy than they are now. Cataviña Boulder Field in central Baja exhibits what is left of a very ancient range—granite boulders strewn in a field. In modern times, Baja's geology show has not run out of steam. Several hot springs imply the presence of very hot rock not far below Baja's landscape. Among these hot springs are one along Highway 3 at Guadalupe about 20 miles (30 km) northwest of Ensenada, and one at Ojos Negros, some 16 miles (25 km) west of Ensenada. A geothermal plant operates at Cerro Prieto 25 miles (40 km) south-southeast of Mexicali.

But Baja is the scene of other kinds of landscape-making besides plate

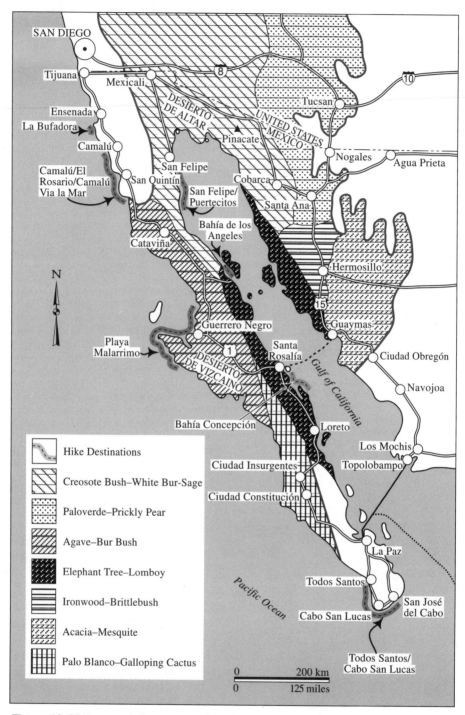

Figure 10 Main vegetation zones of the Sonoran desert

tectonics and vulcanism. In extreme northeastern Baja, the Colorado River finds its outlet into the Gulf of California among vast mudflats and "dry lakes" resulting from the Colorado River's activities. Most of the time this flat, sizzling-hot, salt-encrusted, hard-baked land is honored by *gringos* as an unbeatable setting for high-speed off-road driving, but at other times rains upstream cause flooding that changes the whole region into a quagmire.

In the vicinity of Ciudad Constitución, in the south, Highway 1 often courses atop the gently sloping outwash plain deposited along the eroding Sierra de la Giganta's western flanks. In the Vizcaíno Desert, loose sand is blown by the wind into dunes. Around Santa Rosalía on the Gulf of California coast, both gypsum and manganese have been mined; these are sedimentary minerals bespeaking long periods of evaporation of mineral-rich waters. In many shallow lagoons along Baja's coasts, evaporation vigorously continues, causing salt to precipitate from seawater. Guerrero Negro in central Baja supports the world's largest salt works; evaporation ponds lie along the road to the official whale-watching tower beside Scammon's Lagoon south of town.

Of course Baja's most transfixing feature is its aridity; the central desert usually receives only one to three inches of rain per year. As one drives the 1,050 miles from Tijuana to Cabo San Lucas, water is crossed only once, at Mulegé. Nonetheless, sometimes Baja's air becomes so hot and unstable that storms develop, dumping short and heavy summer rains called *chubascos*. These usually happen during the blistering months of August and September. During the winter, sometimes cold fronts penetrate as far south as northern Mexico and Baja, bringing drizzle or light rain. Thus Baja's weather is different from most of Mexico in that it has two rainy seasons, and thus two growing seasons. Neither of these rainy seasons is very rainy, unless the quirky weather system called El Niño is in place, and then Baja's deserts can become shallow lakes with giant cacti rising from the water's surface.

On Baja's Pacific Coast, pleasant coastal breezes coming off the California Current on hot afternoons are known as *caromueles*. Beaches on the Pacific side generally range 15° to 20° Fahrenheit cooler than those across the peninsula at identical latitudes.

Where the California Current connects with Baja's out-jutting Vizcaíno Peninsula, it deposits whatever it happens to be carrying—sea shells, bottles with messages in them, World War II mines. . . . Some of the world's best beachcombing is here along windswept Playa Malarrimo (see Figure 10). The track leading there is so rugged that only well-equipped four-wheel-drive vehicles can be trusted to make the trip. Hikers unable to reach Playa Malarrimo need not fret; Baja harbors plenty of other exceptional beachcombing beaches. If Baja's coastline were uncoiled, it would stretch from Tijuana to Juneau, Alaska.

Three books deserve mention here because of the special insights they offer into Baja's landscape and natural history. *Into a Desert Place* by Graham Mackintosh describes Mackintosh's hike along Baja's entire coastline, from Ensenada to San Felipe, from April 1983 to March 1985. His narrative, recounting surviving off the sea and desert, including his use of three different kinds of water distilleries, is riveting. Two books often found in public libraries are Joseph Wood Krutch's *The Forgotten Peninsula: A Naturalist in Baja California* and the 1972 Time-Life Book called *Baja California*, by W. W. Johnson, a picture-filled coffee-table book. (See Bibliography.)

Plants

Hikers who know the difference between a stigma and a stipule, and who want to identify Baja's plants, are lucky. The plants of no other part of Mexico are as well documented in English as they are for Baja. Anyone able to locate and pay for I. L. Wiggins's 1,025-page *Flora of Baja California*, which includes 970 drawings, will be able to roam Baja at will, identifying just about every flowering plant encountered.

Moreover, as Figure 9 shows, most of Baja is occupied by the Sonoran Desert, except for the peninsula's extreme northwestern and southeastern corners. Thus the 1940 classic, two-volume botanical work *Vegetation and Flora of the Sonoran Desert* (see Bibliography) becomes handy. Though many Latin names used in this book are out of date, the publication not only helps with identifications but also shows how each species fits into the region's mosaic of plant communities. The first four of the following vegetation zones are based on this publication's treatment, and are shown in Figure 10. (Because the Sonoran Desert extends across the Gulf of California to mainland Mexico, and because there are vegetation zones on the mainland that are not found on Baja, three of the vegetation zones listed in Figure 10 do not occur in Baja and so are not described here: paloverde–prickly pear, ironwood–brittlebush, and acacia–mesquite.)

Creosote Bush–White Bur-Sage

In extreme northeastern Baja, along Highway 5 from Mexicali south along the Gulf of California past Punta Final, creosote bush and white bur-sage sometimes form up to 95 percent of the plant cover. Creosote bush, of the lignum vitae family, is a wiry, much-branched bush usually knee- to head-high, with thumbnail-size, three-lobed leaves. Especially at dawn, creosote-bush thickets smell tremendously of medicine. In fact, this plant's resin contains camphor, which is both an antiseptic and an antibiotic. A scale insect infesting the creosote bush's stem secretes "lac," which can be heated and used as glue and a sealer for waterproof clothing; it is the base for shellac.

Foot-tall white bur-sage, a member of the composite, or daisy, family, grows into a compact maze of slender stems and silvery leaves. In the hottest, driest places, which even creosote bushes avoid, white bur-sage takes over nearly completely. As with most true champions, this plant's outward appearance is very modest.

When arroyos break this zone's monotony, mesquite sometimes appears. Its relatively ample crown and soft-green leaves look extravagant next to austere creosote bush and white bur-sage. Also conspicuous around arroyos are blue paloverde, ironwood, and smokethorn. Mesquite, paloverde, and

A Sonoran Desert scene: the super-spiny, upright cacti are cholla cactus; the bushes with slender, leafless stems are ocotillos.

Two survivors among the Sonoran's sizzling dunes: at top, Mormon tea: at lower right, a dwarf species of evening primrose.

ironwood are all spiny, shrubby members of the bean family. (See appendix B, Key to Thorn-Forest Bean-Family Trees and Shrubs.) Smokethorn is one of those rare bean-shrubs with simple leaves. In fact, most of the year smokethorn produces no leaves at all; it is just a diffuse, "smoky" mass of spiny branches.

Paloverdes have green trunks and branches because they bear chlorophyll, which enable the plant to photosynthesize during long, leafless, droughty periods. Besides blue paloverde, the foothill paloverde, which is even greener than the blue, occurs on many Baja slopes. Another usually leafless, inordinately thorny, green-stemmed tree in the area is referred to as Mexican paloverde, or Jerusalem thorn. Its compound leaves are long and very narrow, like the skeleton of an eel, with flat, green ribs.

Brittlebush, a knee-high shrub in the composite, or daisy, family, has light green, oval leaves, and specializes in rocky or gravelly slopes and mesas. Generally it issues leaves and flowers twice a year, after each of the area's rainy seasons. Where lots of brittlebush occurs, its golden-yellow blossoms sometimes "paint the desert." A sticky, gummy sap exuding from cracks along its stems can be melted and used for varnish or glue, or burned as incense.

Ocotillos of the candlewood family are common in this zone. With twenty to thirty spindly, mostly branchless, leafless stems clumped together, rising ten feet or higher, and with overwintering fruits clustered toward the stems' tips, ocotillo is one of the most distinctive, easy-to-identify desert bushes.

Another eye-catching species is the stately California fan palm, growing in small colonies in desert canyons. Dead, dangling fronds form a brown skirt around its trunk. Fan palms cluster where water is available, so usually their presence announces an island of animal life. In such oases, birds sing and ground squirrels and lizards skitter; the air feels fresh and the greenness pleases the eye. It is impossible to see a squadron of California fan palms without feeling gratitude.

Dunes in northern Baja's Sonoran Desert

A beetle scrambles across Baja's sand.

Elephant Tree–Lomboy

Between Santa Rosalía and the Loreto–Puerto Escondido area, Baja's Highway 1 generally follows the Gulf of California's western coast through a land where plants just get curiouser and curiouser.

For example, there are elephant trees, with outlandishly thick, stubby trunks. Like their close relatives, the gumbo-limbos, large, curling flakes of outer bark exfoliate from their swollen trunks, exposing yellowish under-bark. Elephant-tree leaves are pinnately compound, hinting that the species is yet another bean-bush, but anyone seeing its flowers or fruits will find nothing beanish about them; this tree is a member of the mostly tropical bursera family.

The region's plentiful lomboys, which are shrubs or trees up to twenty feet high, belong to the spurge, or poinsettia, family. Like mainland Mexico's leatherplants, which belong in the lomboy's genus, lomboy's smooth branches are limber, and its grayish, unsubstantial leaves are usually absent. A decoction of lomboy juice has been used as a mordant in dying, as well as a cure for warts and sore throat, and for the hardening of gums!

Maybe the *curiousest* plant here is the boojum. Hikers seeing boojums for the first time generally have to sit down for a while and stare at it. Boojums look like thirty-foot-tall, scraggly rat-tails. Big ones get up to seventy feet tall and curl uncontrollably, sometimes bowing to the ground. They can produce several crops of hardly noticeable leaves a year, each time it rains. From an ethnobotanical perspective, probably the local name *cirio* is better than boojum; the name boojum comes by way of Lewis Carroll, who applied it to a strange, mythical plant on a faraway shore. Boojums are in the same family, the candlewood family, as ocotillos.

In some places, giant saguarolike cacti called cardóns loom sixty feet tall. Closely related, saguaros are not indigenous to Baja, except in the Colorado River area; saguaros are mostly distributed in southern Arizona and Mexico's Sonora state. Usually blossoming in July and August, cardóns are larger, more massive, and, possessing up to thirty arms, much more branched than saguaros.

Both cardóns and boojums are endemic just to Baja and small areas across the Gulf of California in Sonora. This suggests that the species evolved as continental drift tore Baja from the mainland five million years ago. Both boojums and cardóns can be observed at Cataviña.

This zone, being not quite as hot and dry as the creosote bush–white bur-sage zone, welcomes more "generic desert" species than the former zone—especially mesquite, paloverde, brittlebush, ironwood, creosote bush, and ocotillo.

Agave–Bur Bush

Several agave species characterize this zone, the most common being the Shaw's and desert agaves. Early Indians used to eat starchy agave root-crowns. Abundant bur bush is closely related to and similar to white bur-sage, and therefore similarly nondescript and uninteresting—except for its incredible ability to cope with extreme desert conditions.

A characteristic plant in this zone is the fifteen- to twenty-foot-tall, Joshua-treelike yucca called *datilillo*—"little date-tree." Unlike most tree-yuccas, *datilillo*'s leaves cloak most of the trunk's length, instead of clustering toward the top. Sometimes *datilillo* forms veritable forests.

Elephant trees and ocotillos inhabit this zone, as well as a little plant called *heno*, or "hay," whose presence testifies to the fact that, though this is the desert, the air off the Pacific, before it warms up, is humid. Little tufts of *heno* grow epiphytically and spottily on big cacti; *heno* resides in the same family (pineapple family) and genus as Spanish moss. The usual arid-land species already mentioned also are here.

Palo Blanco–Galloping Cactus

Highway 1 enters this zone about 30 miles (50 km) south of Loreto, where it curves inland and climbs into the uplands; it stays within this zone until it hooks to the east some 30 miles (50 km) west of La Paz. This zone's general character is suggested by the fact that the zone's namesake tree, the palo blanco, instead of being a freaky organism super-adapted to a super-hostile environment, is a regular tree. Reaching thirty feet, with a normal trunk, gracefully spreading crown, and plain green, twice-pinnately compound leaves, the palo blanco testifies that this zone receives more rainfall than the ones already mentioned.

Of course, the galloping cactus does not really gallop, but it does manage to creep along the ground, sometimes bending upwards, forming impenetrable thickets up to ten feet high.

The cardón also inhabits this zone, as well as species of cholla and organpipe cactus. Chollas have cylindrical stems and stand waist-high or less; organpipes rise fifteen feet high, have no main stem, and branch profusely from the base, like a menorah with too many hormones. With the extra measure of rain, naturally all the "generic desert" species also inhabit this zone.

Northwestern Chaparral

The term "chaparral" is a slippery one. Some people regard any thicket of scratchy, scraggly shrubbery as chaparral; thorn forests would be chaparral to them. In this book, the word applies to the shrubby zone extending from southern California into extreme northwestern Baja. Because this area is not part of the Sonoran Desert, this vegetation zone is not shown in Figure 10. Ecologists say that fire keeps this kind of chaparral in a shrubby state, even though rainfall may be sufficient for trees to grow. Fires kill trees, but chaparral-zone shrubs burned to the ground simply resprout.

Along Highway 1 between Tijuana and Cataviña, one sees plenty of the chaparral bush par excellence called chamise. A member of the rose family, chamise is a five- to ten-foot-tall evergreen shrub with tufts of small, narrow, heathlike leaves, reddish brown bark, and diminutive, white blossoms appearing in June. When incinerated by dry-season fires, chamise sprouts vigorously from fast-spreading underground roots. These roots hold soil on charred slopes, thus benefiting the entire chaparral biotic community. Chamise's leaves are filled with a bitter resin that keeps cattle from eating it, but also causes the plant to burn in a flash.

In this zone, short trees with reddish brown, smooth, flaking-off bark and thick, leathery, elliptic leaves with entire margins, dark green above and pale below, are madrones. The red-barked shrubs about knee high, with leathery leaves, urn-shaped blossoms, and red berries are manzanitas. Both of these alternate-leaved shrubs are members of the heath family. On dry slopes from 1,500 to 5,000 feet in elevation, the waist-high shrub with opposite, thick, bluish, evergreen leaves is jojoba, of the boxwood family. Jojoba comes in male and female plants, with only the females, of course, bearing fruit. Jojoba nuts are edible.

Southeastern Thorn Forest

This zone is fairly similar to the adjoining palo blanco–galloping cactus zone to the west in the Sonoran Desert, but it receives more rain and lies outside the Sonora Desert proper (and so this vegetation zone is not shown in Figure 10). Palo blanco is the most common tree. The extra rain encourages a thorny forest that is taller and denser than in the true desert.

Beside palo blanco, there is an acacialike albizia called *palo escopeta* (shotgun tree), and a member of the rue family with simple leaves, spineless stems, and a spiny fruit called *palo amarillo* (yellow tree, because of its yellow wood). Also, lomboy grows here.

A visit to the botanical garden just south of Todos Santos can help get a handle on this zone's vegetation. The palms along Playa San Pedrito opposite the botanical garden are fan palms of the genus *Washingtonia*.

Baja's Mountain Islands

Atop Baja's higher mountains there are amazingly moist, cool forests; these forests constitute nothing less than ecological islands. One such forest resides atop Sierra de Juárez in Baja's far north; a rough track off Highway 1 leads to an observatory not far from the 10,157-foot peak called Picacho del Diablo. In the far south, backpackers can climb into a similar forest island atop 7,096-foot Picacho de la Laguna in Sierra de la Laguna Natural Park. (Because both of these areas lie outside the Sonoran Desert, this vegetation zone is not shown in Figure 10.)

In the far north, in the Sierra de Juárez, higher mountains are mantled largely with yellow and sugar pines. In the far south, on Sierra de la Laguna ridge tops, one finds bushy pines called *piñones*, famous for their flavorful "pinyon nuts," sold in *mercados* and by street vendors. The fairly large oak there, with small leaves, is *encina negra*. Also present is a shrubby currant of the gooseberry family, and a hawthornlike shrub that in California is called Christmas-berry. A member of the dogwood family with un-dogwoody-looking flowers is the willow-leaved garrya. A madrone, with smooth, thin bark peeling off in sheets, also grows here.

Baja's Swamps

Not all of Baja's shores are sandy beaches pounded by big waves. Here and there along the coast, lagoons and bays sheltering shallow waters harbor genuine swamps. Extensive swamps occur around the whale-watching area of Scammon's Lagoon southwest of Guerrero Negro, and along Bahía Magdalena's shores, in the vicinity of San Carlos. Baja's two main mangroves are the red and button mangroves, described in Vegetation Zones, Chapter 2, Mexico's Natural Environment.

Animals

Along the Pacific Coast in the chaparral from Tijuana to around San Quintín, two remarkable salamanders occur. One, the arboreal salamander, is the world's champion tree-climbing salamander; in California one was found in a mouse's nest sixty feet up a tree. During long dry spells, this species stays in moist tree cavities and rodent burrows; unsalamanderlike, it squeaks like a mouse and bites. The garden slender salamander is a snakelike species found under rocks and litter around washes and other sandy or gravelly spots. When touched, it goes into convulsions and flips into the air, sometimes breaking off its tail. This behavior probably evolved to confuse predators.

Among frogs and toads, which in general are better adapted to deserts than salamanders, several species extend from the moister United States into northern Baja. Probably the most commonly encountered are the Western, Southwestern, and red-spotted toads. The Pacific tree frog bears a dark stripe through its eye; a closely related species without the dark eye-stripe is the California tree frog.

In Baja, it is the reptiles that shine. Banded geckos—chubby lizards with conspicuous crossbands—spend hot days in rock crevices and under logs. Among the more conspicuous lizards are the desert iguana and the zebra-tailed, leopard, banded rock, side-blotched, coast horned, and desert spiny lizards, as well as the small-scaled tree lizard. The Western whiptail and Western skink both are found throughout much of Baja.

Among the regularly encountered snakes are the coachwhip (Baja's fastest snake), pine-gopher (growing to more than eight feet long), and Western patch-nosed snakes. Enough pit vipers (poisonous) snakes are present that all hikers should stay vigilant when poking about the desert. Sidewinders inhabit northeastern Baja's sandy wastes; these are rattlesnakes often seen in the spring looping themselves across roads after sundown. Also there are Western, red diamond, and speckled rattlesnakes.

All the species just mentioned are illustrated in field guides for the United States. Anyone using these guides should keep in mind that many species are divided into one or more subspecies and, especially important among rep-

A desert horned lizard from the head of Baja's Gulf of California

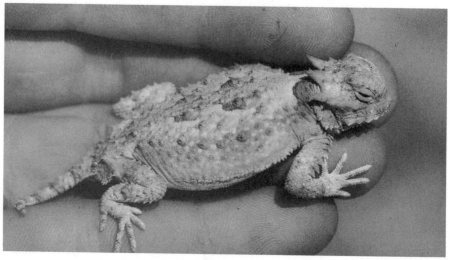

tiles, often these subspecies are colored or patterned very differently from one another. In U.S. field guides, usually the subspecies illustrated is *not* the one found in Baja. I have found it worthwhile to go through my Audubon Society's *Field Guide to North American Reptiles and Amphibians*, tagging all the Baja subspecies descriptions with "BJ."

Raccoons, the same species North Americans know, are found in Baja, as well as the nocturnal ringtail cat, which looks like a cross between a raccoon and a squirrel. Badgers dig den-holes in Baja's deserts, and Baja's main "polecat" is the spotted skunk. There are coyotes and kit and gray foxes. Baja's mountain lions are practically exterminated, but sometimes bobcats are heard of. The most common ground squirrel, a will-o'-the-wisp critter likely to be seen flicking its tail atop a boulder in the middle of the day, is the whitetail antelope squirrel. California's Merriam chipmunk extends into northern Baja's highlands. Long-legged blacktail jackrabbits and the more cuddly-looking desert cottontails and brush rabbits (the former gray, the latter brown) are sometimes spotted. Small deer seen bounding through brushy areas are mule deer; in Baja's wildest, rockiest areas, it is conceivable one might still spot bighorn sheep.

Nearly all of Baja's birds are also found in southern California and elsewhere in the U.S. Southwest; no physical barrier bars them from the north. However, most of mainland Mexico's truly tropical species do not make it across the Gulf of California to Baja's Deep South. Unless subspecies are counted, few birds are endemic to Baja. One exception, fairly easy to spot in the thorn forest during the Sierra de la Laguna hike later in this chapter, is the black-fronted hummingbird, similar to the white-eared hummingbird farther north.

In 1978 President Lópes Portillo presented the Seri Indians with the title to Isla Tiburón, Mexico's largest island, and the adjacent Sonoran coastline, and set up a series of special biosphere reserves covering all the islands in the Gulf of California. Because so many plants and animals are endemic just to these islands, sometimes they are referred to as "The Galápagos of the Northern Hemisphere." On tiny, guano-covered Raza Island in the Gulf of California between Isla Angel de la Guarda and Isla San Lorenzo, 95 percent of the world's elegant terns and Heermann's gulls gather to breed.

Mexico's Guadalupe Island in the Pacific about 225 miles northwest of the Vizcaíno Peninsula's cape (north 29° 00', west 118° 20') has not fared as well. Its ecology has been devastated by introduced goats, house mice, and cats. Several endemic species have gone extinct, such as the Guadalupe fur seal and the Guadalupe caracara, but still it is home to such worthy species as elephant seals, sea lions, and harbor seals. Elephant seals also inhabit Cedros Island and San Benito Island off the tip of the Vizcaíno Peninsula. Both California and Steller sea lions are found along Baja's Pacific Coast; only the California sea lion enters the Gulf of California.

The vaquita is an endemic dolphin restricted to the northern Gulf of California, where only a few hundred survive. Among Baja's cetacean (whale) population are the fin, blue, gray, humpback, and sperm whales. California gray whales spend their summers feeding in the Bering Sea, then migrate 6,000 miles to several warm-water lagoons along Baja's coast, foremost among them

Scammon's Lagoon. Whale pods arrive in December. Some females then give birth and others mate before departing north between March and June.

Other areas good for whale watching include the abandoned dock at Estero San José, 7 miles (11 km) northwest of Guerrero Negro; Punta Banda near La Bufadora across Todos Santos Bay from Ensenada; Punta Baja at the end of the trail leading southwest from El Rosario past Nuestra Señora del Rosario Viñaraco; and Laguna San Ignacio, accessible via the 40-mile (65-km) trail leading southwest from San Ignacio. At the latter location, female whales and their calves sometimes approach fishing boats and permit their noses to be rubbed. In San Ignacio it costs about $25 US per day to accompany an authorized Mexican in his boat, to go out and rub noses.

More than 800 species of fish and 2,000 species of invertebrates live in the Gulf of California. Among the places where tropical fish can be viewed from glass-bottomed boats are Pichilingüe, 10 miles (16 km) northeast of La Paz, and Pelican Rock, near the harbor entrance at Cabo San Lucas, at Baja's southernmost tip. Some of the more interesting fish in the waters around Baja include tuna, bluefish, California barracuda, bonito, dorado, flounder, mullet, swordfish, Pacific sardine, and various sharks.

People

When the Jesuits first explored Baja in 1716, they encountered a population of about 35,000 indigenous people. Smallpox epidemics in 1742 and 1780 decimated the native population; by 1800 only about 10 percent of the area's natives survived. At San Ignacio, from 1743 to 1808 the number of Indians plunged from 2,000 to 100.

At several Baja locations, ancient petroglyphs and paintings survive on cave walls and cliff faces. Hikes to these sites usually require a guide, a bit of preparation, and a decent physical state. Information on such guided hikes can be acquired in San Ignacio at Hotel El Presidente and Motel La Posada, and in Mulegé at Hotel Las Casitas and Hotel Serenidad. La Paz's Museo de Antropología at Calle Cinco de Mayo and Calle Altamirano exhibits photos of a number of cave paintings.

1 ▪ THE 3,000-MILE COAST OF BAJA

Distance: up to 3,000 miles
Difficulty: easy to strenuous
Terrain: beach
Elevation: sea level
Map: ITMP Map No. 201: Baja California, 1:1,000,000

The first hike in this book is an exception. Instead of describing a specific hike, I describe a "general hiking region." This is because *nearly all of Baja's 3,000-mile coast can be hiked.* Baja's day-hike potential is simply unique, so I choose to treat it in a unique way. Nearly anyplace in Baja where one can gain access to the sea, there awaits a potential day hike.

The Pacific and Gulf coasts are very different. Beaches on the Pacific side are cooler, are visited by much larger waves, and gather more diverse flotsam and jetsam than those on the Gulf of California. Tides in the northern Gulf of California can be tremendous—up to thirty feet! Keep this in mind when pegging beachside tents.

Also keep in mind that many places which, on a map, look as if they should at least have a gas station and a general store may consist of nothing but an abandoned shed or two. Never set off for a beach-hiking destination without plenty of water and gasoline. Be prepared for mechanical breakdowns. Often this means that vehicles leaving for isolated beaches should caravan, not go it alone. Baja's heat, aridity, and isolation are not Disneyland concoctions. They can kill the unprepared.

Get a good map of Baja and note some of the beach-hiking options:

- Beginning at Baja's northwestern extreme, across Todos Santos Bay from Ensenada, numerous hiking trails lie in the area around **La Bufadora** blowhole at the end of Highway 23.
- Between **Camalú and El Rosario**, several tracks from Highway 1 provide easy access to the beach. The beach south of El Rosario is magnificently empty for hundreds of miles; trails lead to this area.
- Hikers not willing to stray far off Highway 1 might be intrigued by the "unimproved dirt road" about 1 mile (2 km) long leading to the coast just west of Camalú, to **Camalú Via la Mar**. A "dash-line" track runs along the coast a couple of miles (several km) north from Camalú Via la Mar.
- Two tracks provide access to the Vizcaíno Peninsula's **Playa Malarrimo**, possibly the best beachcombing beach in the world. This is also the location of the "designated whale-watching area" on Scammon's Lagoon (Figure 11), which lies about 20 miles (32 km) southwest of Guerrero Negro, down a sandy road; a viewing tower can be used for a small fee.
- On the Pacific side at the peninsula's very tip, **south of Todos Santos**, many access roads can be spotted leading off Highway 19 to the beach; about a half mile south of Todos Santos, a sign on Highway 19 points down a bumpy road reading ACCESO A LA PLAYA. Keep in mind that the endless beaches **north of Cabo San Lucas** have dangerously strong currents.
- On the Gulf side, Highway 1 hugs the western shore of **Bahía Concepción** south of Mulegé. This is a touristy area and the noseeums can be bad.
- Across from Isla Angel de la Guarda, a spur of Highway 1 cuts to the coast, to **Bahía de los Ángeles**, equipped with an outstanding view of the bay, a rugged upland mantled with some of the earth's tallest cactus forest, and beaches north and south good for day hikes. South of town, a road occasionally touches the coast.
- Paved Highway 5 runs along the coast from north of **San Felipe to Puertecitos**. However, there are so many beachside homes in this area that beach hiking is awkward. South of Puertecitos, the rugged dirt road provides many accesses to the sea.

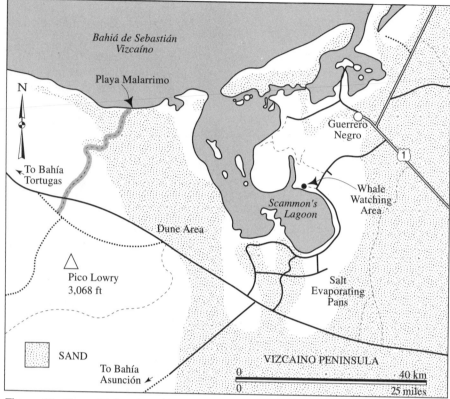

Figure 11 Playa Malarrimo and Scammon's Lagoon, Baja California

Pockets stuffed with field guides for identifying seashells and birds, and binoculars around the neck, guarantee that any beach hike will be interesting. However, on Baja's beaches, usually it is the forbidding isolation, the rhythmic breaking of the powerful surf, and the edge-of-the-continent feeling that make the most profound impressions. This is the right place to remind ourselves that in certain places and at certain times it is more gratifying to abandon usual schedules of birding, note-jotting, and picture snapping, and just let the mind float, soaking up ineffable understandings.

Getting There

With a good map and a vehicle appropriate for Baja's subsidiary roads—often that means a four-wheel-drive vehicle with high clearance and tires capable of floating atop deep sand—there is no reason why literally hundreds of top-notch beach-hiking spots cannot be located and enjoyed.

You can reach Baja by driving south on Highway 1 from Tijuana, by driving west from the mainland on Highway 2 via Mexicali, or by taking ferries from mainland Mexico. Maps usually show more ferry connections than really exist. At this writing, ferries connect the mainland ports of Mazatlán and Topolobampo (Los Mochis) with La Paz, Baja, and also Guaymas, on the mainland, with Santa Rosalía, Baja.

Maps similarly tend to populate central and southern Baja with more civilization than there really is. Two-thirds of Baja's population lives in or near the border towns of Tijuana and Mexicali. South of Ensenada, towns with five-star establishments include La Paz, San José del Cabo, Cabo San Lucas, Buena Vista, and Loreto. More iffy and often more colorful lodging exists in Buena Vista, Santa Rosalía, Guerrero Negro, and San Ignacio.

2 ▪ SIERRA DE LA LAGUNA NATURAL PARK

Distance: 12.5 miles (20 km)
Difficulty: moderate (level terrain but intense heat)
Terrain: dirt road
Elevation: sea level
Map: ITMP Map No. 201: Baja California, 1:1,000,000

Sierra de la Laguna Natural Park lies near the southern tip of Baja, just southeast of Todos Santos. Sierra de la Laguna is capped with a "mountain island" (see the Plants section earlier in this chapter); the peak called Picacho de la Laguna reaches 7,096 feet. However, the hike does not visit that mountaintop forest; doing so requires more than a day hike. This hike follows the one-lane dirt road through the desert from Highway 19 south of Todos Santos to the park's entrance. The road passes through fascinating desert with giant cacti. A visit to the botanical garden just south of Todos Santos can help you get a handle on this area's vegetation.

Giant cacti rise twenty feet high. There are tall tree-yuccas, and species of cholla and barrel cactus. Scrub jays, ladder-backed woodpeckers, cactus wrens, and ash-throated flycatchers are fairly common, and endemic black-throated hummingbirds are not hard to spot.

Getting There
La Paz is on the Gulf side, Todos Santos is about 50 miles (80 km) south on the Pacific side, and they are connected by Highway 19. Several buses from La Paz's *terminal central* (not the one across from the tourist office) serve Todos Santos. Todos Santos's main bus stop is beside Parque los Pinos. From the park, take Highway 19 south over the hill past the well-stocked Super Mercado Hermanos Castro. About 1 mile (2 km) south of town, take a sandy road that departs Highway 19, shooting eastward through the desert. This is the hiking road. Typically the road sees three or four pickup trucks a day; one option might be to hitch in for a distance, then hike back out. Keep in mind that by midmorning this desert can become awfully hot.

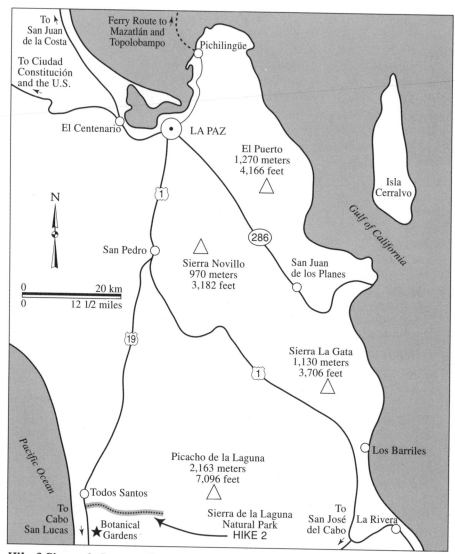

Hike 2 Sierra de Laguna Natural Park

La Paz has numerous lodging opportunities, but pickings are slim in Todos Santos; try the Misión Todos Santos at Juárez y Márquez de León. Most *gringos* camp on the beach; about 1 mile (1.5 km) south of Todos Santos, a sign reading *ACCESO A LA PLAYA*—"beach access"—points to the right.

CHAPTER 4

THE GULF COAST

The Land

The Gulf Coast is similar to the Pacific Coast in that it also is a narrow region running north and south, is hemmed in by a mountain chain on one side and a large expanse of water on the other, and is more arid in the north than the south. One important difference is that the Pacific Coast's Western Sierra Madre are volcanic in origin, but the Gulf Coast's Eastern Sierra Madre are mostly composed of sedimentary limestone. In the Gulf Coast region, the Eastern Sierra Madre's limestone expresses itself eloquently in the character of the foothills between the mountains and the coastal lowlands.

Chapter 2, Mexico's Natural Environment, examines limestone-associated karst topography and explains that sinkholes are depressions in the landscape caused by collapsing caves. The mostly limestone Gulf Coast foothills are home to super-sized sinkholes called *sótanos*. These features are so peculiar and characteristic of this part of Mexico that even English-speaking geologists use the Spanish word *sótano*.

The Empire State Building could be hidden in several of the Gulf Coast's *sótanos*, and there would still be room for King Kong. Among the most spectacular *sótanos* are Gruta del Palmito in Nuevo León just south of Bustamente, and Sótano de las Golondrinas in San Luis Potosí, just southwest of Ciudad Valles. The geological event responsible for the *sótano*'s existence is the ancient uplifting of eastern Mexico's Cretaceous limestone from the ocean bed where it was formed, to the Eastern Sierra Madre mountaintops where it is now.

Here and there across the Gulf Coast region, localized ridges and peaks, apparently independent of the Sierra Madre and the Mexican Plateau, rise from the flatlands. For instance, east of Linares, Sierra Chiquita rises to 5,873 feet; east of Ciudad Victoria, Sierra de Tamaulipas is 4,882 feet high. The most surprising disjunct highlands, however, practically at the ocean's edge, are the volcanic Tuxtlas around San Andrés Tuxtla in southern Veracruz, reaching 6,160 feet.

Plants

The Gulf Coast's ecology has been devastated by humankind. The north's ancient grasslands now have mostly succumbed to vast ranches and fields of corn, sorghum, and beans; often these crops fail because of sporadic rainfall. Even immense tracts of mesquite and thorn forest are being bulldozed to make way for industrial parks and too-dry ranches. Farther south, nearly all the lowland forests have been replaced by ranches and orchards. In the moist foothills, slash-and-burn agriculture has set a patchwork of weedy, rejuvenating fields upon the mountains; white limestone rocks poke through the eroded soil like bones from a wasted body.

The arid north a good distance from the U.S. border is least disturbed. Entering Mexico at Nuevo Laredo, heading south to Monterrey, the first natural vegetation observed is mostly mesquite, huisache, Jerusalem thorn, and prickly pear cactus. Atop low ridges about 20 miles (30 km) north of Vallecillos, on Highway 85, large areas of a low, gray-leafed shrub appear; this is cenizo, one of the Chihuahuan Desert's most characteristic plants. More spectacular but less common are the twenty-foot-high yuccas, looking like the Joshua trees of Arizona and California, but constituting a different species. Between Sabinas Hidalgo and Monterrey, watch silvery waves of cenizo alternate with green lakes of mesquite and huisache.

Farther south, at about the latitude of Tampico, orange plantations appear. Yet farther south, in the very humid lowlands south of Veracruz City, pastures occupy the lowlands, populated with breeds of cattle, particularly zebu, able to withstand unending onslaughts of heat, flies, and ticks. In the moist southern foothills, much of what looks like forest actually is coffee plantations; coffee shrubs usually are grown in the shade of taller trees.

As the Tetlama hike (later in this chapter) passes through Colonia El Sacrificio, something hopeful is seen. The Nahuatl-speaking Indians of this region traditionally grow medicinal herbs, fruit trees, and other plants with beautiful or aromatic flowers around their homes. Today, when young Indians move closer to town, they bring their knowledge of and love for plants with them. On Tamazunchale's slummy, overpopulated slopes, they have created a sophisticated, congenial-feeling agroforestry, the likes of which is usually found only in textbooks.

Several extensive coastal marshes occur along the Gulf Coast. In the south, Highway 175 between the coast and Tuxtepec, Oaxaca, passes through a large marsh along the Río Papaloapan. The *autopista* between Minatitlán and Coatzacoalcos, as well as Highway 180 between Villahermosa and Ciudad del Carmen, similarly skirt impressive marshes.

Animals

In general, the farther south one goes along the Gulf Coast, the greater becomes species diversity, and the more likely one is to see "exotic" species—species not encountered in North America. In the region's northern, arid third, most species also occur in southern Texas. The most conspicuous birds in the northern grassland–mesquite zone include electrical-wire–loving forktailed flycatchers with black, ten-inch-long, scissorlike tails, greater roadrunners that always seem to be disappearing behind a bush, and fence-post–perching crested caracaras; the latter are hawklike birds with flattops.

South of Valles in eastern San Luis Potosí, truly tropical birds begin appearing. At shaded forest edges along the Río Moctazuma at Tamazunchale and in the mountains on the Tetlama hike, for instance, it is possible to spot such Gulf Coast, tropical specialties as the wedge-tailed sabrewing and white-bellied emerald (both hummingbirds), the violaceous trogon, blue-crowned motmot, melodious blackbird, and the yellow-winged and blue-gray tanagers. A good way to spot a large number of Gulf Slope specialties is to stop at different elevations along Highway 174 above Valle Nacional, between Tuxtepec and Oaxaca.

Armadillos and cottontail rabbits—the same species found in the United States—inhabit the entire Gulf Coast zone. In the south there is a rabbit with short ears, tiny tail, and dark-brown legs and head called the tropical-forest cottontail; uncottontail-like, it inhabits humid forests. Gray squirrels sometimes are spotted throughout the zone, wherever real woods occur. In the south the olive-brown, miniature species called the Deppe squirrel might be spotted. Beaver occur along the Río Grande in the north, but not much farther south. Coyotes are especially common in the arid north, as are gray foxes.

Two species of ringtail cat occur in this region, one north of the city of Veracruz and the other south of Tuxpan (thus overlapping a bit). However, ringtails are nocturnal and seldom seen. Their tails are even more conspicuously ringed than the closely related raccoon, which also is present. Long-snouted coati are here, as well as weasels and several weasel-like species; all are nocturnal and rarely seen, except that coatis are learning to go after garbage, so sometimes are spotted around residential areas. Striped and spotted skunks occur throughout the region, as do hog-nosed skunks (one species north of Veracruz, the other south.) Several big cats used to be present but they have been hunted to near-extinction or to extinction; in the northern desert, sometimes at dusk or in the early morning, bobcats still can be spotted.

From Linares, Nuevo León, south, blood-drinking vampire bats inhabit many *sótanos*. At night vampires land near cattle and horses, hobble over to the critters' hooves, and expertly and painlessly cut incisions yielding trickles of blood. A mature vampire weighing about 1¾ ounces drinks its weight in blood every twenty-four hours. Its incision is so clean and shallow that the victim suffers little physical damage. However, vampires can spread deadly diseases among livestock. Humans sleeping outdoors, next to open windows, or with their feet sticking out from beneath mosquito netting are not immune to vampires; vampires can carry rabies.

On the Tetlama hike, several kinds of plants are seen growing on tree limbs. Some of these epiphytes are orchids and others ferns, but the largest, most conspicuous ones are bromeliads, which are members of the pineapple family. Besides their extraordinary appearance and the "tropical feeling" they impart to the landscape, especially larger bromeliads comprise ecological islands among the tree limbs. Water accumulated where the leaves come together attracts entire communities of animals. The Mexican flat-toed sala-mander is an eight-inch-long arboreal species with webbed feet; during dry seasons it lives in one or two bromeliads, eating small insects and spiders drawn to arboreal watering holes, but during the rainy season it roams freely. Any large bromeliad deserves examining.

People

For centuries the coastal cities of Tampico and Veracruz served as the main ports of entry for Spanish settlers; around these towns a certain cos-mopolitan feeling still reigns. In the Veracruz area, even the Spanish lan-guage takes a certain twist—people might say *vos sos* for "you are" instead of *tú eres*.

Traveling down the Gulf Coast from the north, indigenous cultures do not appear until around Ciudad Valles, where a few Huastec villages are found. On the Tetlama hike, several Nahuatl speakers will be encountered; in the roadless mountains around Tamazunchale, there are still many villages of Nahuatl-speaking people living in thatch-roofed huts without plumbing and electricity. Nahuatl is the language of the ancient Aztec. Highway 85 south of Tamazunchale climbs steeply into Otomí territory. Originally farther south along the coast, there were other enclaves of Nahuatl speakers, plus Totonac, Popoluca, and Chontal, but today travelers along the coast miss all hints of indigenous culture unless they look for them.

3 ▪ MAMULIQUE PASS

Distance: 1–2 miles one way (1.5–3 km)
Difficulty: easy
Terrain: old paved road
Elevation: 1,500 feet
Maps: ITMP Map No. 200: México, 1:3,300,000; many maps of Texas

Paso de Mamulique lies in the state of Nuevo León, at about Km 63 on High-way 85, some 30 miles (50 km) north–northeast of Monterrey; it is a "pass" through an imposing escarpment comprising one of the "steps" onto the Mexican Plateau. A nice variety of plants can be observed here, especially thorny shrubs, agaves, and yuccas characteristic of the grassland–mesquite and thorn forest zones.

This is an easy walk on a paved, curvy, gently sloping, abandoned sec-tion of old Highway 85. The hike's main attraction is that it passes through a number of different habitats, so numerous species are seen in a short dis-tance. Plants array themselves on road cuts and at the pavement's edge as if in a garden. This is a good place to look at the region's thorny shrubs and small trees without getting scratched. Unfortunately, truck noise from the

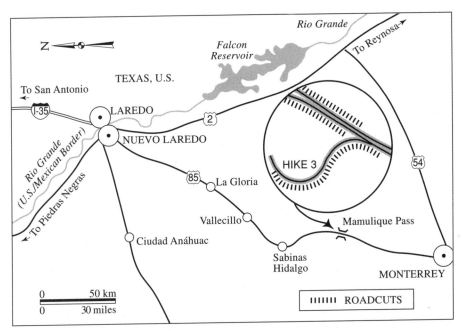

Hike 3 Mamulique Pass

new Highway 85, and the even newer *autopista* between Nuevo Laredo and Monterrey, can be a little bothersome.

About 10 minutes from the walk's beginning, a chain fence appears wearing an *Alto* (stop) sign. Obviously the sign applies only to vehicles because a wide, well-worn path passes around the barrier. It would be lovely to make a circle walk out of this hike, but it is best just to walk downslope for 1.25 to 1.75 miles (2 to 3 km), to about where the ruins of an old gas station are, and head back. In the pass, Highway 85 is too narrow for pedestrians.

One conspicuous, low shrub along the abandoned highway is the Texas algerita, with metallic-blue, hollylike leaves. A member of the barberry family, its small, red, tasty berries make excellent jelly. A yellow dye can be extracted from its stems, and concoctions made from its roots can serve as tonics.

Probably the most common agave here is the lechuguilla, with relatively thin, straight, mostly upward-pointing, bluish green leaves; leaf margins are armored with short, downward-pointing spines. In the Chihuahuan Desert to the west, lechuguilla dominates vast stretches. As far as agaves go, it is pretty scroungy-looking; and anyone who has tried hiking in the Chihuahuan Desert probably has spent ample time extracting lechuguilla spines from feet and legs. On the other hand, peccary are somehow able to eat lechuguilla leaves, and certain birds gather seeds from the lechuguilla's spearlike fruit-spikes.

The second most common agave here, also typical of the Chihuahuan Desert, is sotol. Unlike lechuguilla, its leaves are slender and fairly pliable, and possess upward-pointing spines along leaf margins.

Sotol, with hard spines armoring its leaf margins, graces the roadcut at Mamulique Pass.

Getting There

A steady stream of buses runs between Nuevo Laredo and Monterrey, passing right by this abandoned part of the old highway; Transportes Fronteras and Transportes Zuazua provide most frequent service. Some first-class buses use the *autopista*, bypassing Mamulique Pass. Ticket-sellers may get confused if asked for a ticket to Paso de Mamulique because they do not have the appropriate stamps and rates are not listed. If this is the case, buy a ticket to one town beyond the pass—Ciénega de Flores for those heading south from Nuevo Laredo, Sabinas Hidalgo for those going north from

Monterrey. As you enter the bus, be sure to tell the driver that you wish to disembark at the pass.

The best place to leave the bus is the spacious pull-off alongside Highway 85 at the pass's very top, on the Monterrey side. Here the paved abandoned section of road constituting the hike is clearly visible, to the left, looking north toward Nuevo Laredo. If the bus driver refuses to stop at the pull-off, ask to be let off at Restaurante "La Cuesta" about 0.5 mile (1 km) south of the pass.

Though no formal lodging is available immediately around the pass, Highway 85 is an important north–south tourist drag, so finding a place to stay in nearby towns is no problem. In this area, services wear price. tags more appropriate to the United States than the rest of Mexico.

4 ▪ XOCONOSTLE

Distance: 3–3.75 miles (5–6 km)
Difficulty: easy
Terrain: trail, gravel road
Elevation: 6,600 feet
Map: ITMP Map No. 200: México, 1:3,300,000

Xoconostle (choh-koh-NOHST-leh) is a small town in the state of San Luis Potosí, about 15 miles (25 km) east of the city of San Luis Potosí, on Highway 70. Highway 70 is the main road between the cities of north-central Mexico

Hike 4 Xoconostle / Hike 5 Tetlama

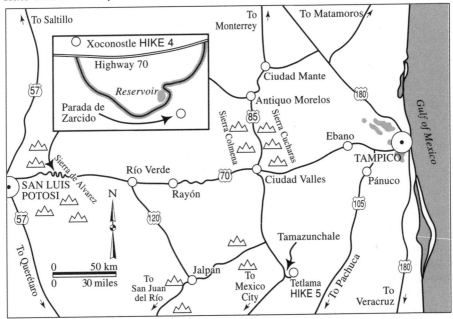

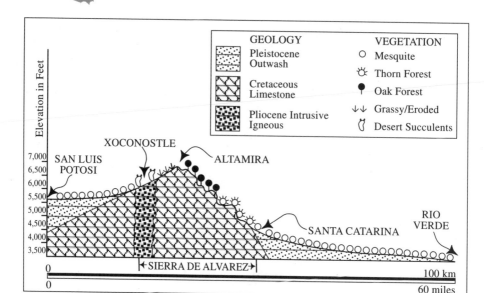

Figure 12 Geological cross-section (showing vegetation zones) of Highway 70 between San Luis Potosí and Río Verde

and the Gulf port of Tampico. Because the 155 miles (250 km) of Highway 70 between Río Verde and the city of San Luis Potosí pass through numerous vegetation zones in El Potosí National Park, and several pull-offs are available for walking around, the bus ride to Xoconostle is described in detail. Though the highway is rather busy, it is generally well paved and offers several opportunities for day hikes en route to Xoconostle. It is particularly scenic and curvy above Santa Catarina. Lots of succulent desert plants occur at Xoconostle; primitive phosphorite mines add a touch of interest.

Beginning in Río Verde, at an elevation of around 3,300 feet, large orange plantations and small truck farms of chili pepper, tomato, and corn occupy the landscape outside of town. As the road heads west, thorn forests dominated by mesquite gradually take over. The highway slowly ascends for about 30 miles (50 km) through the thorn forest. In some places giant organpipe cacti rise like chimneys above the mesquite. The shrub with thrice-compound leaves and vicious recurved spines is *uña de gato* (cat-claw). The desert hackberry looks like a hackberry should, except that it is thorny. *Coyotillo* (little coyote), an opposite-leaved member of the buckthorn family, is famous for its seeds, said to cause paralysis and spasms if swallowed.

During the rainy season (northern summer), the sandy soil below these trees becomes populated with numerous grass species (grama grass, foxtail, lovegrass) and herbs. Wildflowers to look for include a species of salvia, a pokeweedlike plant called rouge plant, a lantana, and the yellow-flowered New Mexico sida, with sepals ornamented with dark, red-brown margins.

Above and just west of Santa Catarina (at about Km 187), the thorn forest becomes dominated by acacias, the main species of which are *gavia*, *espino*, *algarrobo*, and *huajillo*. Another shrub looking like *uña de gato*, but with straight, slender spines, also goes by the name *huajillo*, though it is not an acacia; *campesinos* are not always discerning botanists. At this higher elevation, a second hackberry species joins the desert hackberry, as well as a scratchy buckthorn. Now accompanying the organpipe cactus is a waist-high, much branched, slender jointed cactus called *garambullo*. Ubiquitous prickly-pear cacti are present, as well as the Potosí yucca.

During the rainy season, wildflowers proliferate. As well as the species mentioned for the mesquite-dominated thorn forest, one finds in this thorn forest the brilliant redstar zinnia, a delicate dayflower, a species of prairie clover, a chinchweed, a tiny nama, a portulaca, and a lot more. Toward the thorn forest's higher elevations, a large juniper with drooping branches appears, appropriately named the drooping juniper. Growing epiphytically on the branches of many trees, surprisingly, are dangling gobs of Spanish moss.

The road climbs steeply past picturesque limestone cliffs to the oak-covered peak of Sierra de Alvarez, at about 7,900 feet. Oak forest appears at around Km 211, near a place aptly called Cruz de Encino (Oak Cross). In the oak forest near Km 211.5, there is a pull-off; an even larger one—one with taco stands and *refrescos* for truckers—stands near Km 216. At the latter rest area, trails across the little valley parallel Highway 70 a good bit both above and below the parking area.

It is surely possible to hike from here 3 miles (5 km) all the way upslope to a place called Valle de Los Fantasmas ("Ghost Valley") at about Km 221 on Highway 70. The ghosts in "Ghost Valley" are limestone pillars rising weirdly from the landscape, accessible by a maze of goat trails.

Highway 70 does not climb high enough for pines to appear among the oaks mantling the mountain's upper elevations. However, at least seven species of oak can be found there; these are listed in appendix A under *roble*. The Spanish word *roble* is a kind of generic term used for oaks other than the liveoak kind, which possess evergreen, simple, entire leaves; liveoak-type oaks are called *encinas*. Non-oak trees here include two species of hawthorn, a madrone with reddish, thin bark peeling off in papery sheets, a species of dogwood, and Mexican hickory. Deep in arroyos, North America's Eastern redbud and black cherry make surprising appearances, along with a hairy-leafed walnut called *nogal*.

The oak forest's herbaceous layer becomes lyrical with wildflowers, at least in the rainy season. A dahlia with two-inch-wide heads, red rays, and a yellow center occurs here, as well as two species of geranium, a delicate little flax, species of violet, a gromwell with tiny, funnel-shaped flowers in an inflorescence curled like a scorpion's tail, and species of oxalis. Well, there are too many to list; suffice it to say that there are at least six species of salvia!

Birdlife along this road is interesting, though North Americans with experience in the United States' southwestern deserts will have seen most of the species. In open areas there are turkey vultures, mourning doves, white-winged and scaled doves, loggerhead shrikes, and Eastern meadowlarks. Conceivably the Botteri's sparrow might show up, or more likely be heard singing. A bird

Prickly-pear cacti mount the stone wall along the Xoconostle hike's old oxcart trail.

list from this slope's oak forest looks like one from the oak forests of the Rockies of Arizona and New Mexico. There are acorn woodpeckers, gray-breasted jays, rufous-sided towhees, and, if one is sharp, maybe a Hutton's vireo.

On the mountain's western slope, the landscape becomes much more arid. Highway 70 passes through a fascinating cactus desert, which is the focus of the hike at Xoconostle. The hike leaves from one point on Highway 70 and returns to another. This is a fairly easy stroll, though immediately after a rain the first half, which follows an old oxcart trail, may be slippery. The trail's second half follows a small gravel road back to Highway 70, where either a bus can be caught, or the hike can be continued alongside Highway 70 back to Xoconostle, about 2 miles (3 km) down the road. There is plenty of space along the road for hiking; usually there is even a path.

The old oxcart trail on which the hike begins departs from Highway 70 heading southeast 150°. The trail's first stretch passes below tall, stately, droopy-branched, feathery-leaved peppertrees. Though peppertrees, members of the sumac family, are upland Mexico's favorite shade tree, they are not native Mexican species; they hale from Peru.

The very spiny prickly-pear cactus forming impenetrable, yards-high thickets along the trail is *nopal cardón*. In the Nahuatl language, *xoconostle* is the name of this cactus's edible fruit. Another cactus common along this part of the hike is *garambullo*, a dense, much-branched, waist-high cactus with arm-

A scene along the Xoconostle hike; next to an órgano *cactus, a cow enjoys a peppertree's diffuse shade.*

thick joints. The area's main Joshua tree–like yucca is the one called *izote*.

In the oak forest on the east side of Sierra de Alvarez, dangling Spanish moss was observed on the bus ride to Xoconostle. On this walk on the west side of the Sierra, atop some cacti and on tree branches it is possible to spot tiny, scaly, gray, tufted plants looking like Spanish moss, except that they do not form dangling strands. This is *heno*, which means "hay," and is in the same genus as Spanish moss. Both are members of the pineapple family. Central Mexico is home to four species of this genus.

About 600 yards from the trail's beginning, the road veers to the left and widens. Notice the interesting population of leatherplant—slender, unbranching, usually leafless, gray-brown, succulent, knee-high members of the poinsettia or spurge family; they look like dark, skinny witch's fingers poking from the ground.

After the left turn, the trail continues uphill. At the crest, the village of Parada de Zarcido becomes visible. Continue downhill toward town, passing to the right of the tiny school with a metal fence around it. Pass onto the big levee and stay atop it as it curves to the left and enters the wooded area on the lake's far side. Just past the lake, the road makes a sharp right, then a minute later it ends at a T; go left and proceed northeast 45°.

At the first Y, about 700 yards up the road, go left, upward; this leads into a good succulent area. At the next Y, maybe 500 yards farther, again go left and upwards. Miners working in the strip mines along this stretch say that they are mining phosphorite. Phosphorite is a white, powdery form of the mineral called apatite; the phosphorite mined here is used in animal feed as a nutritional supplement for phosphorus. Apatite often forms in metamorphosed limestone. Therefore, this phosphorite probably formed when the igneous intrusion shown in Figure 12 invaded the region's limestone bedrock.

Soon after the second Y, a road comes in from the left; continue straight at northeast 30° all the way back to Highway 70. In this area, notice the six-foot-tall, succulent, stiff-looking plant with straight stems conspicuously ornamented with old leafscars, and leaves that, if present at all, look like maple leaves clustered at the stem's very tip. During early spring, yellow flowers exactly like those found on North America's groundsels may be present. In fact, this plant, called *candelero*, *is* a groundsel. To North Americans accustomed to thinking of groundsels as spring wildflowers occupying moist places, seeing this tough, succulent groundsel is nothing less than mind-boggling.

The conspicuous agaves on this slope are wild, rather runty magueys. The conspicuous, low, clumpy cactus with cylindrical joints and a heavy armament of vicious-looking, pale spines is a cholla cactus; in Texas it would be called devil's cholla.

Birds in this area are fairly typical for arid areas—mostly black and turkey vultures, mockingbirds, curve-billed thrashers, brown towhees, and black-throated sparrows.

Once you reach Highway 70, either continue to hike alongside Highway 70 back to Xoconostle, about 2 miles (3 km) down the road, or catch a bus on to San Luis Potosí. Below the cactus zone at Xoconostle, Highway 70 returns

At Xoconostle, from left to right: a starved-looking maguey agave; a cholla cactus; and candelero, *the succulent groundsel.*

to mesquite-dominated, immoderately thorny forest. The road levels out on the arid floor of the San Luis Potosí Valley, at about 5,900 feet. This gain in altitude represents a "step" onto the Mexican Plateau.

Getting There

Numerous buses run on Highway 70, but most first-classers do not stop at pull-offs or small places such as Xoconostle. However, bus riders who have stopped for a day hike should not be stranded for more than an hour or two before a second-classer deigns to stop. Bus riders coming from the east can take a first-classer to Río Verde, then change to a second-class bus in Río

At Xoconostle, some maguey agaves have escaped from cultivation. Fermented maguey sap becomes pulque, a traditional Mexican alcoholic drink.

Verde, before the vegetation begins to get interesting. Riders originating in San Luis Potosí should take a second-class bus headed for Río Verde or beyond, and disembark where they wish.

The village of Xoconostle is spread out along Highway 70. The old oxcart trail that is the trailhead for this hike lies on the western side (the San Luis Potosí side) of town, where electrical lines cross the highway and a concrete culvert runs beneath it. Located on the highway's southern side (on your left as you face San Luis Potosí), below tall peppertrees, the entrance to the trail is picturesquely framed by ancient stone walls overgrown with cactus. The usual stopping place for second-class buses seems to be right across from the trail's entrance. Plenty of space is available for parking.

Every kind of lodging is available in San Luis Potosí, but only a bit in Río Verde. Xoconostle has no hotels.

5 ▪ TETLAMA

Distance: 4 miles (7 km) one way
Difficulty: moderate
Terrain: trail, gravel road
Elevation: 1,000 feet
Map: ITMP Map No. 200: México, 1:3,300,000

The mildly strenuous road to Tetlama lies right above the town of Tamazunchale, in the extreme southeastern corner of the state of San Luis Potosí, about 100 miles (175 km) as the crow flies north–northeast of Mexico City. Of all the hikes in this book, probably none offers a better chance to meet Native Americans—in this case, Nahuatl-speaking descendants of the Aztec. Indians from isolated villages walk this one-lane dirt and gravel road to reach Tamazunchale's market.

From Tamazunchale the road climbs steadily and sometimes steeply to the Nahuatl village of Tetlama. Two accesses to the road are described, one passing through Tamazunchale's "Colonia el Sacrificio," a slope densely populated by people and interesting plants. The second access bypasses the Colonia. Vegetation along the road is mostly weedy but, in this hot, humid environment, even weeds are spectacular!

Approach via Colonia el Sacrificio: One reason for passing through Colonia el Sacrificio is to see traditional Indian agroforestry—people living intimately with many diverse trees and other useful plants. On the upslope side of the main street passing through Tamazunchale, Avenida 20 de Noviembre, find Callejón del Aguacate (Avocado Alley) next to the store called Comercial Reforma, more or less across from the army barracks; the alley's street-sign is a small one, high on the Comercial's wall.

After you pass through the alley, take the first left and begin climbing, always staying on the most-used part. Soon the wide sidewalk deteriorates into a much-used mud and rock trail, but then a long series of steep, irregularly constructed concrete steps appear. Climb these all the way to where the trail makes a hard right onto approximately five yards of level ground; a fine view of the valley opens to the right, and a little *refresco*-and-cracker kiosk stands to the left, with the number 755 neatly painted at the corner. Here turn left, to south 190°, and continue directly up the steep slope to the ridge top. Here the steps end, a few feet of mud must be crossed, and finally the ridgetop trail is reached, which is part concrete and part mud.

At this point, if you want to be guided around the area, feel free to contact Don Alejandro, the father in a family with which I once stayed. At the ridge top, turn back around and briefly descend the steps you just climbed, to the first right (on your right as you are heading down the steps). At this right, follow the mud trail as it bends around to the left, and at the gate of the first house, one standing atop a gray, cinder-block wall, stand and call "Don Alejandroooooooooooo...." The family is used to odd-hour visits from random *gringos*, but the dog finds it hard to get used to; do not pass through the gate until someone offers an invitation to come up. No one here speaks a word of English—but in Spanish, Don Alejandro, who spoke Nahuatl as a child, can point out a plethora of slope-grown edible and medicinal herbs.

The most common fruit trees on Colonia el Sacrificio's slope are mango, banana, papaya, guava, lemon, and orange. Dark-leafed coffee shrubs often grow in the shade of taller trees. Probably the most common "weed tree" on the slope, with alternate, pinnately compound leaves, is the *cocuite*, a member of the bean family, looking like a black locust with pink flowers. Sometimes it is known as mouse killer because its bark and leaves, when ground with cooked corn, kill mice. Other times it is called *madre de cacao* (mother of cacao), because cacao, the chocolate plant, grows best in shade, and *cocuite* often serves as the shade producer.

To continue on to Tetlama after you have been guided around Colonia el Sacrificio, at the ridge top, turn right and follow the path for 3 or 4 minutes, to the large Cross of the Santa Misión. Here take a left across the rocky ridge crest to the dirt trail on the other side. Go right for another 3 or 4 minutes, until it ends. During this walk, a gravel road becomes plainly visible below, on the left; this is the road to Tetlama. Follow this gravel road as it heads toward the hill across the valley, bearing southwest 230° (see the third section, The Road Beyond Colonia el Sacrificio, below).

Approach via Pickup Truck: The pickup-truck approach enables hikers to ride upslope to Tetlama and then walk back downhill to Tamazunchale. Once a day a pickup usually leaves from downtown Tamazunchale, going beyond Tetlama, all the way to the road's end at Tamacor, another Nahuatl village. (The pickup truck's route also can be hiked.) The pickup's schedule depends on the season and the driver's mood. At this writing, the truck leaves at noon, which is unfortunately late because it places hikers on the road in the afternoon heat. However, there is usually a nice breeze at these elevations, and you will be heading downhill.

Look for the pickup shuttle on the downslope side of Tamazunchale's main street, Avenida 20 de Noviembre, next to the Mini-Super Rubio and the Expendio de Carnes "Mendoza," across the street from the entrance to Callejón del Aguacate.

Follow Highway 85 south of town to about 300 yards south of the Quinta Chilla (a small motel), and take the only gravel road leading upslope, to the left. Just stay on this gravel road all the way to Tetlama. At first, nothing but weedy pastures can be observed, but things become more interesting higher up.

The Road Beyond Colonia el Sacraficio: Hikers taking the first approach, through Colonia el Sacrificio, meet up with the gravel road taken by those who take the second approach by getting a ride in a pickup truck (or hiking on the pickup's route). Regardless of one's approach, follow this gravel road the rest of the way to Tetlama; beyond the Colonia, there are no turnoffs to confuse matters.

Along this road to Tetlama, hacked-up *cocuites* grow in straight lines; just stick a *cocuite* twig into the ground and it grows into a fence post! Another strange and conspicuous tree to look for bears foot-long, pale, waxy fruits on

Near Tetlama, "cow okra" pods hang bizarrely from a tree's trunk; an epiphytic Rhipsalis *cactus dangles beside it on the left.*

its trunk, instead of on branches like normal trees. This is *chote*, a member of the bignonia family, in which is also found the northern catalpa and trumpet creeper. English speakers in Belize call it cow okra. Cows do love the fruit and humans eat it if nothing better is handy. Local Nahuatl speakers esteem the

Mala mujer *looks soft and gentle, but its stem is covered with stinging hairs.*

The passion flower bears a curious, three-forked stigma above five reflexed stamens.

cooked fruit as medicine for the kidneys, and they swear that a flower stuffed into the ear cures earaches.

After about 2 miles (3 km), pass a tin-roofed, open-walled storage *palapa*; across the road a nice rock beneath a shade tree affords an agreeable gaze onto the steamy Gulf lowlands.

About halfway to Tetlama the road passes a stately grove of fan palms. In the few forest remnants along the way, be sure to notice the abundant epiphytes—plants living on tree limbs but not parasitizing them. Probably the most conspicuous epiphyte is an air-conditioner–size bromeliad looking like a maguey with elongated spikes of flattish flowers. Often accompanying this bromeliad is an epiphytic cactus called rhipsalis. Uncactuslike, rhipsalis is composed of abundant, much-branched, slender, pencil-like stems.

An interesting, and common, head-high weed along the road bears foot-wide, soft, hand-shaped leaves and small white flowers. It is *mala mujer* (bad woman), so called because its seemingly soft vegetative parts sting like a nettle.

One of the most beautiful blossoms along the road is that of the passion flower, a vine. In the center of its three-inch-wide blossoms, the style branches into three parts, each bearing a stigma; five anthers spread below this. The ovary is mounted on a pedestal above the stamens but below the three-forked

Along the road to Tetlama, a beetle exits a morning-glory blossom.

style. The three-forked style accounts for the passion flower's name; looking like a cross, it reminds Mexico's faithful of Christ's Passion.

The slopes traversed by the hike are occupied by weedy pastures, orange plantations, and fields of nopal cactus. Nopal is a spineless or nearly spineless cactus with elongate, edible joints. Outside Tamazunchale's Mercado Municipal, Nahuatl women sit slicing nopal joints into tiny slivers which, stir-fried with onions and garlic, become soft and a bit slimy, but with a pleasing, lemony taste. Nopal is big business; sometimes large trucks are seen chugging up the Mexican Plateau, hauling what must be a ton or more of nothing but neatly stacked nopal joints.

Morning-glory vines along the road to Tetlama put on a real show. So do butterflies, the prettiest of which are the giant, iridescent-blue morphos and, with narrow, often striped wings, the heliconiids. Usually at least one line of leaf-cutter ants slices across the road, each little critter toting its leaf shred. These leaf tatters are carried underground to subterranean compost heaps where fungus grows on them. The ants eat cauliflowerlike knobs that develop on the fungus.

Near Tetlama, two of the author's old friends, working in a field of nopal cactus, want their picture taken.

Birds along this trail are mostly "weed species." However, there is such variety that an early-morning hike should provide an interesting list. Almost always chachalacas can be heard, and frequently seen; these are raucous birds looking like streamlined turkeys. In pastures the large, black birds with Jimmy Durante beaks are groove-bill anis. Tiny, sparrowlike birds wearing bandit masks are white-collared seedeaters. During the northern winter, a surprising number of Wilson's warblers flit among the trees.

After another 2 miles or so (about 3 km), after passing along a ridge for a few minutes, another pleasant sitting-boulder appears beneath a small shade tree on the right, offering a restful view back toward Tamazunchale. At this

Cordoncillo, *a member of the black-pepper family, bears hundreds of tiny, very simple flowers in slender, recurving spikes.*

point, Tetlama's roosters can be heard crowing and its turkeys gobbling. Usually a *refresco* stand is open in Tetlama; otherwise there is little to see, so this might be a good place to turn back. It is also possible to continue through Tetlama to Tamacor, about 1 mile (2 km) farther.

Getting There

Tamazunchale, the base town for this hike, lies on the busy north–south-running Pan American Highway, Highway 85. Many buses pass through town, especially those of the Flecha Roja line. Just south of Tamazunchale, Highway 85 becomes curvy and steep as it climbs onto the Mexican Plateau.

Tamazunchale has several hotels of various colors, most too close to noisy streets to be restful. For a quieter place, try the Quinta Chilla, a shady motel about 0.5 mile (1 km) south of town next to a river, with some bungalows behind a wall, and with plenty of camping space. Look for its name on the wall, on Highway 85's river side.

CHAPTER 5

THE MEXICAN PLATEAU

The Land

The Mexican Plateau is shaped like a slender, deformed wedge of pie tilted onto its nose, with the top skewed hard to the left, the west. The whipped-cream swirls at the wedge's edges are the Western and Eastern Sierra Madre mountains. In general this is a very dry piece of pie, except in the vicinity of the whipped cream.

Torreón, Coahuila, in the pie-slice's north-central zone, lies at about 3,800

Wild begonias along the road to Tetlama

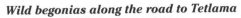

Aptly named allthorn, this common Chihuahuan Desert species conserves water by dropping its tiny leaves when the rains end.

feet in elevation and receives approximately ten inches of rain per year. About 400 miles (645 km) farther southeast, at San Luis Potosí, S.L.P., the elevation is up to 6,000 feet, and rainfall increases to about fifteen inches per year. Mexico City, 250 miles (400 km) even farther southeast, continues the trend by showing up at 7,370 feet, with about twenty-five inches of annual rain. This compares with approximately thirty-four inches in a typical year in St. Louis, Missouri. South of Mexico City, below where the two Sierra Madre chains connect, the plateau's physiography becomes so complex that general trends are hard to peg down.

One of Mexico's many species of prickly-pear cactus—this one can be found in northern Coahuila.

In northern Mexico's Chihuahuan Desert, old, woody skeletons of cholla cactus such as this one can be found.

One prominent feature of the southern area is the Transverse Volcanic Belt, a neat line of volcanoes running east and west, passing just south of Mexico City. On rare clear days in Mexico City, toward the southeast, it is possible to see Citlaltépetl, also called Orizaba, claiming the title of Mexico's highest peak by rising to 18,855 feet. Just west of Citlaltépetl comes Malinche (14,636 feet), then farther west there's Popocatépetl (17,888 feet), then Ixtaccíhuatl (17,343 feet), Nevado de Toluca (15,036 feet), Cerro Tancitaro (12,661 feet), and Nevado de Colima (14,236 feet) . . . all lined up like ducks in a row.

South of the Transverse Volcanic Belt, the Mexican Plateau (as defined here) includes some mountains in Oaxaca and, in the state of Guerrero, the Southern Sierra Madre. The Southern Sierra Madre are nearly cleaved from the rest of the highlands by the vast valley of the Río Balsas, extending from the coastal border between Michoacán and Guerrero south of Mexico City, practically all the way to Puebla.

The Western and Eastern Sierra Madre are fundamentally different from one another; the Western chain is volcanic in origin while the Eastern is mostly, but not entirely, composed of uplifted sedimentary limestone. Thus the Western Sierra Madre are dark, rugged, and physiographically youthful; the Eastern range, with its dignified layers of limestone outcropping as majestic white cliffs, on a foggy morning can remind one of a placid Chinese watercolor. Both ranges are in most places six or seven ridges across.

Between the two ranges the Mexican Plateau drops to a still-high, arid plain. In the north, as explained in Chapter 2, Mexico's Natural Environment, *bolsons* form, the most extensive of which is Bolsón de Mapimí southeast of Ciudad Camargo, Chihuahua. About 175 miles (300 km) to the east of Bolsón de Mapimí, a series of hot springs flows into a depression creating an extensive marsh just west of Monclova, Coahuila, called Cuatrociénegas ("Four Swamps"), famous for its abundant wildlife. Inside several of the region's *bolsons*, evaporation outpaces rainfall so gypsum crystals precipitate out and dry into blindingly white salts. Sometimes wind whips these crystals into white dunes that migrate across the landscape. A good place to see regular sand dunes is where Highway 45 crosses the Médanos de Samalayuca just south of Ciudad Juárez, Chihuahua.

The farther south one travels on the plateau, the more rain falls, and the more likely that permanent lakes replace *bolsons*. Often these lakes have no rivers leading from them; their average permanent levels represent states of equilibrium between local rainfall and evaporation rate. These lakes, verdant oases in an otherwise dusty, eroded landscape, include such much-beloved tourist destinations as Lagos Pátzcuaro, Yuriría, Chitzeo, Sayula, Atotonilco, and what is left of Lago de Texcoco.

Plants

The Chihuahuan Desert occupying most of the northern Mexican Plateau is fundamentally different from Mexico's other big desert, the Sonoran. The Chihuahuan lies higher in elevation than most of the Sonoran—usually above 3,500 feet—so summer temperatures there average 10 to 20° Fahrenheit lower than those of the Sonoran; in winter hard freezes can occur. Good looks at the Chihuahuan are afforded by Highways 45 and 49 between El Paso, Texas, and Gómez Palacio, Durango, and Highway 40 between Saltillo, Coahuila, and the Continental Divide west of Durango, Durango.

One of the Chihuahua's most distinctive plants is the lechuguilla, a scrawny-looking agave with spearlike fruiting spikes and needle-tipped leaves that stab hikers' legs. Yucca of various species abound throughout the Chihuahuan, the most common being the soaptree yucca, from whose large roots soap can be made. Also fiber can be produced from its leaves, and its flowers and fruits can be eaten.

Other typically Chihuahuan plants include yuccalike sotol and nolina. Candelilla of limestone areas looks like dense clusters of long, slender, leafless, wax-covered fingers sticking from the ground. Numerous cactus species exist here, but not as many as in the Sonoran Desert. Creosote bush and ocotillo are common in many places but giant, columnar cacti are rare. Trees are small and restricted to areas such as arroyos; mesquite sometimes takes over.

Plant identifiers should not forget that many plants of the northern half of the Mexican Plateau are included in Correll and Johnston's *Manual of the Vascular Plants of Texas* and Robert Vines's *Trees, Shrubs and Woody Vines of the Southwest* (see Bibliography). In the plateau's southern region, Oscar Sánchez Sánchez's *La Flora del Valle de México* is useful far beyond the limited area of the Valle de México. These are technical guides.

Animals

Located less than 250 air-miles (400 km) south of the U.S. border, Sky Ranch is a research station operated by Brownsville's Texas Southmost College in the Sierra de Guatemala, in the Eastern Sierra Madre south of Ciudad Victoria, Tamaulipas. Birdwatchers at Sky Ranch have spotted around 255 bird species in the general vicinity; this compares to about 296 species listed for the state of Kentucky.

Though the vast majority of these species also can be spotted in Texas, a few are restricted to the northern Mexican Plateau, such as spotted wrens in arid areas and striped sparrows in meadows and open pine forests. In relatively humid oak–pine forests at higher elevations, mountain trogons appear, as do top-knotted tufted flycatchers, brown-backed solitaires with hauntingly beautiful songs, nervous little slate-throated redstarts, and plain-looking but endemic rufous-capped brush-finches.

At higher elevations farther south, a few extra "exotic" species appear, such as green violet-ears (hummingbirds), endemic gray-barred wrens, inquisitive flocks of gray silky-flycatchers, endemic collared towhees, and bright red warblers. For North Americans used to Dendroica-type, mostly yellow warblers, seeing shockingly red red warblers is exciting stuff!

Walking through the plateau's grassland–mesquite and desert zones, one often sees on the ground abundant marble-size, dry, yellowish spheres of compacted grass clippings; these are rabbit droppings. Two common species of rabbit with white sides occur here: black-tailed jackrabbits specialize in dry lowlands north of Mexico City, while cottontail rabbits dominate higher

At dusk on Lago Catamaco in southern Veracruz, this epiphyte-filled tree provides safe haven for several roosting herons.

Left: Native to Central and South America from southern Mexico to Paraguay and Argentina, the black hawk-eagle, *Spizaetus tyrannus,* hunts in dense rain forests and cloud forests of lower mountains.

Below: Several species of horned lizards, also known as "horny toads," are common in Mexico's deserts.

Right: A tiny mouse, *Reithrodontomys sumichrasti,* feeds on fallen monarchs on a bed of fir needles. In the caterpillar stage, monarchs consume milkweed plants and absorb toxins from the plants that remain in the adult monarch body. Mice and birds that eat the monarchs prefer the abdomen, where the concentration of toxins is the lowest.
(Photo: © Gregory G. Dimijian)

Below: Spectacled caimans, *Caiman sclerops,* are distinguished from crocodiles, also native to southern Mexico, by their shorter, wider snouts, and a bony ridge in front of their eyes.

3

Left: In upland San Luis Potosí, large bromeliads (pineapple family) and a cactus with drooping, pencil-like stems live epiphytically in trees next to a field of *tuna,* or edible cacti.

Below: In the skies above "The Snail," or El Caracol, at Chichén Itzá, an afternoon storm is brewing.

Below right: A roadside altar dedicated to Santa Lucía

Left: Settlers in lowland Chiapas show off a recent harvest of root-crops, extremely important items for tropical American farmers. The plant with large, arrow-shaped leaves, sometimes known as "elephant's ear," is taro; the dark tubers tapering at both ends are wild yams, similar to sweet potatoes; the woody shrubs leaning against the fence, with leaves similar to those of marihuana, is manioc, sometimes called cassava, tapioca-plant, and yucca.

The Pacific shore near Salina Cruz, Oaxaca

In Tabasco, this enormous ceiba or kapok tree, *Ceiba pentandra* (closely related to the African baobab) has shed its leaves during the dry season to reveal a host of other plants living on its trunk and limbs; among these are bromeliads, orchids, strangler fig vines, and a semiparasitic relative of the northern mistletoe.

Right: Near the ruins of Palenque in Chiapas, these cascades must have pleased the ancient Maya as much as they do today's visitors.

Left: Wild plaintain, *Heliconia* sp., is a common weed in the humid lowlands of southern Mexico; it is closely related to Africa's bird-of-paradise.

Below: A tree trunk in Veracruz is home to several epiphytes. The largest one, with spines, is a cactus; the curled-up ferns are *Polypodium* sp.; the slender, grasslike leaves at the far right belong to a bromeliad; in the lower left corner is an orchid; also present are lichens and mosses.

Brown pelicans on a fishing boat at Mazatlán (Photo: Dr. Sigrid Liede)

elevations elsewhere. Desert cottontails occur in most arid zones, and the Mexican cottontail appears in highlands south of Mexico City. The volcano rabbit is an extraordinary, tiny, uniformly brown, short-eared, almost tailless critter of mountain forests where tall bunchgrass occurs between widely spaced pines. Volcano rabbits are narrowly endemic, existing on Popocatépetl and Iztaccíhuatl, and a few other slopes near the Valley of Mexico.

Mexican free-tail bats spend their summers around Tucson, Arizona, and overwinter in Jalisco. Several species of gray and red squirrel occupy the plateau's mountainous oak–pine forests; in the northern Western Sierra Madre, tuft-eared Abert squirrels can be spotted. Coyotes survive throughout much of the plateau, and originally so did wolves, which now barely hang on in the northern Western Sierra Madre and in mountains south of Big Bend. Kit foxes sometimes are spotted in the arid north and gray foxes rarely show up throughout. Black bears are occasionally reported in the plateau's northern highlands. Raccoons and their cousin the ringtail cat are fairly common throughout. Coatis are just in the highlands but badgers are found in the plateau's lower, arid zones. Striped and hog-nosed skunks occur throughout; there is both a northern species of spotted skunk and a southern one. At least formerly, bobcats roamed the entire region north of Mexico City.

Originally, piglike collared peccaries occurred in all but the driest part of the plateau. Today mule deer still are common in certain of the plateau's northern, isolated arid zones, and white-tailed deer can show up any place not close to human settlement. In the plateau's most rugged, isolated, northernmost mountains, lucky hikers might spot pronghorn antelope or even bighorn sheep.

People

The farther south one travels on the Mexican Plateau, the more "Indiany" it gets. In the north, the main group with some of their traditions intact are the Tarahumara in and around Chihuahua's Copper Canyon, also known as Barranca del Cobre.

In contrast, the highlands south of Mexico City are home to hundreds of small villages composed mostly of Native Americans. The smaller the village and the farther it lies from major thoroughfares, the less is the probability that people there speak Spanish and "think Mexican." Especially in the uplands of Oaxaca and eastern Guerrero, villagers still speak Native American languages, and Catholicism mingles promiscuously with ancient spiritual insights. In Guerrero the main indigenous groups are Nahuas (150,000 people), Mixtecs (70,000 people), and Tlapanecs (60,000 people). In Oaxaca there are Zapotecs (375,000 people), Mixtecs (325,000 people), Mazatecs (120,000 people), and numerous smaller groups. Isolated Ixcatlán 50 miles (80 km) northwest of Oaxaca City is home to all 200 surviving Ixcatecs.

In *mercados* of Mexico City, Oaxaca City, and practically any other fair-size town in the southern plateau uplands, one sees Indians coming to town to buy and sell. Some, especially the women, still wear colorful traditional dress; usually men (depending on the group) wear typical Mexican *campesino* clothes. A while back at Oaxaca's second-class bus station, I struck up a conversation with a man who looked like a local but spoke Spanish with an accent. It turned out that his native language was the little-known tongue of Chinantec, and the man came from the very isolated village of Ayotzintepec about 50 miles (80 km) northeast of Oaxaca.

One thing the Chinanteco mentioned about his home region was that a great deal of marijuana was cultivated there. This reminds us that, especially in the southern Mexican highlands, it is not a good idea to wander too far into isolated places looking for rustic settlements. Michoacán is considered Mexico's marijuana-growing capital.

6 ■ MEXIQUILLO FALLS

Distance: 1.5 miles
Difficulty: easy
Terrain: dirt road
Elevation: 8,600 feet
Map: ITMP Map No. 200: México, 1:3,300,000

This hike lies just south of the timber town of La Ciudad (sometimes shown on maps as Ciudad), Durango, on Highway 40 between Durango City and Mazatlán. Mexiquillo is a small waterfall that after rains can be photogenic, but during the dry season may amount to no more than a trickle of exceedingly black runoff from a nearby sawmill. The walk follows a one-lane logging road and passes through cool pine forest and a very interesting geological setting to the falls. From there the hiker can either return or embark upon an abandoned railroad right-of-way (no rails or cross ties) that in one direction leads down the vertical wall of a tremendous canyon, and in the other runs for a few peaceful miles (several km) among low hills of pine.

During the pine-hill walk, several timber roads shoot off to the left (north), where soon they meet Highway 40, which parallels this section of the hike. The abandoned railroad right-of-way passes through several tunnels; anyone judging them safe enough to hike through will be grateful for a flashlight.

Because this area has a history of robbery, do not hike this trail alone. Think twice about carrying expensive cameras and other precious items and, by all means, do not succumb to the urge to camp in the deliciously fresh pine forest. Camping overnight is simply begging for trouble.

The trail leaves Highway 40 on the south side of La Ciudad—the Mazatlán side. Take the only paved road leading southeast from the highway and follow it for about a minute, then embark on the dirt road to the left, to the east-northeast. Follow this through pines for a bit more than 10 minutes, until arriving at the sawmill.

A sign on the metal fence surrounding the sawmill may say that everyone

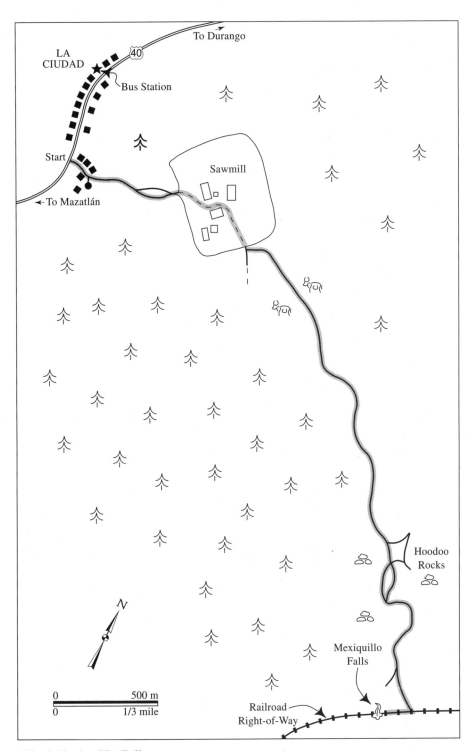

Hike 6 Mexiquillo Falls

not affiliated with the sawmill must stay out, but the guard at the entrance assured me that during work hours visitors to Mexiquillo are expected to walk through the sawmill to the access road on the other side. Nonetheless, one should ask the guard for permission to pass through: "*¿Está bien si pasamos a Mexiquillo?*" (Walking through the sawmill can be avoided—and thus also the attention of dozens of hard-working, hormone-filled, loud, and sometimes impudent young men—by following the fence around to the sawmill's south-southeast side, to the only opening.)

As you go through the sawmill area, piles of sawdust and slabs come and go inside the site, so your passage may be different from the one shown in the map. The main idea is to get past the first buildings, then look for the clearly visible opening in the fence on the far side. Saying "*¿Mexiquillo?*" to anyone standing around should result in a finger being pointed in the right direction.

At the south-southeast exit gate, a one-lane, dirt/gravel road heads straight away from the sawmill, to the south, but another follows the fence for a while to the east, then bends off toward the southeast; follow the route along the fence, to the southeast. Mexiquillo Falls lies about a mile down the road.

About midway, the logging road enters a strange and lovely landscape of widely spaced pines, and a museum of monumental-sized column-, pillar-, pedestal-, and toadstool-shaped rocks. Sometimes such rocks are called hoodoo rocks.

It is interesting to put one's nose right up to these rocks and, using a magnifying glass, examine the rocks' composition and texture. The main part of the rock—the pinkish, fine-grained "groundmass"—has mixed into it white to gray grains clearly visible to the naked eye. Volcanic rock with large grains mixed into the fine-grained groundmass is said to have porphyritic texture, and such rocks are sometimes called porphyrites.

The hoodoo rocks themselves are worth thinking about. This area's "balanced rocks" and chimneys were not moved into their precarious positions; they simply developed there as the rock around them eroded away. Once, at the level of the geometric plain defined by the tops of all the area's hoodoo rocks, a stratum of resistant rock existed. Wherever this stratum was eroded through, the relatively soft rock below was quickly (in geological terms) eroded away, down to the stratum on which the hoodoo rocks stand today, which itself must be fairly resistant. Today the upper layer of resistant rock exists only as hard "caps" atop the hoodoo rocks. Once they are finally eroded away, the hoodoo rocks will vanish. The many rock chimneys and razorback ridges seen from Highway 40 west of La Ciudad owe their existence to similar strata of hard rock overlying relatively softer rock.

Naturally, the hoodoo-rock area is a favorite picnicking spot for locals, so here the trail branches and rebranches, making a maze among the hoodoos; keep an eye on the map and your compass. The area is not large enough to really get lost in. All roads to the north soon connect with Highway 40; all trails to the south inevitably intersect with the abandoned railroad right-of-way.

When the road reaches the abandoned railroad right-of-way, Mexiquillo

Falls lies immediately to the right. To see it, pass through the rock cut on the right. Upon exiting the corridor and entering an elevated section of the right-of-way, Mexiquillo Falls should roar magnificently, or dribble piteously, to your right.

At this point, several options are available. The quickest is to return the way you just traveled. A spectacular extension is to continue following the right-of-way west-southwest past the falls until a canyon of stomach-churning proportions opens to the left. Besides offering an awe-inspiring view, the right-of-way along the canyon wall creates an interesting microhabitat; several interesting agaves and cacti occur here. The right-of-way does not course along the canyon wall for long before the first of three tunnels is reached. Good judgment is needed here to determine whether to pass through them; the third tunnel is definitely unsafe. Years ago, avalanches and tunnel rockfalls put an end to blasting for this ill-fated railroad track just beyond the third tunnel. At the last tunnel you are willing to pass through, just turn around and walk back to the falls, and retrace the route from there.

Another option once you reach Mexiquillo Falls is to extend the hike by following the abandoned railroad right-of-way in the other direction, toward the west-northwest. Access roads regularly come in from the north, from Highway 40, which is often within earshot. About 2.5 miles (4 km) from Mexiquillo Falls, a regular gravel road crosses the right-of-way. A left here brings you to Highway 40 in a couple of minutes.

About 2 miles (3 km) farther down the right-of-way, a short tunnel is encountered. Most hikers will find it safe enough to walk through. However, about 0.5 mile (less than 1 km) beyond that tunnel, a second tunnel maybe 300 yards long occurs, and that one deserves prudent circumspection. During the rainy season, the low end can be flooded; certainly a flashlight is needed. The railroad right-of-way itself crosses Highway 40 about 1.5 miles (2.5 km) beyond this tunnel, right above the little village of Las Adjuntas. Do not take chances with these tunnels; they may have deteriorated since my visit.

Anyone itching to continue beyond Las Adjuntas can do so, for across the highway the right-of-way continues paralleling Highway 40 all the way to El Salto, 9 miles (15 km) away. However, this stretch is much less scenic, often runs close to loud Highway 40, passes through uninteresting ranchland, and, if it has been raining, may be marshy where bridges are out. About 2 miles (3 km) before reaching El Salto, a stream must be crossed by walking along a hair-raising trestle—just some planks less than a yard wide wired atop the metal structure, and no handrails. . . . The last mile before El Salto, however, is quite nice, edging along the rim of yet another colossal canyon.

Birds in this area's nearly pure pine forest are very similar to those found in mountaintop ponderosa pine forests in Arizona and New Mexico. The olive warbler is surprisingly common; keep on the lookout for Hutton's vireo. One of the few species found here but not in the United States is the tufted flycatcher. This species, unlike most tropical flycatchers, which usually are small, mousy creatures, is easy to identify because of its tufted crest and cinnamon-brown underparts.

Getting There

This hike lies just south of the timber town of La Ciudad, Durango, on Highway 40 between Durango City and Mazatlán; by road, La Ciudad is 28 miles (46 km) west of El Salto, which is itself 62 miles (100 km) west of Durango City. Several buses run each day in each direction between Durango and Mazatlán, especially the Estrella Blanca line. Though maps show La Ciudad almost midway between Durango and Mazatlán, reaching La Ciudad from Durango takes about 1½ hours, but from Mazatlán travel time is about 4 hours. Highway 40 between La Ciudad and the Pacific lowlands is scenic but twisty, and usually the 10-minute break at the midway point lasts a half hour or longer.

In La Ciudad—as muddy- and rough-looking a town as one wants to see— across Highway 40 from the Estrella Blanca bus station stands a fairly unsavory-looking hotel. Much of La Ciudad's population appears to consist of young sawmill workers temporarily away from home, and very fancy women favoring plenty of makeup. In El Salto, right beside the highway bus stop, there is another hotel that looks a bit better. Just downslope from Km 222 on Highway 40, about midway up the Mexican Plateau's wall near the town of Portrelillo, there is a small, clean-looking motel. If none of these options appeal, a good strategy might be to stay in Durango, take the early bus to La Ciudad and do the hike, then take the late bus to Mazatlán.

7 ▪ LOS AZUFRES PARK

Distance: 1.5–2.6 miles (2.5–4 km)
Difficulty: easy
Terrain: paved road
Elevation: 9,200 feet
Maps: ITMP Map No. 200: México, 1:3,300,000; ITMP Map No. 204: México South, 1:1,000,000

Los Azufres Park lies in the high mountains of the southwestern state of Michoacán about 15 miles (25 km) north of Ciudad Hidalgo by road, some 100 air-miles (180 km) west-northwest of Mexico City. Because no regular public trails exist in the park, the map shows the park's road system, which, at least during the week when traffic is light, makes for very pleasant walking through the pines and sacred firs. Hiking within the park is rather limited, and off the pavement it is hard to know for sure whether one is trespassing. The best day hiking may be between the park and San Pedro, which lies 6 miles (10 km) below the park, on the valley floor on the way to Ciudad Hidalgo.

Several awe-inspiring, thunderous, steam-venting, electricity-producing geothermal wells can be visited in Los Azufres Park, as well as a few hissing fumaroles, sputtering mudpots, and simmering hot springs. If cool sunlight happens to grace the hike, the experience is simply delicious. All the park's big geysers have been capped; there are no Yellowstone-like attractions.

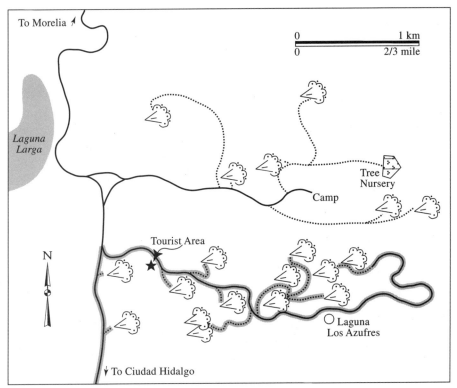

Hike 7 Los Azufres Park

The park's entrance originates at the first traffic triangle as you come from below on the main highway; inside the triangle, two maps of the park are accompanied by explanations of how geothermal steam is converted to electricity.

The park's officially designated "tourist area" lies about 500 yards around the entrance road's first bend, on the right; Laguna Los Azufres is about 1.25 miles (2 km) farther, also on the right. Laguna Los Azufres, announced by a sign referring to it as LOS AZUFRES, is less a lake than a muddy pond flanked by a few gurgling hot-water springs and hissing fumaroles. Though swimming here is free, the bathrooms are ruined beyond use.

Steam-venting wells raise the decibel level of parts of Los Azufres to that of Kennedy Airport's Runway One. Most of the vented steam originates when surface water seeps into the earth, meets with very hot rocks, and vaporizes. Small quantities of gases from deep inside the earth escape from the area's fumaroles, carrying trace elements. Thus yellow rims of native sulphur form around many fumaroles; when reddish streaks appear in the yellow, that is probably selenium. Grayish streaks generally denote arsenic. The heavy rotten-egg odor sometimes smelled at Los Azufres is hydrogen sulfide.

The most abundant gases vented in fumaroles usually are nitrogen, hydrogen, and carbon dioxide, the basic ingredients of the earth's atmosphere. The issuance of these gases by volcanoes and fumaroles over billions of years has essentially defined the makeup of the earth's present atmosphere. Therefore Laguna Los Azufres's hissing, spitting, and gurgling fumaroles deserve a tip of the hat for their fundamental role in biosphere-making.

Inside Los Azufres Park, the main conifers are false white and Michoacán pines. The false white pine, like North America's "true" white pine, bears five straight needles per cluster. Sacred firs, with their crosslike, "religious" branches, appear only at higher elevations; Lindley's cypresses, typical of oak–pine forest zones, are common on the lower slopes. A pretty lupine with dark violet flowers grows along the roadside.

Many bird species here are typical of the western United States' pine forests—American robins, white-breasted nuthatches, brown creepers, Eastern bluebirds, and chipping sparrows, for instance. Nonetheless, Los Azufres is far enough south to have bird species never spotted in North America. Large, noisy flocks of gray silky-flycatchers, related to cedar waxwings, are common. The main warblers are the crescent-chested warbler, with its monotonously repeated *tcherrrrrrrrrrr*, and the slate-throated redstart, which loves to flash its white outer tail feathers.

Less frequently seen red warblers always are a treat to see, and plain-looking brown-backed solitaires raise goose bumps with their majestic, echoic, intricate, haunting songs. Tufted flycatchers display cardinal-like head tufts and cinnamon-brown underparts. The wren strikingly barred with black and white stripes across its back is the gray-barred wren, an endemic species found only in the mountains of Mexico's southern plateau. One has to be fast to spot green violet-ears, all-green hummingbirds with violet ear-patches. Maybe the most "exotic" bird to look for is the mountain trogon, with bright-red underparts and a *tucka-tucka-tucka* call.

Squirrels similar to North America's gray and fox squirrels, but different species, scamper among the oaks at lower elevations.

The road continues another mile (1.5 km) or so upslope past Laguna Los Azufres, makes a big bend, passes several footpaths into the woods, and dead-ends at a gate. One might assume that the *Alto* sign halfway to the gate, like most other Mexican *Alto* signs, means "Hey, wake up!" rather than really "Stop." The gate at the end of the road is easy to pass by and no sign says not to, and tempting, well-worn footpaths lead downslope from the gate, past some fumaroles and hot springs. However, at the trail's end a sign facing the opposite direction says flatly to stay out, so do not pass beyond the *Alto* sign on the gate.

Getting There

Ciudad Hidalgo, the gateway to Los Azufres Park, is richly served by buses cruising between Morelia and Mexico City. In Ciudad Hidalgo, next to Hotel Suzy on the main street, two to five mini-buses make the run to Los Azufres each day; frequency of departure depends on demand. Whatever itinerary you plan, check the current schedule between Hotel Suzy and Los Azufres the day before if possible, because of its frequent changes.

A fairly continuous stream of mini-buses shuttle between Hotel Suzy and the village of San Pedro, which lies about 6 miles (10 km) south (downslope) from the park. The stretch between Ciudad Hidalgo and San Pedro passes through a flat agricultural area, but between San Pedro and the park it is all forest and steep slopes. Therefore, one pleasing option is to take an early bus from Ciudad Hidalgo to Los Azufres Park, tour the park, then hike downslope to San Pedro. Or you could bus from Cuidad Hidalgo to San Pedro and hike uphill to Los Azufres. Heavy bus traffic between Ciudad Hidalgo and San Pedro can be counted on year-round.

Ciudad Hidalgo offers plenty of lodging possibilities. Closer to the park, at Km 14, mid-slope between San Pedro and the park, Balneario "Erendira" is a privately operated thermal swimming pool open to the public. About 2 miles (3 km) higher, the sizable Motel Tejamaniles stands near the first encountered big plumes of steam.

Inside the park at the "tourist area" designated on the map, a cabin accommodating six people costs about $50 US nightly; six-person tents can be rented for about $8.00; tent sites go for about $3.25. Swimming in the nearby hot-spring–fed concrete pools costs about $2.75. A sign next to the restaurant and small grocery advertises horseback riding, but often the horse owner seems to be unavailable.

8 ▪ MONARCH BUTTERFLY ECOLOGICAL RESERVE

Distance: 8 miles round trip (13 km)
Difficulty: moderately strenuous
Terrain: cobblestone and gravel road
Elevation: 8,000–10,000 feet
Map: American Automobile Association map of Mexico's inset for Mexico City and vicinity

The Monarch Butterfly Ecological Reserve lies on the border between the states of Michoacán and México, right above the town of Angangueo, Michoacán, some 70 air-miles (110 km) east-northeast of Mexico City. During "butterfly season," between late October and mid-April, millions of overwintering monarch butterflies drape the reserve's mountaintop boreal-forest trees.

A very steep, curvy, one-lane gravel road connects downtown Angangueo with the reserve; if you hike slowly and take occasional breathers, about 3 hours are needed to hike it. Though one sees more cornfields than forest, this can be a pleasant hike; the people are friendly and talkative, and the cool, crisp air just makes fine walking. During butterfly season, trucks shuttle non-hikers between Angangueo and the reserve.

To protect the monarchs and their forest habitat, unguided hiking inside the reserve itself is prohibited. To prevent erosion of overused trails and to keep up with ever-changing concentrations of butterflies, the reserve's trails constantly change. It is typical that inside the reserve visitors must walk a

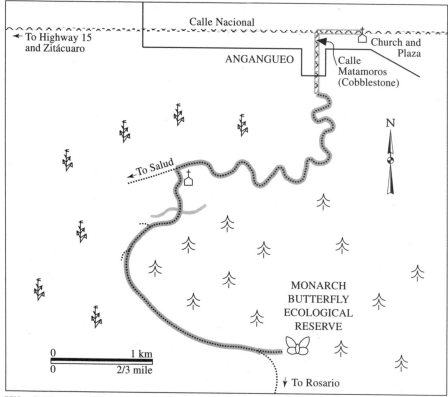

Calle Nacional

← To Highway 15
and Zitácuaro

ANGANGUEO

Church and
Plaza

Calle
Matamoros
(Cobblestone)

← To Salud

N

MONARCH
BUTTERFLY
ECOLOGICAL
RESERVE

0   1 km
0   2/3 mile

↓ To Rosario

Hike 8 Monarch Butterfly Ecological Reserve

little over 1 mile (2 km) before reaching the main butterfly populations.

Starting at Angangueo's plaza, follow the main street, Calle Nacional, downslope (west) for about 350 yards to Calle Matamoros, which is a substantial cobblestone street on the left that heads up very steeply (due south). Turn onto Calle Matamoros and, without taking any rights or lefts, keep trudging up this slope; the cobblestone surface becomes gravel after 500 yards.

The road curves around for about 2 miles (3 km), after which a gravel road and an altar with a cross appear on the left, while the main road continues straight into the village of Salud; go left. During the rest of the walk, two Y's are encountered; go left at both, staying on the main road. The reserve's entrance stands next to the village of Rosario; its visitor center and fenced-in steps are impossible to miss.

Plants and animals here, except for the monarch butterflies, are essentially the same as those of the pine and pine–sacred fir forests described in hike 7, Los Azufres Park. The monarchs themselves are not hard to find; they smother trees with orange and black flutterings, and a few land on visitors' shirts and heads. Listen to the rushing-water sound caused by myriad dainty wingbeats.

During the northern summer, monarch butterflies are found in much of the United States. Two or three generations may hatch and die before fall arrives. When fall approaches, the year's last generation of monarchs begin feeding voraciously, putting on fat. Before the first frosts occur, mostly in October, the vast majority of monarchs migrate south to Mexico. Most other butterfly species do not migrate at all; when spring comes, they hatch from overwintered eggs, or metamorphose from overwintered pupae. One of the great mysteries of nature is how these insects manage to return to the same few Mexican mountaintops used by their ancestors since time immemorial. A few monarchs may overwinter in the United States, and many others settle on mountaintops other than the one occupied by the reserve.

Only about one-sixth of the monarchs overwintering in Mexican forests are protected by the sanctuary. Even inside this reserve, local people have managed to cut one-fifth of the trees during the last decade. Not enough is being done to save the monarch butterfly. The more money that eco-tourists pump into the reserve area, the more likely it becomes that the monarch's winter habitat will be more effectively protected.

Getting There

The main city near the reserve is Zitácuaro, Michoacán, about 60 miles (100 km) west of Mexico City, on Highway 15. The reserve's main entrance road departs from the town of Angangueo, about 30 miles (50 km) north of Zitácuaro. Coming from the west on a second-class bus (first-classers probably will not stop), you might want to disembark at San Felipe, a tiny settlement consisting mostly of *comedores*, fruit stands, souvenir stalls, et cetera, at the juncture of Highway 15 and the road to Angangueo. Because the main highway north of Angangueo is in poor repair, the road between Angangueo and San Felipe serves as Angangueo's umbilicus to the outside world. A fairly steady stream of second-class buses runs throughout the day between Angangueo and San Felipe, many continuing to Zitácuaro.

The large mounds of mining tailings around Angangueo are left from abandoned silver mines. Lodging is available in both Angangueo and Zitácuaro, but a much larger selection is available in Zitácuaro. Campers arriving at the reserve's entrance wearing backpacks usually are approached by kids offering tent sites.

9 ▪ VOLCAN MALINCHE

Distance: 12 miles round trip (20 km)
Difficulty: strenuous
Terrain: paved and unpaved roads, trail
Elevation: high point 10,500 feet
Map: ITMP Map No. 204: México South, 1:1,000,000

Malinche is a 14,636-foot volcano mostly in the state of Tlaxcala, about 19 air-miles (30 km) northeast of Puebla. Puebla is 47 miles (75 km) from Mexico

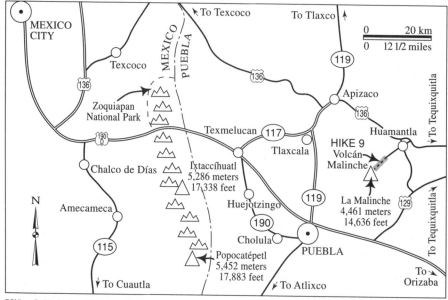

Hike 9 Volcán Malinche

City, and because the bus ride from Mexico City to Puebla and on to Volcán Malinche is interesting in its own right, it is also described here. The four-lane, limited-access Mexico City–Puebla Toll Road, or *autopista*, lies east of Mexico City in the states of México and Puebla. Sometimes the highway goes by the number of 190 D. The most interesting section of the highway crosses the mountain called both Sierra Nevada and Sierra de Ahualulco. The higher elevations of this stretch lie within Zoquiapan National Park.

Beginning in Mexico City at an elevation of 7,380 feet, the highway crosses arid desert, climbs through oak forests into cypress, pine, and fir forests at 10,660 feet, and then descends through similar zones to Puebla, at 7,050 feet. Several exits and parking areas along the highway provide limited access to forested areas. Hikers need to exit the *autopista* to find decent places for walking around.

Volcán Malinche is also known as Matlalcueyetl. This strenuous hike covers 6 relentlessly steep miles (10 km) to the tree line at about 10,500 feet. At such elevations, even seasoned hikers get out of breath and feel their hearts pounding like crazy. People with heart conditions should avoid this hike.

Nor should novice hikers climb Malinche; at higher elevations, the main trail breaks into several interconnecting footpaths, and route finding can be a challenge. On the other hand, experienced hikers able to navigate by compass and keep their cool and backtrack when a trail leads to a precipice may find the hike up Malinche to be this book's most exciting. On rare, smogless days, the view west, down the line of snow-capped volcanoes constituting the Transverse Volcanic Belt, is simply breathtaking.

When one reaches the tree line, there is temptation to continue on to the peak. Local fellows swear that they can hike from Alta Mira to Malinche's peak, and return home again in time for supper. Probably they are not exaggerating. Hikers in great shape who arrive at the tree line early in the day feeling good, and confident about finding the way back to Alta Mira before dark, may decide to go ahead. In determining whether to attempt the peak, do not underestimate the weather's importance. Storms build fast here and can be violent. One would not want to be on Malinche's treeless upper slopes with lightning striking all around.

Eucalyptus trees, easy to recognize from their splotchy bark, are native to Australia. Here they grow fast and make good shade.

I took 8½ hours, lugging a heavy backpack and spending plenty of time birdwatching, photographing, and sitting on rocks breathing hard, to hike from Alta Mira to the tree line and back.

Mexico City–Puebla Toll Road: Right outside Mexico City the landscape was once green with dense oak–pine forest, but now it looks like desert. At Km 37, the tall, handsome trees with diffuse, feathery leaves are peppertrees, introduced from South America; the trees with blotchy bark are eucalyptus, introduced from Australia.

Remnants of oak–pine forest, in which Lindley's cypress is a prime component, appear at Km 43. The main oaks are the wrinkle-leaf and Mexican oaks, the latter a bushy species. As elevation increases, at Km 48 pines take over from oaks. At Km 50, notice dark basalt rocks derived from ancient lava flows. By Km 53, the road has climbed so high that oaks completely drop out, leaving pure pine. The most characteristic pine here is the Montezuma pine, with five (sometimes four) drooping, twelve-inch-long needles per cluster.

The mountain peak is reached at the exit at Km 56.5. At these elevations, sacred fir is common. Other pines to look for are the timberline Montezuma pine, with needles only half as long as the Montezuma pine, and the Aztec pine, a famed source of turpentine, possessing three or four medium-size needles per group.

At Km 59, a small tree forms a dense understory along the roadside; this is the alder called *aile*. Two other common roadside bushes are both members of the composite family. The one with glossy, leathery, blackjack-shaped leaves tufted at the end of branches is charcoal shrub; the other, closely related to North America's groundsel and bearing opposite, serrated leaves, is *hilo*.

At the boundary between the states of México and Puebla at Km 63.8, the highway enters a boulder-strewn desert fairly suddenly. By Km 70, the highway dips back into the lowlands, where agriculture dominates and only a few pines survive. By Km 75, the vegetation deteriorates into a jumble of Lindley's cypress, eucalyptus, peppertrees, cornfields, and maguey.

Most flowering plants along this highway are described and illustrated with line drawings in the book *La Flora del Valle de Mexico*, listed in the Bibliography.

Volcán Malinche: In Puebla, catch the bus to Alta Mira. In Alta Mira, minibus service ends in front of a small store. From here, hike upslope to the forest's edge, turn left, and skirt the forest for about 4 minutes, until you arrive at a paved road. At this point, a radio tower is visible at northeast 40°. Cross the paved road onto the gravel road heading south 190°. Walk for 1 minute and take the first right, a dirt logging road leading upslope and into the forest at southwest 230°.

The logging road continues unambiguously for about 1 mile (1.5 km)—some 33 minutes. Then a Y is encountered; go right, south-southwest 210°. Then, hiking at a fairly leisurely pace, pursue this itinerary:

After 3 minutes, a road comes in from northeast 50°; ignore it. After 3 more minutes, at a Y, go left, southeast 140°. After 10 more minutes, at the next Y, go right, west 270°. After 10 more minutes, take a path leaving the road

Sacred firs proclaim their piety with outer branches that form crosses.

at southwest 220°. After 4 more minutes, at the next Y, go left, upslope. After 13 more minutes, at the next Y, go left, upslope. After 45 more minutes, at the next Y, go left, upslope.

At this point, the trail comes and goes fitfully, but by now hikers should have a good idea where the peak is—at about southwest 210°—because it has loomed into view several times. Until the tree line is reached, hiking strategy amounts to following an interlocking maze of livestock trails upslope through clumpgrass and widely spaced pines.

At the tree line, it is easy to see that in most places Malinche's upper slopes are rocky cliffs too steep for anyone but well-equipped mountain climbers. However, one slope comprises a continuous, grassy, exceedingly steep incline right to the peak. . . . During the entire hike toward the tree line, keep in mind that the peak usually lies at about southwest 220°; returning downslope, Alta Mira lies at a bearing of northeast 40°.

The forest here is similar to that seen on the bus ride from Mexico City. Birds are essentially the same as described in hike 7, Los Azufres Park.

Bunchgrass grows thickly among the pines of Malinche's lower slope.

This thistle-like eryngium, a member of the carrot family, is common on Malinche's middle slope.

Getting There

Take a bus from Mexico City to Puebla. In the city of Puebla, buses of the Autobuses Surianos line leave every 10 to 20 minutes for Huamantla. The town of Huamantla (wah-MAHNT-la), Tlaxcala, is the closest city to Malinche; the

Related to mistletoe but leafless, **injerto** ***parasitizes pine trunks on Malinche's lower slope.***

village of Alta Mira is closer still. In Huamantla, mini-buses to the village of Alta Mira leave about every 20 minutes or so from the intersection of Calle Morelos Poniente and Calle de La Reforma. Both of these streets are well known, and anyone can point you to them. The first micro-buses from Huamantla to Alta Mira usually leave between 7:00 A.M. and 8:00 A.M., depending on demand, and the last bus to leave from Alta Mira for Huamantla takes off at around 7:00 P.M. or 8:00 P.M., again depending on demand. Alta Mira lies only about 3.5 miles (5 to 6 km) upslope from Huamantla, and the road there is good all the way.

During my visit, all mini-bus drivers swore that Alta Mira was very far away and excessively difficult to get to, and that the ticket there cost a hefty $10 US. However, when I refused the price and began the journey on foot, the drivers quickly lowered the price to 50 cents. I could not determine whether this was good-natured kidding, which might have been the case, or evidence of a smoothly functioning scam for travelers.

No formal lodging is available in Alta Mira, but some can be found in Huamantla; much more of a variety is found in Tlaxcala.

10 ▪ ZAPOTITLAN

Distance: about 2 miles one way (3 km)
Difficulty: easy (intense heat)
Terrain: gravel road
Elevation: 4,600 feet
Map: ITMP Map No. 204: México South, 1:1,000,000

The town of Zapotitlán lies on the eastern end of the state of Puebla, on Highway 125 between Tehuacán and Huajuapan, about 12 air-miles (20 km) southwest of Tehuacán; it is approximately midway between the cities of Puebla and Oaxaca. Situated far beyond Mexico's two main deserts, the Sonoran and the Chihuahuan, this small, isolated patch of desert contains an extremely interesting and scenic community of cacti, yuccas, agaves, and other succulents and hot-desert plants.

Just east of Zapotitlán, a botanical garden with a small network of well-maintained trails is worth visiting. Unfortunately the same few species are labeled again and again, leaving others unidentified. The hike itself, 3 to 4 miles (5 to 6 km) east of Zapotitlán and its botanical garden, passes by some evaporation ponds where salt is produced as it must have been during ancient times. The walking, along a one-lane gravel road with a few steep inclines, is easy, but heat here can be hellish.

As you leave Tehuacán on the bus ride on Highway 125 to Zapotitlán, the agaves on the first desert hill are the ones sometimes called *gallinas*. From around Km 8 to Texcala, the big columnar cactus is an *órgano*.

At about 0.5 mile (1 km) before Zapotitlán, at Km 25, lies the Jardín Botánico y Vivero de Cactaceas, the botanical garden. If you want to take this short hike, get off the bus here. The well-maintained, pretzel-shaped trail is only 200 to 300 yards long, but lies on a steep hillside. Identified stars of the Jardín include such locally common species as the giant, branched, saguarolike cactus called *teteche* (provides firewood and edible fruit) and a similar but smaller species called *garrambullo*. A dark green, knee-high, columnar cactus with downward-pointing spines often planted as living fences is *baboso*. The main local prickly pear cactus, with edible fruits and whitish spines, is *nopal crinato*. A small barrel-cactus with star-shaped spine clusters

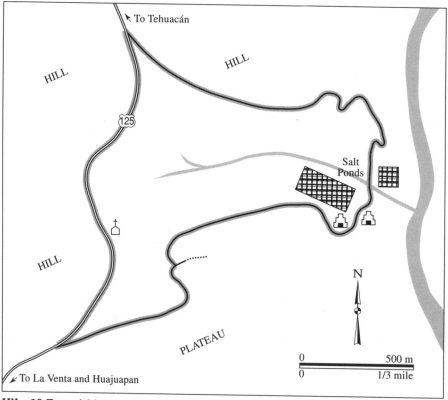

Hike 10 Zapotitlán

dominated by one recurved, vicious-looking spine is the *biznaga ganchuda*; another *biznaga* is smaller, but forms dense thickets, and its spine clusters lack the domineering barb. There are at least two spherical cacti not more than three or four inches high, with spine clusters rising atop little titlike bumps. The one with spines in groups of about twenty is a *Coryphantha*; the one with only three or four spines atop each tit is *biznaga lechuda*. The *leche* ("milk") part of this name reflects the fact that if one of the tits is pricked, white, milky latex bleeds forth.

Two agaves inhabit the slope. The one with wide leaves often imprinted with spiny margins of the leaves above it is *pichomel*, reputed to have medicinal value; the agave with slender leaves and leaf margins unprotected by large spines is *gallina* (hen). The only tree identified in the botanical garden is the one with smooth, greenish bark and locustlike leaves; it is *manteco* (lard).

The trailhead for the Zapotitlán hike lies about 3 miles (4 to 5 km) east of the botanical garden, at Km 20, about 500 yards east of the hilltop village of La Venta. From this point just east of La Venta and facing east (toward Tehuacán), take the one-lane gravel road leading to the right immediately before the road cut. Do not drive this gravel road, because halfway down a chain usually barricades the way. No KEEP OUT signs are posted and a man living in the valley near

The Zapotitlán hike passes through this landscape of giant órganos.

the salt ponds assured me that hikers are welcome. Though usually no one is encountered during the entire hike, if you meet someone, it might be a good idea to ask permission to pass through: "*¿Podemos pasar?*"

After about 11 minutes' saunter from the trailhead, the road makes a Y; take the left to northwest 300°. At the end of the road's descent, it curves toward the north, continues between some adobe ruins and salt ponds, and

At Zapotitlán, barrel cacti dwarf the author's cap.

crosses a stream. Beyond the stream, the hike embarks upon a new gravel road heading north and upslope. Stay on this road, identical to the first, as it curves around and climbs through fine cactus territory all the way back to Highway 125.

Zapotitlán's cacti are simply a joy. Beside the *teteche* labeled in the botanical garden, which can grow to thirty feet, the local pachycereus has been known to grow nearly twice that high. *Órganos*, the common unbranched, columnar cactus, grow to about thirty feet and are slightly pointed toward the top. Other cactus species in the area standing ten feet or higher, for which common names have not been found, include *Neobuxbaumia macrocephala*, *Cephalocereus chrysacanthus*, *Lamaireocereus hollianus*, and *Senocereus stellatus*.

Among the cacti in the prickly-pear genus, *Opuntia*, are *Opuntia imbricata*, *O. depressa*, *O. hoffmanni*, *O. macdougaliana*, and *O. pilifera*. Of these, the first is the familiar tree cholla, the second is a flat-pad, *nopal*-type cactus, and the last three are "tree prickly pears." Also there are five species of mammillaria, four species of barrel-shaped cacti, and several other cacti of various forms! Serious students of botany may be interested in visiting this area with a copy of C. E. Smith Jr.'s 1965 article "Flora of the Tehuacán Valley" (*Fieldiana Botany*, 4:107-143).

Succulents put on a real show here. Non-cactus succulents in this area include six agaves, all listed in appendix A, Scientific Names, under agave. The local yucca has an unbranched trunk. The local nolina is called palmita; also there is a local sotol. Certainly the star of the non-cactus succulents is Mexican ponytail, in this area standing twenty feet high, with bulbous trunks as big as good-size hippopotami.

Besides mesquite, in this area there is a good variety of common desert plants such as ocotillo, tree cholla, leatherplant and yellow trumpet. However, it is estimated that about 29 percent of the species in this small patch of isolated desert are endemic just to this particular desert where the states of

One of many cacti species at Zapotitlán; note size compared to a one-peso coin.

An agave along the trail at Zapotitlán

If leaf margins of a large, rosette-forming plant bear curling fibers, rather than spines, it is a yucca, not an agave.

At Zapotitlán, Mexican ponytails such as this one possess water-storing trunks as big as refrigerators.

Puebla, Oaxaca, and Veracruz meet. Thus, here serious flower sniffers delight in such Tehuacán-area specialties as a borage-family member called *anaqua*, with the Latin name *Ehretia tehuacana*, and a composite-family montanoa, *Montanoa tehuacana*.

The area's more common trees and shrubs include palo dulce, a legume-family member with vetchlike leaves, and hopseedbush, a soapberry-family member with willowlike leaves and half-inch-wide fruits with papery longitu-dinal wings. *Canelillo*, a low shrub in the euphorbia family, is covered with star-shaped hairs; *gallitos* is also in the euphorbia family, though it looks like a cactus. The lantana-leaf salvia bears reddish flowers and leaves with densely hairy undersurfaces.

At Zapotitlán, this bromeliad, called heno *(hay) grows epiphytically on a bush.*

Birds around Zapotitlán, except during the cool hours of dawn and dusk, are scarce and not nearly as interesting as the plants. Two endemic species found here are the gray-breasted woodpecker and the bridled sparrow. Other common "desert birds" include the phainopepla, Say's phoebe, Bewick's wren, brown towhee, and curve-billed thrasher.

At trail's end there awaits a stunning experience. A hacked-up, trunk-charred, absolutely abused mesquite tree twelve feet high stands beside the gravel road, atop a knoll, just a few yards before the road meets Highway 125. A boulder beneath the mesquite invites a sitting session. The aforementioned delicious experience is simply that of sitting on the boulder, enjoying the hilltop's meager breezes and the diffuse-leaved mesquite's even meagerer shade. What is nice is discovering how, in such sizzlingly hot, blindingly bright desert, one tree can make such a difference. At road's end, one can catch a green Línea Zapotitlán bus to Tehuacán, or walk back along the highway to the trailhead.

By the way, one of the world's most important archaeological finds took place in an unimpressive-looking cave near Coxcatlán, 25 miles (40 km) southeast of Tehuacán; the oldest ears of corn known to humans were found there. Corn seems to have originated in the Tehuacán Valley. Just 2.5 miles (4 km) from Zapotitlán, atop the mountain called Cuthá or Cerro de la Máscara, there are some small pyramids, apparently from the Monte Albán Civilization.

In colonial times the "Zapotitlán Road" was important because it connected the Gulf port of Veracruz with Oaxaca. One famous traveler of the old highway was Thiery de Menoville, sent here in 1777 by France to collect *nopal* cactus and the cochineal insect parasitizing it. The natural red dye called cochineal is obtained from an extract derived from female cochineal insect bodies, which look very much like red mealybugs covered with white, waxy plates. Before de Menoville's trip, the Spanish enjoyed a cochineal monopoly; afterwards the French dominated its production, cultivating Mexican prickly-pears and cochineal insects in the Antilles. Those scarlet capes worn by dandies and church bigwigs in old paintings speak of squished female mealybugs.

Getting There

The main city in the area is Tehuacán, Puebla, midway between the cities of Puebla and Oaxaca. Though Tehuacán is richly served by buses, it has no central terminal. Moreover, few if any of the many first-class buses traveling Highway 125 stop at Zapotitlán; in Tehuacán a local second-class bus line must be ferreted out. At this writing, Línea Zapotitlán leaves from near the intersection of Calle 3 Oriente and Calle 1 Sur. Remember that *oriente* means "east" and *sur* is "south." Look for green mini-buses parked along the street, leaving every half hour or so.

Plenty of lodging is available in Tehuacán, but not in Zapotitlán.

CHAPTER 6

THE PACIFIC COAST

The Land

The Pacific Coast region is bone dry in the north, but rainfall increases toward the south. North and west of Ciudad Obregón, this region is occupied by part of the Sonoran Desert; the desert's most arid, isolated, and starkly beautiful section is the Desierto de Altar, at the head of the Gulf of California. Here rainfall usually amounts to three inches or less a year, and the wind heaps sand into dunes. Gran Desierto de Pinacate Natural Park, lying about 30 miles (50 km) northeast of Puerto Peñasco, is established around 4,560-foot Pinacate Peak.

Farther south, resort- and port-city Mazatlán receives about thirty-five inches of rain a year; even farther south, Acapulco averages nearly sixty. Usually all but two or three inches of Acapulco's rain falls from June through October. Figure 4 shows that along the southern Pacific Coast occasional islands of aridity interrupt the gradual march toward raininess. Some areas of the Pacific Coast do not look as dry as they really are; irrigated fields often bestow upon the landscape a deceptively verdant look. Notice the razor-sharp borders between irrigated green fields, and adjoining low, scraggly, spiny natural vegetation. Some years' rainfall statistics are turned on their head when hurricanes blow off the Pacific, as was the case with Hurricane Calvin in 1993.

The California Current (see Figure 4), streaming south from the coast of Alaska, lies at the heart of the Pacific Coast's dryness. Chilly, east-blowing winds off the current heat up drastically when they hit the Mexican coast; because warm air holds more moisture than cold, relative humidity plummets, and air with low relative humidity produces little rainfall.

Plants

Between Mexicali and Caborca, Highway 2 travels through the Desierto de Altar, affording a good view of the creosote bush–white bur-sage plant

141

community described in Chapter 3, Baja California. Though mesquite is not dominant in this plant community, be on the lookout for sand dunes that seem to be populated by numerous young mesquite switches, because there is a good story behind such dunes.

When dunes shift atop mesquites, instead of suffocating, the trees just sprout new shoots above the sand's surface. Once the new shoots are established, they break the sand-laden wind blowing across the desert, more sand accumulates around the sprouts, and so the sprouts must grow some more to keep above the sand. Therefore, the seemingly independent, young mesquite switches sometimes observed occupying mounds of sand often are the tips of single, sand-blanketed mother-mesquites doing their parts against shifting sand and desertification in general; they are the desert counterparts of red mangroves, which stabilize coastal areas by gathering silt. Old-timers in south Texas's mesquite country used to joke that "you dig for wood (mesquite's subterranean stems and roots) but climb for water (windmills)."

It is not uncommon to find animals centering their life cycles around magnanimous, mostly buried mesquites. I once spent a day observing courtship rituals of the roundtail ground squirrel, which took place around an extensive system of burrows dug among a mesquite's smothered maze of branches.

Around Santa Ana on Highway 15 between Nogales and Hermosillo, dominant plants of the open desert are paloverde and prickly pear cactus. This zone extends far to the north, into the United States' Arizona uplands; Interstate 10 northwest of Tucson runs through it. Though paloverdes and prickly pear cacti dominate, most travelers think of this zone as the home of giant saguaro cacti, which can reach forty feet in height and weigh seven or eight tons.

In Spanish *palo verde* means "green tree," which alludes to the fact that paloverde trees possess chlorophyll in their trunks and twigs, imparting to them a green color. During droughty periods this enables paloverdes to shed their water-transpiring leaves, yet continue photosynthesizing food in their woody parts. Two species of paloverde inhabit this zone, the blue and foothill paloverdes. The co-dominant prickly-pear cacti are low, usually reclining species with beaver-tail–shaped pads.

As Highway 15 heads south from Santa Ana toward Hermosillo, the more undisturbed parts of the landscape gradually become dominated by the bushes called ironwood and brittlebush. Ironwood is a spiny tree in the bean family that during the flowering season sports purple pea-blossoms; brittlebush is a member of the composite family, producing golden-yellow flowers. Hikers in North America see many yellow-blossomed composites, but not many woody ones.

Between Guaymas and Ciudad Obregón, Highway 15 traverses an area where remaining thorn forest is dominated by mesquite and acacia. In this case the main acacia is a flat-crowned one with sparse foliage and, with abundant thorns, aptly called *espino*—"spine."

South of Culiacán, Sinaloa, all the way to Tehuantepec, thorn forests of various species compositions occupy most land not devoted to ranches and farms. Often seen rising above the thorn forest's low canopy is a giant, much-branched cactus up to forty feet high, bearing three-inch-thick fruits copiously covered with yellow wool and long yellow bristles. This is the comb cactus. Seeing the long bristles, one wonders whether anyone really ever used the fruits as combs; better documented is the fact that Indians once ground this cactus's seeds into a nutritious meal from which a kind of cake was baked.

Here and there along the Pacific Coast marsh–savanna lands appear, the most extensive being the Marismas Nacionales (National Swamps) in northern Nayarit between Mazatlán and Tepic. Swamp lovers can explore this area by taking Highway 23 southwest from Acaponeta through Tecuala and subsequent marshes to the ferry across Laguna Agua Brava to Novillera.

Except in the northern desert area, along most of the Pacific Coast anytime a road heads eastward from the coast toward the Mexican Plateau, the following vegetation zones are passed through as the highway climbs in elevation:

Thorn Forest➤   Tropical Deciduous Forest➤   Oak–Pine Forest

These vegetation zones form rather narrow but very long bands more or less paralleling the coast. The ribbon of thorn forest along the coast, usually about 50 miles wide (80 km), receives on the average between fifteen and thirty-five inches of yearly rainfall. Tropical deciduous forest, or at least its much chopped-on and scorched remains, mantles foothills where rainfall averages twenty-five to sixty inches. In the north, oak–pine forest may appear on the plateau's slopes as low as 4,000 feet, but in the south it may hold out until 6,500.

Animals

The farther south one travels along the Pacific Coast, the easier it gets to spot animal species not found in North America. For example, at Mazatlán, less than halfway to the Guatemalan border, in gardens, orchards, and woodland edges near resorts it is possible to see cinnamon hummingbirds and happy wrens. Birders able to find scrubby woods in this area might be lucky enough to see orange-fronted parakeets, lilac-crowned and white-fronted parrots, elegant quail, and rosy thrush-tanagers.

Farther south in the wooded hills above Acapulco, the list of "exotics" skyrockets. There are banded quail, citreoline trogons, pale-billed woodpeckers, spot-breasted orioles, orange-breasted buntings, ruddy-breasted seedeaters, and magpie jays. In contrast, most shorebirds even this far south also can be seen in the United States, one exception being the collared plover. The situation is similar for lagoons and riversides, a nice exception being the mangrove swallow.

Armadillos constitute a considerable part of roadkill along Highways 15 and 200. The cottontail species seen between Mazatlán and Tehuantepec is the Mexican cottontail; north of Culiacán, it is the desert cottontail. Several species of gray squirrel inhabit forested parts of the zone. Coati are found throughout the region, except in the most arid areas; in the desert, there are badgers. In lazy rivers farther south, look for river otters. Once the Pacific

Coast was home to jaguars, ocelots, margays, jaguarundi, and bobcats, but now these big cats are nearly or entirely exterminated. In isolated thorn forests, collared peccaries still can be glimpsed. Mule deer inhabit the northern desert, and white-tailed deer, at least originally, occurred throughout. In the most isolated parts of Gran Desierto de Pinacate Natural Park, one can always cherish the hope of spotting pronghorn antelope and bighorn sheep.

The American crocodile is the star wildlife feature in the Playa Ventanilla hike later in this chapter. By the way, American alligators do not occur in Mexico. Spectacled caimans, often confused with crocodiles and occurring in southern Mexico, are distinguished from crocodiles by bony ridges in front of their eyes. Caimans grow up to six feet long; American crocodiles become twice that large.

People

On long-haul, second-class buses along the Pacific Coast, it is fascinating to watch the kinds of people coming aboard. On coastal Highway 200 near the border between the states of Oaxaca and Guerrero, folks enter who obviously have some or a lot of African blood in them. In 1553 two boatloads of Bantu slaves escaped their masters before reaching Acapulco, so today about 80,000 descendents of black Africans live in and around the towns of Ometepec and Cuajinicuilapa in extreme southeastern Guerrero. By the way, these escaped slaves were not the first Africans to arrive in Mexico; five Africans accompanied Cortés on his march to conquer the Aztecs in Tenochtitlán in 1519!

Though a rich mosaic of indigenous cultures once populated the Pacific Coast—from Papago and Seri in the northern desert, to Cora and Tecual around Puerto Vallarta, and Zapotec and Huave around Tehuantepec—today travelers along most of the Pacific Coast detect little Indian influence. However, especially in Oaxaca, side roads into the foothills sometimes lead into villages of Native Americans. At *mercados* such as the big one in Tehuantepec, *indíginas* from isolated Indian villages can be seen selling their produce and handicrafts.

11 ▪ TEQUILA

Distance: 3 miles (5 km)
Difficulty: easy
Terrain: paved road, trail, gravel road
Elevation: 4,000 feet
Map: ITMP Map No. 200: México, 1:3,300,000

Tequila, the home of tequila liquor, lies in the state of Jalisco, on busy Highway 15 between Guadalajara and the Pacific Coast, about 30 air-miles (50 km) west-northwest of Guadalajara. With Tequila's elevation of around 4,000 feet

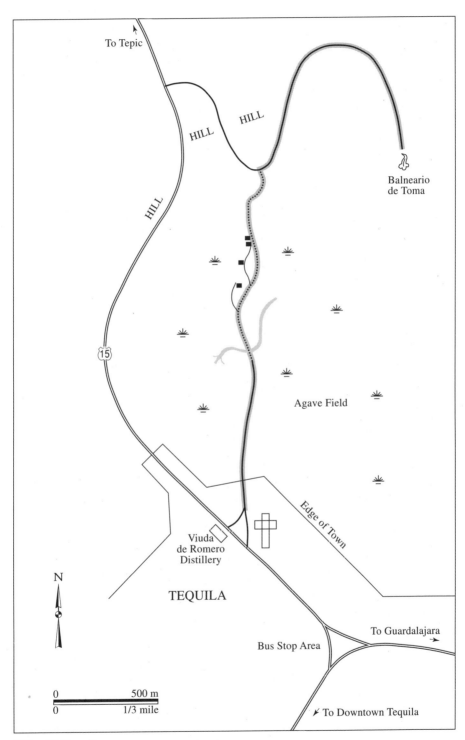

To Tepic

HILL

HILL

HILL

15

Balneario
de Toma

Agave Field

Edge of Town

Viuda
de Romero
Distillery

N

TEQUILA

To Guardalajara

Bus Stop Area

0   500 m
0   1/3 mile

To Downtown Tequila

Hike 11 Tequila

and its proximity to Guadalajara, which lies unmistakably on the Mexican Plateau, it is a close call as to whether Tequila's plants and animals belong to the Mexican Plateau biota or that of the Pacific Coast. Probably it is accurate to say that the walk begins on the Mexican Plateau's western rim, then descends onto the slope of the Pacific Coast.

The easy hike begins across from a large tequila distillery's visitor center, follows an old oxcart road between ancient, picturesque stone walls, passes through large tequila agave plantations, and after about 3 miles (4 to 5 km) descends on a gravel road to an exceedingly pleasant *balneario*, or spring-fed swimming-pool area. The *balneario* perches on the southern slope of the Río Verde Valley, which extends from the coast all the way inland to the Aguascalientes–León area. Elements of Pacific Coast biota range up this valley from where it empties into the Pacific in Nayarit, past Tequila, clear to the vicinity of Guadalajara.

To reach the distillery serving as the hike's trailhead, from the entrance road to Tequila on Highway 15 (where the buses stop), walk northwest, away from Guadalajara and downtown Tequila, along Highway 15 for about 7 minutes. Look for an office building on the left with large, blue letters atop it announcing the Viuda de Romero tequila distillery. The distillery's visitor center is clearly marked EXPOSICIÓN Y VENTA. A free tour of the plant and some souvenir-buying is available here (see Getting There, below).

The hike begins exactly opposite the Viuda de Romero building, across Highway 15. On the street leading directly away from the visitor center, east-northeast, walk 2 minutes until you come to the wall around the cemetery, then turn left. For the next 13 minutes, continue northward, usually with a venerable stone fence to the left. Judging from the fence's antiquity and how the trail is sunken below the surrounding landscape, long ago this must have been an important thoroughfare—possibly the main route to the coast. The gigantic shade trees along this section of the hike are guanacastes, of the bean family. Guanacastes are famed and treasured throughout the New World tropics for the cool shade they cast.

Little native vegetation is to be seen in this area, except for a few cactusy areas atop ridges where the ground is too stony to plant agaves. Hikers will see that the agave being grown around Tequila is not the huge, thick-leafed maguey typically seen in Mexico's arid uplands. From maguey comes *pulque*, the poor man's drink, not tequila. In Spanish the agave around Tequila is called *mezcal de tequila*, or just *tequila*. The tequila agave's leaves are much smaller, thinner, and straighter than those of maguey; it is the *azul* (blue) variety.

After seven or eight years of cultivation, the first step for turning the *mezcal de tequila* plant into tequila is to trim the plant's lower leaves. Not only does this remove spiny tips, which tend to skewer workers, but it also causes the plant's bole, or "inner stem," to grow more. The bole is used for making tequila, not the leaves. Cropped *mezcal de tequila* plants look like giant pineapples. Once the trimmed boles have matured they are cut and sold by the ton to distilleries. Part of the plantations seen around Tequila are privately owned, but several of the big ones are owned and operated by the distilleries themselves.

The birds are not spectacular in this area, though for northerners it is always fun to see such common tropical species as scaled doves, vermilion flycatchers, curve-billed thrashers, lesser goldfinches, brown towhees, and the like. In fields away from town, one might spot a Cassin's kingbird or, in the winter, the clay-colored sparrow. The little falcon zipping around is the American kestrel.

At the trail's low point, it crosses a tiny stream that, at least during the dry season, flows almost entirely with the stinking residues of Tequila's various distilleries. Cross the stream on the rickety platform provided and continue north-northwest. After about 6 minutes, at the Y, continue to the right past the small community of scattered houses. In another 13 minutes, ascend a slope and meet with a gravel road. Highway 15 lies to the left; the *balneario* awaits to the right.

Follow the gravel road to the right for 15 minutes, until it ends at Balneario La Toma. Entrance here costs about $2 US per day. Concrete pools are fed by natural springs, and inside the establishment reigns a pleasant, cool, shaded atmosphere. There is a cafe with an expansive view of the valley and a congenial family atmosphere. Sometimes oompah-type Latin music is played, evoking the feeling of a very mellow Bavarian spa. At the *balneario*'s second pool, the one fed by a waterfall, be sure to pay homage to the venerable strangler fig.

From the *balneario* it is an easy half-hour walk along the gravel road to Highway 15. However, second-class buses willing to stop at odd places are surprisingly rare along this highway. Anyone wanting a bus after visiting the *balneario* probably would save time by returning to Tequila's entrance-road triangle instead of waiting where La Toma's gravel road intersects Highway 15.

Getting There

Tequila is easily accessible, especially from Guadalajara; several bus lines serve it. Tequila's downtown area lies just south of Highway 15; the town's main entrance road, where buses stop, forms a small triangle as it intersects with the highway. Some small hotels are available in downtown Tequila.

Viuda de Romero is only one of several distilleries in Tequila, and it is a rather modern one. Visitors wanting to see a traditional operation should drop by Tequila's Orendain Distilleries. Sr. Arturo Gonzalez Luna, who speaks some English, operates a small grocery/souvenir shop next to Tequila's traffic triangle, and may be able to help arrange a visit. Look for Don Arturo next to the triangle in the shop that says LICORES on it.

Inside a modern distillery, the tequila agave boles are cooked in fourteen-ton autoclaves at temperatures of 212° to 221° Fahrenheit. From the autoclaves, the cooked boles ride belts to big "squeezers" that press out the boles' sweet juice. Sweet juice lost during the cooking process is now added to the fresh-squeezed part. At this point the sweet juice is fermented for 48 hours. The distillery's own unique strain of yeast, which is a fungus, is employed, imparting to the tequila a flavor characteristic of the distillery.

After fermentation, the alcohol is separated from innumerable incidental byproducts and contaminants by the process of distillation. Though Viuda de Romero distills its fermented liquid three times at three different heats, this thrice-distilled 90-proof tequila is still only 45 percent alcohol.

Several spots around Tequila deserve special mention. For instance, on Highway 15 between Tequila and Ixtlán del Río, several towns are famed for their opals; at least one sign in this region claims, in English, THE BEST OPAL IN TOWN. The town making the most fuss about opal seems to be Magdalena, just west of Tequila. Since opals are made of quartz, the most abundant of all the earth's minerals, and plain water, it is surprising that opals can be so pretty. Opal comes in colorless forms as well as in all light colors; there is even a special form called precious opal, displaying a rainbow effect. Fire opal is a clear orange-red.

Opal occurs in a variety of geological contexts, especially around recent volcanoes, near hot springs, and in sediments. Opal can appear in veins and seams running through rocks, and at Juxtlahuaca Cave (see hike 12), opal stalactites might even be spotted. One of the most curious forms of opal is the opal pseudomorph. Opal pseudomorphs start out as pieces of wood, shell, or bone. Then molecules of quartz and water seep into the object, displacing the original molecules. Thus opal pseudomorphs are fossils.

Just west of Ahuacatlán, about midway between Tequila and Tepic, Nayarit, Highway 15 crosses an area blanketed with very dark, jagged, jumbled-up boulders. This is a lava field originating from 7,600-foot-high Volcán Ceboruco, which rises in full view on the highway's northern side. This field's dark rocks and boulders are basalt, the main rock formed from most lavas. You might be able to glean a smidgen of information from the neglected and vandalized information station beside Highway 15 inside the lava field.

Just south of Tequila, Tequila Volcano rises over town to an elevation of about 9,800 feet. The road to the peak is 11 miles (18 km) long. A nice day hike probably can be worked out with a taxi driver who would drive part way. As Mexican volcanoes go, Tequila is a modest one, but on a clear day the view from its summit should be outstanding.

12 ■ JUXTLAHUACA CAVE

Distance: about 5 hours' duration
Difficulty: moderately easy
Terrain: underground trail
Elevation: 3,400 feet
Map: ITMP Map No. 204: México South, 1:1,000,000

Juxtlahuaca Cave, or Grutas Juxtlahuaca, lies in the state of Guerrero right above the little town of Colotlipa, some 30 miles (50 km) east-southeast of Chilpancingo and more or less 150 air-miles (250 km) south of Mexico City.

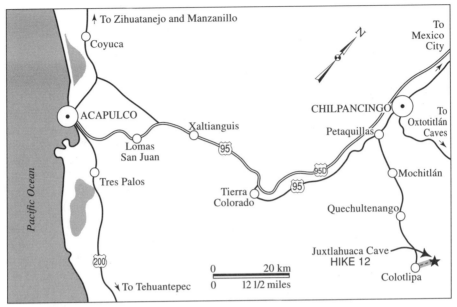

Hike 12 Juxtlahuaca Cave

The hike takes place in an extensive cave system with stalagmites, stalactites, dripstone, crystal "flowers," underground lakes, and other typical cave features. Some 3,000-year-old wall paintings in Olmec style—the oldest known such art in the Americas—are more archaeologically important than artistically spectacular.

A certified guide is required for the walk; the fee is a bit more than $25 US for any group of ten people. Of course the larger the group, the less it costs the individual; probably individuals and small groups stand a greater chance of teaming up with others if the visit is on a weekend.

The cave is chilly, clammy, and sometimes muddy; carry rain clothes to protect against underground waterfall spray and to avoid becoming chilled and wet. Water may need to be waded, so having shorts handy is a good idea. Several organisms live in the subterranean lakes and streams, and pale, ghostly crickets are fun to see.

Getting There

The nearest city to Juxtlahuaca Cave is Chilpancingo, on busy Highway 95 between Mexico City and Acapulco. Every half hour or so during the day, minibuses shuttle between Chilpancingo and Colotlipa, the little town below the cave's entrance. In Chilpancingo, minibuses are based across from the university, known locally as Escuela UPN, on Calle 18 de Marzo. If you bus up from Acapulco, there is no need to continue north into Chilpancingo. Disembark at Petaquillas and wait at the intersection for the Colotlipa minibus. Most minibuses from Chilpancingo passing this intersection end their trip in Petaquillas, so look for the ones with Colotlipa written on their windshields.

The road from Petaquillas to Colotlipa is paved but rather narrow, and with only a few potholes. In Colotlipa, minibuses park at the town square.

Everyone around Colotlipa's plaza knows to automatically point visitors toward the cave-guide hiring place; it is a private residence with no house number on it, on Calle Hidalgo, which has no sign identifying it, but which runs from the plaza. It is the fifth door down from the park; the wall next to the door says BILLARES PLAYA AZUL. The guides belong to a sort of union and do not seem at all willing to negotiate smaller fees for smaller groups.

Lodging is plentiful in Chilpancingo, but iffy in Colotlipa. For visitors with sleeping bags, the guide probably can work something out with a local family. Because Colotlipa is far, far off the beaten path in a really pretty part of the country, and because a couple of little towns between Petaquillas and Colotlipa support very colorful *mercados*, staying with locals might be a good idea.

13 ▪ PLAYA VENTANILLA

Distance: 4–5 miles round trip (6–8 km)
Difficulty: moderate
Terrain: sandy beach
Elevation: sea level
Map: ITMP Map No. 204: México South, 1:1,000,000

Playa Ventanilla is a tiny cluster of huts along the state of Oaxaca's coast about 6 miles (10 km) west of Puerto Angel, midway between the major beach resorts of Huatulco and Puerto Escondido. Hikers may walk to Playa Ventanilla from any of several small towns along the beach between Puerto Angel and Mazunte, thus extending their hike. From Playa Ventanilla, the hike follows a sand beach where very large waves crash just a few yards away. Lagoons just inland from the beach harbor crocodiles that sometimes can be spotted sunning themselves. About 2 miles (4 km) up the beach a lake is reached, famous

Hike 13 Playa Ventanilla

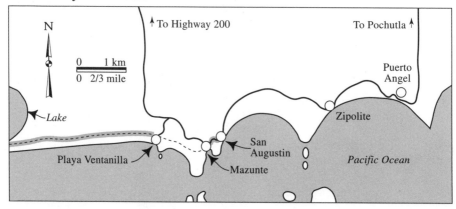

among the locals for its fine fishing and abundance of birdlife. From the lake one must return via the beach to Playa Ventanilla.

Blustery wind, sizzling temperatures, and intense sunlight parch unprotected lips and skin, so lip balm, sun screen, and sunglasses are needed. Walking beyond reach of the bigger waves can be tiring because the sand is loose and one sinks; by midmorning this dry sand becomes so hot that it cannot be hiked barefoot. On the other hand, hiking on firm, wet sand closer to the sea requires unremitting vigilance against occasional "rogue waves" that can engulf the unwary—especially risky for those with cameras. In fact, because of the damaging effects of wind-borne salt spray and sand grains, it may be wise to not carry a camera on this hike.

Playa Ventanilla can easily be reached by walking from Mazunte. Heading north from Mazunte, the gravel road to Playa Ventanilla is the first side road to the left. A sign points the way; a huge guanacaste tree offers shade at the junction. From Playa Ventanilla, there is no trail; the hike heads west on the sandy beach. From Don Paustino's hut (see Getting There, below), just walk to the beach, turn right, and keep walking.

The American crocodile is Playa Ventanilla's star wildlife feature. As the hike toward the lake begins, watch for the first lagoon on the right. On the far bank, leading into the water, there will probably be one or more narrow trail-like corridors through the weeds, possibly muddy and with the vegetation matted down. That is where crocodiles come and go. In this lagoon, any log spotted floating low in the water might actually be a croc—especially if it possesses a pair of nostrils and unblinking eyes.

Tremendous waves pounding the beach keep away shorebirds; here no sanderlings play tag with the water's edge. Among the water birds at the big lake are neotropic cormorants, green herons, American and snowy egrets, wood ibises, and maybe some roseate spoonbills. The slender-necked birds with outlandishly large feet treading atop waterlily pads are northern jacanas. Both least and pied-billed grebes can occur here, as well as both ringed and green kingfishers. The violet-green swallow with white patches on both sides of its rump is the mangrove swallow.

At the lake, no shelter from the wind and sun is available. This is a raw, wild place that singes the skin as it comforts the spirit. From the lake, one must return via the beach to Playa Ventanilla.

Getting There

The nearest city to Playa Ventanilla with regular first- and second-class bus service is Puerto Angel, which is easily accessible from Oaxaca City. A steady stream of buses flows along Highway 200 between Acapulco and Tehuantepec, but most of them bypass Puerto Angel, which lies 7 miles (12 km) south of the east–west-running highway. However, most second-class buses on Highway 200 stop in Pochutla, at the entrance to the road to Puerto Angel. Therefore, bus-riding visitors coming from either Acapulco or Tehuantepec may find that they need to buy tickets for Pochutla, then in Pochutla search out Autobuses Estrella del Valle bus line, which operates

A future occupant of the sea-turtle museum at Mazunte.

from a small courtyard next to Hotel Posada San José on the town's main street.

About twenty buses a day shuttle between Pochutla and the small coastal village of Zipolite, passing through touristy Puerto Angel on the way. Playa Ventanilla lies about 4 miles (6 to 7 km) from Zipolite. At this writing, no buses pass Mazunte or the road to Playa Ventanilla, but cheap taxis can be found by asking around. The friendly locals are nicely amenable to giving rides to hitchhikers.

Non-camping hikers need to spend the night in Puerto Angel, Zipolite, or Mazunte, then the next morning either hike or take a taxi all or part way to Playa Ventanilla. Puerto Angel is relatively five-star territory. At Zipolite, the hammock-renting tradition is alive and well, and many rustic rooms are available; this is a favored destination for nakedness-loving, beach-flopping northern Europeans. At Mazunte, several private landowners rent rooms, but one must ask around to find them.

Playa Ventanilla is fairly un-*gringo*ed territory. At this writing it amounts to no more than a cluster of huts near the beach, comprising the private domain of Paustino Escamilla Silva and his wife Doña Rejina. On a very informal basis, they serve *refrescos* and fix visitors at least one real meal a day. They have a *palapa* or two and speak of someday renting hammocks. Once or twice, North Americans have visited in RVs, staying for weeks at a time. Enjoying one of Don Paustino's home-grown, chilled, super-sweet coconuts after the long hike back from the lake rates as one of the Pacific Coast's premier experiences, but anyone disdaining grungy, recycled straws (for sipping chilled coconuts) should bring along their own. In short, at this writing, Playa Ventanilla is virgin territory.

"At this writing" is a phrase that regrettably must be used too much. The area from Puerto Angel to Mazunte is being built up fast, as is the entire Mexican coastline, especially in the vicinity of Huatulco. The Mexican government plans (threatens) to develop Huatulco into something "even larger than Cancún"; Playa Ventanilla should be experienced before it is absorbed by generic touristry.

In fact, at Mazunte an impressive-looking sea-turtle museum probably will be on-line by the time this book is available. Not long ago this entire beach area was best known as a sea-turtle slaughtering ground. As recently as 1990 ghastly heaps of remains of endangered sea turtles lined the roads here. At least officially, during recent years the hunting of sea turtles was managed. Mexican soldiers were stationed here to protect eggs removed from slaughtered females. However, I know a *señora* who cooked for the soldiers, and she says that their favorite dish was . . . sea-turtle eggs pilfered from the hatchery. Anyone interested in learning about sea-turtle politics should look into Tim Cahill's article "The Shame of Escobilla," included in his book *Jaguars Ripped My Flesh*.

CHAPTER 7

CHIAPAS

The Land

Mexico's highlands peter out at the Isthmus of Tehuantepec. East of the isthmus, in Chiapas, the highlands reappear and continue as exuberantly as ever through Guatemala, El Salvador, and Honduras, until a brief hiatus appears in southern Nicaragua. From the point of view of Chiapas's upland biota, the Isthmus of Tehuantepec's lowlands constitute a barrier for migration to and from the Mexican Plateau, but no such barrier hinders migration toward the south. Biologically, then, Chiapas's flora and fauna show stronger affinities with Central America than they do with "mainland Mexico." Even for naturalists who know "mainland Mexico's" natural history, Chiapas is a whole new story.

The map in Figure 13 shows that Chiapas's landscape can be divided into seven distinct physiographic regions, each region with its own characteristic plant communities.

Pacific Coastal Plain

The lowlands and several ranges of low hills along the Pacific Coast constitute Chiapas's Pacific Coastal Plain. Outcropping rocks are mostly metamorphic and intrusive igneous rocks of Precambrian and Paleozoic age—Mexico's oldest. The foothills are mantled with hacked-up tropical deciduous forest. Here and there, coastal strand, palm forest, marsh–savanna, and thorn forest emerge, and certain areas next to the ocean are occupied by extensive mangrove swamps, such as those seen in the Manglar Zapotón Ecological Reserve southwest of Escuintla. Adjoining this reserve to the southeast is the marsh called Pampa La Cantileña, accessible by a rough track from Tapachula to Barra San José.

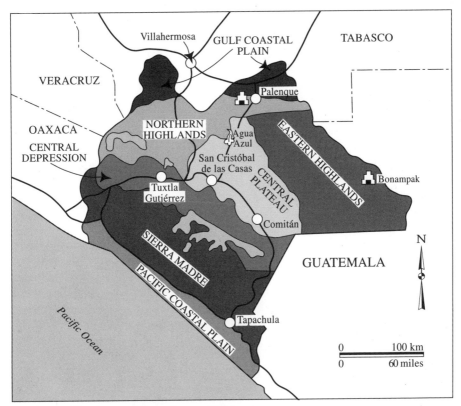

Figure 13 Physiographic regions of Chiapas

Sierra Madre de Chiapas

This is a mountain range extending into Guatemala, rising to about 13,000 feet on the Guatemalan border. The mountains are volcanic and steep-sided. Tropical deciduous and tropical evergreen forests at lower elevations give way to oak–pine forest and cloud forest on the middle and upper slopes. Several endemic species inhabit these forests, such as the two oak species *Quercus ovandensis* and *Q. paxtalensis*.

Central Depression

The Central Depression is a giant, sloping basin, in the bottom of which is pooled the huge, man-made lake called Presa La Angostura, formed by damming the Río Grijalva. The Grijalva exits the almost boxed-in depression through El Sumidero, a canyon with sheer walls rising more than 3,000 feet high; El Sumidero National Park lies just north of Tuxtla Gutiérrez. Outcropping rocks are mostly marine limestones and slates. This hot, arid basin, almost completely surrounded by humid highlands, is home to a high percentage of endemics. Farming and ranching has converted most of the earlier tropical deciduous forest to thorn forest and marsh–savanna.

Chiapas Plateau

Also called the Central Highlands, the Chiapas Plateau is a highland composed mostly of limestone, with extrusions of volcanic rocks at higher peaks. A few pinnacles reach 9,500 feet. On the drier western side, tropical deciduous forest and oak–pine forest dominate; on the moister eastern side, oak–pine–sweetgum such as that seen on the Yerba Buena Reserve hike (later in this chapter) occurs. Little original forest is left.

Eastern Highlands

Mostly low foothills and even some lowlands occur in this "highland," ranging in elevation up to 5,000 feet. Outcropping rocks are mostly limestone, but some sandstone and volcanic extrusions are found. Lower elevations are mantled with tropical evergreen forest interspersed with marsh–savanna and palm forests. Small patches of tropical rain forest occupy certain valleys along the Río Usumacinta.

Northern Highlands

The Northern Highlands are a series of steep, not very high ranges of volcanic origin. The Río Grijalva traverses the area, often cutting high vertical cliffs. The low foothills are covered by tropical evergreen forests in lower elevations and oak–pine–sweetgum forest in the higher.

Gulf Coastal Plain

The Gulf Coastal Plain consists of lowlands along the Gulf Coast. Underlying rockstrata are geologically young Cenozoic deposits. Most of the tropical evergreen forest and tropical rain forest once occupying this area has been converted into ranches and plantations. Here and there marsh–savanna occurs, along with secondary forests of various shades and occasional palm forests.

Plants

Most visitors to Chiapas eventually travel Highway 199 between San Cristóbal de las Casas and Palenque. On this road, be sure to notice how the vegetation evolves from lowland Palenque's lush broadleaf forest to pine forests around high-elevation San Cristóbal. Characteristic roadside plants of the lowlands north of Ocosingo include banana trees, coffee shrubs and the slender-trunked, small tree with umbrellalike, deeply lobed leaves, called cecropia; south of Ocosingo and at higher elevations, oaks and pines appear. By the time Highway 199 joins Highway 190 between Tuxtla Gutiérrez and Comitán, the air is chilly and the forests are almost purely pine. Do not forget to take a look at Dennis Breedlove's *Introduction to the Flora of Chiapas* (see Bibliography).

Animals

Campers at Maya Bell near Palenque Ruins often awaken to the morning roarings of howler monkeys; during the Palenque hike (later in this chapter), spider monkeys might be spotted atop the hill between the ruins and Naranjo. Typically one *hears* big-chested howlers but *sees* long-armed spiders. Armadillos occur throughout Chiapas, as do cottontail rabbits. The rarely seen, tiny tropical-forest cottontail is missing from the Sierra Madre de Chiapas and the Central Depression, but is found elsewhere. Three species of gray squirrel inhabit Chiapas, and the small Deppe squirrel occurs in the Northern and Eastern Highlands, and a small area on the Pacific side. What appear to be porcupine gnawings may be just that; throughout Chiapas there is an arboreal, nocturnal "prehensile-tail porcupine." Both pacas and agoutis have long been favored game for Chiapan hunters. Sometimes coyotes are spotted, as well as gray fox. Both raccoons and ringtail cats make it to Chiapas, as well as coatis. Any critter looking like a cross between a fat cat and a thick-tailed monkey, with a little bit of bear thrown in, is a kinkajou.

A host of weasel-like creatures inhabit Chiapas, but they are mostly nocturnal, very secretive and shy, and are seldom seen. Striped skunks range the state's southern two-thirds, and the spotted skunk occurs throughout, as probably is the case with the hognose skunk. River otters can be spotted in rivers and lagoons on the Pacific Coastal Plain. Five species of big cat once roamed Chiapas, but now they are restricted to the most isolated places, mainly in the Eastern Highland region. Collared and white-lipped peccaries have been overhunted in most regions. White-tailed and brocket deer were treasured game for Chiapas's early indigenous people, but now they also have declined.

People

The same rambunctious landscape that spawned Chiapas's rich flora and fauna also produced many indigenous cultures; Chiapas is Mexico's "most Indian state." Most of Chiapas's native people speak languages belonging to the Chiapan Group of the Mayan family of languages—Tzeltal, Tzotzil, and Chol are the most commonly encountered. Clusters of Zoque speakers inhabit the Grijalva Basin, and Zapotec can be heard along the Pacific Coast; Zoque and Zapotec are not Maya languages. Many indigenous refugees fleeing turmoil in the Guatemalan uplands have settled in Chiapas; in these settlements one never knows what language will be heard.

Visitors to Na Bolom, the museum/art gallery/pension/knicknack store/pilgrimage-destination-for-people-who-know-about-Lacandóns, in San Cristóbal de las Casas will become well sensitized to the Lacandóns, known as Mexico's "most aboriginal people." Usually a few Lacandóns hang around Na Bolom wearing traditional knee-length, white tunics, and long, black hair. While some of the Lacandóns—those at the entrance to the well-known Maya ruin of Bonampak—know all about outsiders' worldly ways, a few still live in isolated pockets of the Eastern Highlands, and thoughtful people worry whether too many contacts with the outside world will erode their culture.

Here is an idea for anyone fascinated by anthropology, and intrigued by the possibility of settling someplace otherworldly for an extended period. Indian-rich San Cristóbal de las Casas on Chiapas's high-elevation Central

Hibiscus blossoms bear many stamens that grow together in a cylinder surrounding the flower's style, which terminates in five stigmas.

Plateau is laid-back, inordinately pleasant, and used to outsiders. Here one can find lodging ranging from the most elegant to the most basic. What could be more pleasant than using San Cristóbal as a base and spending several weeks in the area exploring, using the following titles for inspiration?

See the Bibliography for complete information on *The Great Tzotzil Dictionary of San Lorenzo Zinacantan*; *Zinacantan: A Maya Community in the Highlands of Chiapas* (Zinacantán lies about a half-hour microbus ride east of San Cristóbal); *Illness and Shamanistic Curing in Zinacantan: An Ethnomedical Analysis*; *Tzeltal Folk Zoology: The Classification of Discontinuities in Nature*; and *Principles of Tzeltal Plant Classification: An Introduction to the Botanical Ethnography of a Mayan-Speaking Community of Highland Chiapas*.

14 YERBA BUENA RESERVE

Distance: 200 yards
Difficulty: easy
Terrain: trail
Elevation: 5,580 feet
Map: ITMP Map No. 205: Yucatán Peninsula, 1:1,000,000

Yerba Buena Reserve lies on curvy Highway 195 in the Northern Highlands, between Tuxtla Gutiérrez and Villahermosa; it is about 0.5 mile (1 km) north of Pueblo Nuevo Solistahuacán, and 90 miles (145 km) north-northeast of Tuxtla Gutiérrez.

This is a short hike on a forest footpath up a moderately steep slope in a fairly mature oak–pine–sweetgum forest. It takes less than 15 minutes of non-stop walking to traverse the forest, but the idea is to take one's time and really look at things. The hike is worthwhile because this type of forest is seldom available to unannounced visitors who want to walk unhurriedly and in peace and quiet. Oak–pine–sweetgum is a relatively rare vegetation type, harboring numerous species of fairly restricted distribution.

The trail begins right behind the rusty, abused sign announcing RESERVA ECOLÓGICA LA YERBABUENA, in the vicinity of Highway 195's Km 166 marker. Just get on the trail and follow it through the forest until it ends at a steep hillside cornfield.

When I first began visiting this reserve in the early 1980s, hikers up this slope did not need to stop after a 15-minute stroll. The Seventh Day Adventists who owned the reserve, and still operate the little backcountry clinic just below the slope, wanted to keep the entire area above the clinic intact in order to protect the clinic's water supply. In those days one could hike from the highway to the peak at 7,482 feet. At the peak there existed a magnificent cloud forest of stunted trees covered with thick accumulations of lichens, mosses, ferns, and other epiphytes; sunlight, when the peak was not cloaked in clouds, was brilliant and surreal in its intensity. Resplendent quetzals lived here before the missionary's son took to shooting them for mounting.

In Pueblo Nuevo a large number of farmers, mostly of native stock, resented Yerba Buena keeping their slope in forest when it could be planted in corn. Ultimately the farmers banded together and invaded Yerba Buena's forest, chopping some down before authorities ran them off. For years tensions continued and similar invasions took place. Chiapas's governor promised to send guards. Men with guns faced one another.

In the early '90s, Yerba Buena's elderly missionary founders no longer retained the energy needed to dominate the situation. During my last visit, a new cornfield blocked the old trail to the peak and woodchoppers hacked incessantly and illegally in the cloud forest at the peak. It is quite possible that, of all the hikes in this book, what the little Reserva Ecológica la Yerbabuena has to say about natural history in Mexico is the most compelling, relevant, and sad.

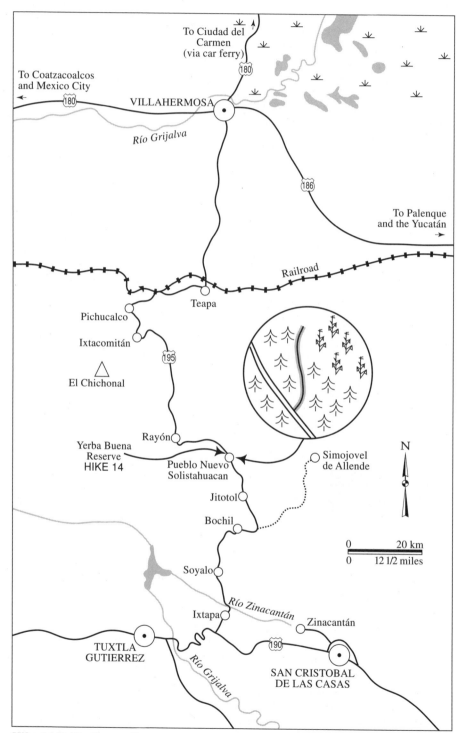

To Ciudad del
Carmen
(via car ferry)

To Coatzacoalcos
and Mexico City

180

180

VILLAHERMOSA

Río Grijalva

186

To Palenque
and the Yucatán

Railroad

Teapa

Pichucalco

Ixtacomitán

195

El Chichonal

Rayón

Simojovel
de Allende

Yerba Buena
Reserve
HIKE 14

Pueblo Nuevo
Solistahuacan

Jitotol

Bochil

N

0   20 km
0   12 1/2 miles

Soyalo

Río Zinacantán

Ixtapa

Zinacantán

190

TUXTLA
GUTIERREZ

Río Grijalva

SAN CRISTOBAL
DE LAS CASAS

Hike 14 Yerba Buena Reserve

Green-leafed plants rooted in soil accumulated on tree limbs are epiphytes.
They aren't parasites—they photosynthesize their own food.

Despite the tensions between Yerba Buena and local farmers, outsiders visiting the reserve have never experienced problems; ancient tradition holds that trails such as this are available to everyone. However, it would be unwise to enter the new cornfield, or to show much interest in it.

One special feature of what is left of Reserva Ecológica la Yerba Buena's forest is that several epiphytic species—orchids, ferns, peperomia—grow upon the tree's outspreading branches. The forest understory here—shrubs, vines, wildflowers, et cetera—also is exceptionally diverse. There is a shrubby hibiscus with hairy, three-lobed leaves and three-inch-long, purplish flowers, and a four-leaf senna more than six feet tall; most North American sennas

White roots snaking across a tree's bark identify this epiphyte as an orchid;
bromeliads, ferns, and other epiphytes don't have white roots.

seldom reach knee-high. Also there is a shrubby cestrum and a shrubby fuchsia, and at least two shrubby composites (a baccharis and a verbesina); North Americans think of all of these as herbs, not woody shrubs.

At least a dozen orchids have been found here, including four species of the genus *Encyclia*, and other species of *Coelia*, *Nagelietta*, *Physosiphon*, *Pleurothallis*, and *Malaxis*. Epiphytic orchids can be distinguished from bromeliads and other tree-borne plants by their thick, *white* aerial roots.

The oaks in this oak–pine–sweetgum forest are confusing and hard to identify. Students from England's University of East Anglia working in this area (see Bibliography) have identified four oak species as *chiquinív*, *cantdulán*, *tzaquioco*, and *palo de arbol*; two other oak species just could not be identified. The students found seven families of ferns and fern allies, but could identify only one fern—bracken—which grows worldwide. There is a begonia here worth seeing, too.

The two pines identified by the East Anglians go by the local names of *ocote colorado* and *ocote blanco*. This area's sweetgum is the same sweetgum that is so common in Eastern North America, with star-shaped leaves turning crimson in the fall. Other trees here include ash, coralbean, dogwood, viburnum, blackgum, hornbeam, and hophornbeam. This forest's surprising similarity to Eastern North American forests is considered in the cloud forest section of Vegetation Zones, Chapter 2, Mexico's Natural Environment.

North American hikers visiting during the northern winter may be surprised at the number of familiar bird species seen in the reserve and along Highway 195. Among them are the yellowthroat, yellow-throated warbler, yellow warbler, black-and-white warbler, hooded warbler, American redstart, Eastern wood peewee, Northern bobwhite, whippoorwill, American kestrel, and red-tailed hawk. How poignant to walk in this forest hearing the songs of overwintering birds mingling with the upslope choppings, even as every year new, shocking statistics come out showing that the numbers of migrating songbirds continue to plummet. Of course we Northerners can't feel too self-righteous, because new studies show that many of the above species also are disappearing because in North America large forests are being broken into smaller parcels, removing the "deep forest" needed by many species, and exposing these species to predators that penetrate only forest edges, such as suburban housecats.

Among the birds found here that are distributed only in southern Mexico and Central America are the garnet-throated, sparkling-tailed, and beautiful hummingbirds, and the slender sheartail. Other "exotics" include the blue-throated and russet-crowned motmots, blue-and-white mockingbird, rufous-browed peppershrike, slaty flower-piercer, and black-headed siskin.

During their 1987 expedition, the University of East Anglia students identified several mammals living on these slopes, including the giant, piglike rodent called paca, the raccoonlike coati, and the wildcat called jaguarundi. More familiar species included the opossum, raccoon, gray fox, gray squirrel, and hog-nosed skunk.

At the end of the trail, simply retrace your route back to the highway.

Getting There

Numerous buses run between Villahermosa and Tuxtla Gutiérrez, and second-classers stop any place they are asked to, including "*Reserva Yerba Buena, un kilómetro al norte de Pueblo Nuevo.*" If the Yerba Buena destination throws the ticket seller for a loop, buy a ticket for Pueblo Nuevo and walk the half mile to the reserve. Usually it is easy to get buses out of Villahermosa, but Tuxtla often is a hassle because there is no central terminal. During my most recent visit, Tuxtla's first-class ADO line refused to sell tickets to Pueblo Nuevo. If this policy persists, look for AUTOTRANSPORTES IXTAPA, SOYALO, BOCHIL Y PICHUCALCO at 4° Oriente Sur No. 544.

Lodging of all kinds is available in both Tuxtla and Villahermosa, but in the smaller towns along Highway 195—Pichucalco, Ixtacomitán, Jitotol—it can be rudimentary, unpredictable, and very colorful. A parking area lies about 200 yards south (Pueblo Nuevo direction) of the reserve's sign.

15 ▪ SAN CRISTOBAL'S PRONATURA RESERVE

Distance: about 1.25 miles (2 km)
Difficulty: strenuous, but with several resting seats
Terrain: trail
Elevation: 7,400 feet
Map: ITMP Map No. 204: México South, 1:1,000,000

PRONATURA Reserve, also called Reserva Ecológica PRONATURA and Estación Biológica Huitepec, lies just outside the colorful, tourist-oriented town of San Cristóbal de las Casas in central Chiapas's uplands. PRONATURA is Mexico's foremost environmental group. Entrance into the reserve costs about one dollar, and the reserve is closed on Mondays. The signs that read *SENDERO* [name] mean "trail [name]."

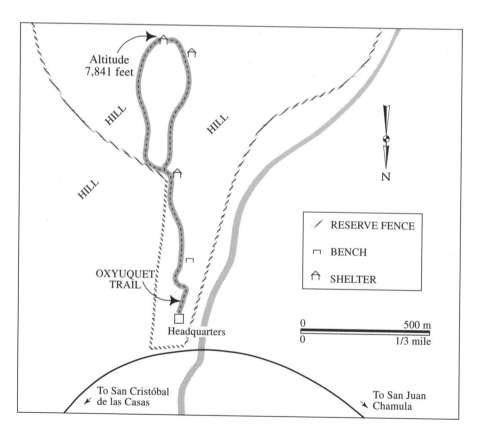

Altitude
7,841 feet

HILL   HILL

HILL

N

OXYUQUET
TRAIL

RESERVE FENCE

BENCH

SHELTER

Headquarters

0 ————————— 500 m
0 ————————— 1/3 mile

To San Cristóbal
de las Casas

To San Juan
Chamula

Ten-foot-tall castor-bean plants, natives of Africa, are common all through tropical America.

Hierba santa's *spicy-smelling leaves are used both as medicine and as wrappers for hot tamales.*

The hike, known as the Oxyuquet Trail, passes through a regenerating oak forest on a steep mountain slope. At the hill's peak, numerous bromeliads, orchids, and ferns live epiphytically on tree limbs. Along the trail, several signs in Spanish describe the slope's ecology. Steps are provided on steeper grades, and four pleasant resting spots are equipped with seats—three beneath thatched roofs.

A sign bearing the following is mounted on the reserve's entrance gate:

A LI TE'ETIK XCHI'UK LI SAT VO'ETIK LI'E SK'AN
JTUK'ULANTIK TA JKOTOLTIK
A LI TE'ETIK XCHI'UK LI SAT VO'ETIK LI'E SK'AN
ME JK'ELTIK TA JKOTOLTIK

The first two lines say the very same thing as the last two; the first lines are in the San Cristóbal dialect of Tzotzil, while the second are in the Chamula dialect. Here is a word-for-word translation of the first two lines:

A LI - TE'ETIK - XCHI'UK - LI - SAT - VO'ETIK - LI'E - SK'AN
(The - trees - with - and - well - water - here - love)
JTUK'ULANTIK - TA JKOTOLTIK
(Take care - everyone)

In other words, "Let's all love and take care of our trees and water."
The reserve's information signs refer to the ridge-top oak forest with its

Lichens are composite plants made of algae cells enmeshed in a network of fungus filaments.

An epiphytic fern in San Cristóbal's PRONATURA Reserve produces unfernlike, tongue-shaped fronds.

epiphytic plants as cloud forest. My opinion is that this is borderline cloud forest at best; full-fledged cloud forests have many more epiphytes and more lichens and mosses on the ground than are found here.

The two main oak species on the reserve's slopes are the wrinkle-leaf and thick-leaf oaks. A conspicuous shrub or small tree below the oaks, with reddish brown, smooth bark peeling off in large, papery plates, is the madrone. Greenish yellow, beardlike plants dangling three to six inches from tree branches are lichens—extraordinary plants actually composed of algal cells living mutualistically with a matrix of fungal cells. The alga photosynthesizes, producing food for itself and the fungus, while the fungus supplies the lichen's physical support and shape, and handles water distribution.

About midway up the slope, notice the cordlike plant creeping along the ground, looking somewhat like an emaciated green hand with recurved, pencil-thin fingers. This is an extremely primitive plant that lived 300 million years ago, before flowering plants evolved. Though it reproduces by spores, it is not a fern or moss. In English it is referred to as a ground pine, though it has nothing to do with pine trees; it is its own kind of thing, a sort of living fossil.

Growing epiphytically in the trees, the bushel-basket–size, agavelike plant consisting of tongue-shaped leaves with red bracts arising in its center is a bromeliad. Bromeliad flower clusters look like large grass flowers; most bromeliads are epiphytic, but pineapples are terrestrial bromeliads. Non-flowering orchids usually can be distinguished from bromeliads because orchids possess conspicuous white "roots" that creep across the bark of tree branches. Several ferns, which also reproduce by spores, grow epiphytically here, including one with tongue-shaped blades with regularly spaced, brown dots on the lower surface; the brown dots are clusters of spore capsules.

During the northern winter, several overwintering bird species familiar to North Americans as summer migrants inhabit the PRONATURA Reserve. These include ruby-crowned kinglets and black-throated green and Townsend's warblers; also there are Northern flickers, acorn woodpeckers, and Steller's jays. The reserve is home to several nice "exotics," such as crescent-chested warblers, ruddy-capped nightingale-thrushes, blue-throated motmots, brown-backed solitaires, green violet-ears, and black-throated jays.

Getting There

PRONATURA Reserve lies about 3 miles (4.5 km) west of San Cristóbal de las Casas; San Cristóbal is amply served by buses. In Mexico City, *directo* service is available on the Cristobal Colon line, which leaves from the Eastern Terminal, at the San Lázaro stop on the Observatorio/Zaragoza Metro run. From San Cristóbal, the reserve is on the paved road (designated on some maps as Diag. R. Larrainzar) to Zinacantán and San Juan Chamula.

Combis (minibuses) from San Cristóbal leave from the big *mercado* area for Zinacantán and Chamula every 10 to 20 minutes. To reach the *combis*, starting at San Cristóbal's Zócalo, or central park, walk about 10 minutes north on the busy street called Gral. Utrilla. After the crowded, hectic, and very colorful market area, with its multitudinous fruit stands, meat stalls, et cetera, appears on the right, continue downhill past the market and turn right at the first major street, called Edgar Robledo. Walk eastward for 2 or 3 minutes to the large parking lot where numerous Volkswagen vans—the *combis*—are parked. Usually at least one van is loading; look for one parked near the lot's entrance, possibly with its door open, with "San Juan Chamula" written on the door. The question, "*¿Donde está el servicio a Chamula?*" can be helpful.

Lodging in San Cristóbal covers the spectrum. The closest lodging to PRONATURA Reserve lies about 1 mile (1.5 km) toward town from the reserve; there Restaurante el Campestre has a spacious campground and some cabins. Pitching a tent costs about $2 US; inexpensive hookups are available for RVs. Ask about the steam bath there.

16 ▪ AGUA AZUL NATIONAL PARK

Distance: 4.5 miles (7 km)
Difficulty: moderate
Terrain: trail
Elevation: 1,000 feet
Map: ITMP Map No. 205: Yucatán Peninsula, 1:1,000,000

Agua Azul National Park lies near Highway 199 between San Cristóbal de las Casas and Palenque, about 40 miles (65 km) south-southwest of Palenque. Agua Azul is a mildly touristy spot; most people spend a day here swimming among pretty cascades, then return home at night.

Few visitors realize that approximately 2 miles (3 km) below the rather tame "tourist cascades," there are three seldom-visited, fairly spectacular waterfalls. This hike leads to those falls. The trail passes through a landscape drastically altered by slash-and-burn agriculture; one sees a lot of cornfields and weeds, with a few patches of remaining forest. However, the climate is so hot and humid that even the robust, exotic-looking weeds are fun to see. Agua Azul National Park is just a tiny parcel of land around the cascades; the Mexican government has allocated all the land between the "tourist cascades" and the falls to an *ejido*.

Many more *campesinos* and their horses use the trail than hikers. In some low spots, horses chop the trail into mud mush or ankle-crunching clods, depending on when the last rain occurred. The three waterfalls the hike visits are too big and turbulent for swimming and wading, and the slopes around them are too steep for anything other than looking.

At Agua Azul's entrance road, one must hike, hitchhike, or drive 2.5 miles (4 km) downhill to the park. After descending from the highway and passing Agua Azul's ticket booth, take the dirt lane to the right, down toward the river, past the row of *palapas*. Continue past the last building to the edge of the Río Paxilhá, turn right, and follow the river downstream. After about 3 minutes, a small but deep stream must be crossed. If the very rickety pole bridge is out, just snoop around and see how the locals reach the other side. Across the stream, the trail climbs onto a hill's eastern slope. Then both trail and river meander fairly consistently toward the north.

About 5 minutes after the deep, narrow stream, the trail is enlarged by a small road coming in from the right. After continuing along the slope for about 0.5 mile (1 km), the trail descends onto the valley floor and embarks through a landscape of weedy cornfields. Here be on the lookout for one of the area's most beautiful "weeds"—a plant that would be prized in most any North Ameri-

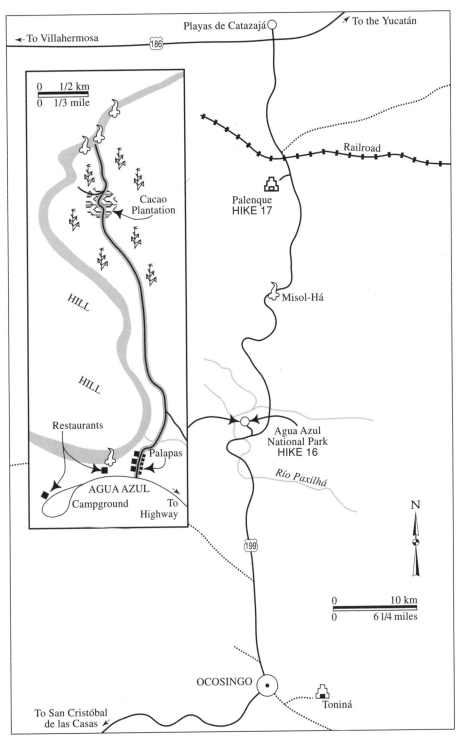

Hike 16 Agua Azul National Park

The "tourist cascades" at Agua Azul

can greenhouse. It is the wild plantain, related to banana trees and African bird-of-paradises. Just like a banana tree, wild plantain leaves are broad and glossy, and its flowers curiously constructed. The wild plantain's individual blossoms are cradled in bright red and yellow, scooplike spathes, which in turn are stacked in spectacular triangular spikes held stiffly above the leaves.

After about another 0.5 mile (1 km), the trail enters a shadowy cacao plantation. Cacao is the tree that produces cacao beans, from which chocolate is manufactured. The curious thing about cacao trees is that their flowers and fruits, instead of appearing at the ends of branches, sprout directly

At Agua Azul, Manuel Cruz López captures cicadas for fishing.

from the tree's trunk. Inside each cacao fruit, twenty-five to thirty-six one-inch-wide seeds are embedded in a white, mucilaginous, edible pulp; some people make a fine jelly from this pulp. When cacao seeds are properly fermented and processed, chocolate results. Chocolate is an invention of Mexico's native people; the conquistador Hernán Cortés learned about chocolate from Montezuma.

The cacao plantation is traversed in about 5 minutes. On the plantation's northern side, the trail comes to a not-too-obvious intersection; go right, toward the east, where less than a minute of walking remains before the trail returns to weedy cornfields—belonging to the local *ejido*. I asked several *ejido* members if there was any problem at all with hikers crossing *ejido* land to reach the lower falls, and everyone assured that there was none; in truth, established footpaths through *ejido* land generally are considered public thoroughfares. Nonetheless, by no means should a hiker ever leave the trail and enter the fields—not even for one step. If someone along the trail looks concerned, it would be appropriate to ask, "*¿Está bien si pasamos por aquí a las cascadas grandes?*" and proceed only when assurances are given that it is OK.

Soon a sinkhole is passed in a cornfield on the right, and another steep slope must be descended. Finally the trail enters a small, riverside forest. Here the first waterfall can be heard. The second one lies not far downstream; the third and final lies 7 or 8 minutes farther below.

Getting There

Many buses run between San Cristóbal and Palenque, and most stop at Agua Azul's entrance. In both Palenque and San Cristóbal, travel agencies dispense bus service to Agua Azul—some of it luxurious and expensive. Arriving by regular bus at Agua Azul's entrance road, one must hike or hitchhike 2.5 steep miles (4 km) downhill to the park. Agua Azul lies so near Palenque that it is possible to take the early bus from Palenque, spend the day at Agua Azul, and return that night.

Next to the cascades at the end of the short dirt trail along which the *palapas* stand, eight no-star rooms are available, each with two beds and each costing about $10 US. Most overnight visitors shell out around $3 for a hammock in a *palapa*, or erect a tent for the same price. A fellow usually hangs around the cascades offering horseback rides to the falls. He says he charges about $7 US per hour, which sounds a bit stiff; negotiate. A round-trip ride to the falls can easily be made in 2 hours, though this would leave little time for bird-watching and flower-sniffing.

17 ▪ PALENQUE

Distance: 7–8 miles (11–13 km)
Difficulty: moderately strenuous
Terrain: trail, gravel road
Elevation: near sea level
Maps: ITMP No. 204: Mexico South, 1:1,000,000; ITMP No. 205:
Yucatán Peninsula, 1:1,000,000

Palenque lies on Highway 199 about 60 air-miles (100 km) east-southeast of Villahermosa, Tabasco, in extreme northeastern Chiapas. The name "Palenque" is used both by a smallish town with a good tourist infrastruc-

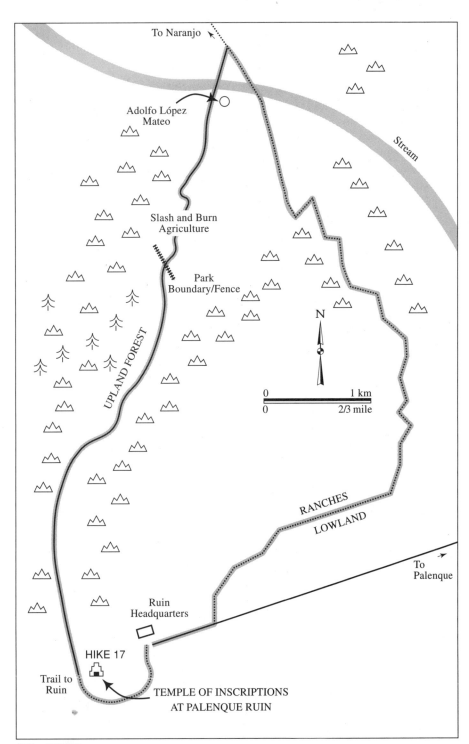

To Naranjo

Adolfo López
Mateo

Stream

Slash and Burn
Agriculture

Park
Boundary/Fence

N

UPLAND FOREST

0   1 km
0   2/3 mile

RANCHES
LOWLAND

To
Palenque

Ruin
Headquarters

HIKE 17

Trail to
Ruin

TEMPLE OF INSCRIPTIONS
AT PALENQUE RUIN

Hike 17 Palenque

ture, and a spectacular Maya ruin, which lies about 10 microbus minutes west of town. Of all the hikes in this book, this one provides the best chance for experiencing plants and animals typical of tropical rain forests—the "jungle." The forests around Palenque survive only in small, disturbed patches. However, the species there are largely "jungle species."

Not only do Palenque's forests share many species with tropical rain forests or "real jungles," but also certain structural features are shared. For example, in these forests there are many lianas (woody vines) and epiphytes, such as bromeliads, orchids, and peperomias. The forest floor is densely populated with a dense thicket of spiny palms and shrubs. Spiny palms are characteristic of tropical American forests in the same way that bamboo is characteristic of Southeast Asian jungles. It is hard to identify trees along the forested part of this hike simply because leaves, flowers, and fruits usually grow too high to examine. However, be sure to notice one common, very conspicuous, easy-to-identify tree; the strangler fig's gray, smooth bark and immense trunks with wide, flaring buttresses are unmistakable.

This is a fairly rigorous hike, half of which follows an ancient Indian trail up and down steep slopes through forest and field, the other half following a seldom-used gravel road passing partly through hills and partly through lowland ranch country. Soon after rains, the limestone rocks over which the Indian trail passes become mud-smeared and treacherously slippery.

This hike's trailhead lies inside the Palenque ruin itself, so a ticket must be bought. Locate the Temple of Inscriptions—the pyramid inside which, in 1952, the Mexican archaeologist Alberto Ruz discovered one of the world's most fantastic burials and treasure troves. Starting in the plaza facing the pyramid's steep series of steps, pass to the structure's left, to where a well-used trail ascends the steep, densely forested slope. Embark on this trail, ignoring the exit that almost immediately appears to the right, which leads on to the pyramid.

Follow the trail as it climbs, parallelling a deep valley on the left. After 4 minutes a small ruin is passed by; this is a wonderful place to sit and watch for birds in the wooded valley below. On the upland half of this hike, the birds are like Christmas candy. If a field guide to Mexican birds is at hand, look up some of the species as you read the following list, and just marvel at the fantastic colors and forms.

Around the ruins themselves, it is possible to see citreoline and violaceous trogons, and fast-moving white-bellied emerald and rufous-tailed hummingbirds; collared araçaris and keel-billed toucans are fairly common, the latter croaking like a raspy-voiced frog. There are yellow-winged, crimson-collared, scarlet-rumped, and blue tanagers, and red-crowned and red-throated anttanagers. Red-legged honeycreepers really have red legs, dot-winged antwrens have dots on their wings, and barred antshrikes do wear bars. There are white-breasted woodwrens, yellow-bellied elaenias, masked tityras, yellow-throated euphonias, bananaquits, black-headed saltators. . . .

Actually, these species are denizens of forest borders. Step into the forest itself and even more wondrous species appear. Often one hears the clear, tremulous whistle of the little tinamou, related to flightless rheas and ostriches, and the quavering, screech-owl–like call of the hard-to-see tody motmot. The spotted wood-quail, a sort of jungle bobwhite, has a low-high-low *grouww-chow-lo* call. Like enormous brown creepers, tawny-winged and barred wood-creepers flutter heavily onto giant tree trunks. Well, the list goes on and on.

Even casual birders without binoculars can see interesting species on this hike. On barbed-wire fences in ranch areas, the scarlet birds with bandit masks are vermilion flycatchers; the black birds with Jimmy Durante beaks and long tails are groove-bill anis. Vultures always can be spotted soaring through the sky. The ones with widely flaring tails, and wings bearing white "windows" when seen from below, are black vultures; the completely black species with narrow tails are turkey vultures. Something looking like a turkey vulture but flying a bit more buoyantly may turn out to be the rare lesser yellow-headed vulture.

Despite the birds putting on such a show, the star animal at Palenque is the howler monkey. During the first part of this hike, there is a good chance that, off toward the east, howlers will be heard roaring. "Roaring" is an apt description, because that is what they do. Having a daydream shattered by one of these critters letting go nearby is enough to curl toenails. Some years ago, near the famous Maya ruin of Bonampak in southeastern Chiapas, I verified that when a troop of howlers is approached from below, they are likely to defecate. The tumbling excreta splatters and scatters in tree limbs, elegantly conveying the message to go away.

Beyond the tiny temple the trail climbs rather steeply for about a half hour before reaching the ridge crest. Follow the trail along the undulating ridge for about 25 minutes before arriving at a fence at the forest's edge; this is the park's boundary. Pass through the gate and proceed downhill, to the southwest, through very weedy slash-and-burn territory. After a half hour of following the main trail, reach the Chol-speaking village of Adolfo López Mateo. Keep heading south through town. Children and women usually run from their huts offering *refrescos* and local handicrafts.

Upon reaching the wide gravel road serving as the town's main street, you have two options. The first is to turn right at the gravel road, follow it for a couple of minutes, and, upon reaching the larger gravel road, turn right again; this road runs directly back to the Palenque ruins.

The second option is to continue southward on the footpath, crossing Adolfo López Mateo's gravel road, and after 3 or 4 minutes you reach a very pleasant stream perfect for wading and equipped with plenty of boulders to sit on. Beyond the stream, the trail continues southward a couple of minutes to the main gravel road. At this intersection, almost immediately to the left lies the Tzeltal-speaking village of Naranjo. Follow the gravel road to the right back across the little stream and on to Palenque to complete the remainder of this hike.

For a couple of miles the road back to Palenque proceeds in a generally northwesterly direction. When another road comes in from the west (left), continue straight, to the northeast. After about 2.5 miles (4 km), the gravel

During the Palenque hike, note the fifteen-foot-tall tree ferns that grow along the road; they are real ferns, reproducing by spores.

road meets the paved road just northeast of the park's museum and the ruins' entrance.

The original forest mantling the hills through which this road passes must have been magnificent. Even what is left is interesting. For example, it is easy to find wild plantain, so similar to the house plant from Africa called bird-of-paradise, and closely related to banana trees. Also there are fig-family cecropias, slender-trunk trees with deeply lobed, umbrellalike leaves; remember the story about cecropia stems and ants in the tropical evergreen forest and tropical rain forest section of Vegetation Zones, Chapter 2, Mexico's Natural Environment. Look for gigantic, ferny leaves issuing from very rough, polelike trunks pockmarked with scars of old frond stalks. It is hard to believe that these ten-foot-tall plants are actually ferns—tree ferns—until you notice that the plant's fronds unfurl fiddleheadlike, exactly like the most delicate woodsia, and that the fronds are equipped with spore-producing sori. During the Devonian Period about 400 million years ago, tree ferns dominated much of the middle story of the world's forests, but today they are essentially "living fossils."

Often during the last mile or so of hiking through the ranchlands, children appear selling plastic bags of dried mushrooms—"magic mushrooms," as the young people at Maya Bell call them. Magic mushrooms, belonging to the genus *Psilocibe*, grow in the area's pastures on drying-out cow poop, and are hallucinogenic. Lacandón Indians have been documented using this mushroom in their rituals, as have the Mixtec, Zapotec, and Mixe in Oaxaca.

Probably it is not a good idea to experiment with these. Apparently one can survive the mushroom's hallucinogenic compound, a toxin called psilocybin, of the lysergic acid (LSD) family of compounds, but there are many potentially dangerous chemicals in these fungi besides psilocybin. Andean Indians who eat moldy peanuts (mold is a fungus, like mushrooms) suffer a high incidence of liver cancer. Eating a mushroom off a cowpat is like walking into a chemical lab and downing the first vial of chemicals seen, not knowing what is in it.

Two tree species are planted in straight lines next to several ranches along this road. The one with diffuse, pinelike needles is Australian pine, which is not a pine at all, but a member of the casuarina family, indigenous to Australia and the Pacific Islands. Australian pine is planted throughout the tropical and subtropical world because it grows quickly, is a good firewood producer, and when it is cut down it just sprouts back again. The other straight-line, roadside tree is *cocuite*, in the bean family, with locustlike leaves, pink clusters of flowers, bark that is ground with cornmeal to make a mouse poison, and the wonderful propensity for growing into a fence post if a branch of it is stuck into the ground.

Getting There

The main city in the area is Villahermosa, Tabasco, where it is not unusual to arrive at the big, first-class ADO terminal to find that no tickets to Palenque are available for several more hours. In such cases, usually it is quicker to walk a few blocks to the bustling second-class terminal, where service to Palenque is more frequent. Just ask directions to the *terminal de autobuses de segunda clase*. In the town of Palenque, minibuses to the ruin depart from a parking lot on Calle Allende just north of the main street, Av. Juarez, every 10 minutes or so.

In Palenque, abundant lodging of every kind is available. Campers and hammock-renters often gravitate to the Maya Bell Campground on the road between town and the ruins, within easy walking distance of the ruins' entrance.

CHAPTER 8

THE YUCATAN PENINSULA

The Land

Unlike most of Mexico, the Yucatán Peninsula's geological evolution had little to do with vulcanism and metamorphism. Twenty million years ago, during the Miocene epoch of the Tertiary Period—fairly recently in geological time—the Mexican uplands were in place, but the Yucatán existed as the marly, calcium-rich bottom of a warm, shallow sea. Regional uplifting and dropping sea levels now have bared the Yucatán as a massive slab of limestone. The unique karst topography that develops upon limestone bedrock, as described in the limestone geology section of Geology, Chapter 2, Mexico's Natural Environment, is characteristic of the Yucatán.

Offshore of northwestern Yucatán, waters remain fairly shallow for 150 miles before plunging into the 12,300-foot-deep Mexico Basin in the Gulf of Mexico's center. This shelf of warm, shallow water is as large as the Yucatán Peninsula itself, and supports an enormously important fishery and ecosystem referred to as the Campeche Bank. During the Celestún National Park hike later in this chapter, stand at the water's edge, gaze toward the northwest, and contemplate not only the Campeche Bank's vibrant biodiversity, but also the super-spectacular event that occurred there 65 million years ago, mentioned in Geological Zones, Chapter 2, Mexico's Natural Environment.

Plants

On the Yucatán Peninsula, the farther northwest one travels, in general, the drier it gets. While Xpuhil on Highway 186 in the south, between Chetumal and Escárcega, can receive more than five feet of rain in a year, at Mérida in the northwest, the annual rainfall is about half that. The peninsula's vegetation reflects this gradient very clearly. In the Yucatán's southeastern corner, forests are fairly high and "forestlike"; around Mérida, what forest remains is exceedingly dense, thorny, and scrubby, and averages only fifteen to thirty feet tall.

Starting in the Yucatán's southeastern corner and moving toward the northwestern corner, these are the plant communities one passes through: Tropical Evergreen Forest→ Tropical Deciduous Forest→ Thorn Forest

Animals

Along the Yucatán's shores, some of the more conspicuous birds include the brown pelican, often diving headfirst from twenty to fifty feet above the water. The magnificent frigatebird has a long, forked tail and hooked bill, and there are laughing gulls and the least, royal, and black terns, the latter only during the winter. Also during the winter, the spotted sandpiper is abundant. For the most part, North American birders wanting new species for their life lists will see few species here that cannot also be seen on the shores of Texas and Florida. One exception is that over lagoons and estuaries, mangrove swallows often can be spotted.

Inland, things become more exotic. For example, step into the scrub around Chichén Itzá or some other Maya ruin, and one might spot the black-throated bobwhite (the northern bobwhite also is here), ruddy ground-dove, turquoise-browed motmot, masked tityra, black-and-blue jay, white-lored gnatcatcher, rufous-browed peppershrike, and blue-black grassquit.

On any island separated from the mainland for many millennia, it can be expected that some organisms will have evolved into forms unique to that island. That is the case with Cozumel Island, off Yucatán's northeastern coast. Cozumel is home to at least two endemic bird species—the Cozumel thrasher and the Cozumel vireo. Along the dirt road parallelling the beach north of Cozumel City, the Cozumel vireo is rather common and easy to attract with the *shhh-shhh-shhh* hiss. Other species are found on Cozumel and certain Caribbean islands, but not elsewhere in Mexico. For example, gray kingbirds occur mostly in the West Indies, southern Florida, and Cozumel. Stripe-headed tanagers live in the Bahamas, Greater Antilles, and Cozumel. White-crowned pigeons inhabit the Florida Keys, West Indies, the Caribbean islands, and Cozumel. Caribbean elaenias occupy the Lesser Antilles and islands off the Yucatán's coast.

Originally, both howler and spider monkeys occupied most of the Yucatán, but now hunting and habitat destruction restricts them to a few places in the south. The Punta Laguna hike later in this chapter visits a very special spider-monkey population in northern Quintana Roo. Armadillos occur throughout the Yucatán, as do cottontails and tropical-forest rabbits, the former mostly in the north, the latter mostly in the south. In trees around ruins in the south, often there are gray squirrels; Deppe squirrels are tiny, olive-brown squirrels native throughout the region. Prehensile-tailed porcupines are listed for all of the Yucatán, though they are seldom seen, being both arboreal and nocturnal. It might be interesting to ask hunters met on hikes about these porcupines; often they go by the name of *zorro espín*, or "spiny fox."

Both pacas and agoutis might be found in isolated areas; these are pig-sized rodents famous for their "better-than-pig" taste. Sometimes gray foxes are spotted throughout Yucatán, as are raccoons and their close cousins the ringtail cats. Coati have been known to knock over a few trash cans; they look like raccoons with monkey tails. There are several nocturnal, weasel-like creatures in the Yucatán. Striped and hog-nosed skunks occur in the north, and spotted skunks throughout. At Celestún, one might spot river otters; the boatmen may call them *perros de agua*—"water dogs." Five of Mexico's six species of big cats originally were found throughout the Yucatán; even today at Celestún, hikers along muddy shores find jaguar and ocelot tracks. Tracks of both collared and white-lipped peccaries might be detected in isolated areas in the south. At one time, both the white-tailed and brocket deer were common here, but they have been overhunted; brocket deer are smaller than white-tails, and their horns are just raspy nubbins.

The Campeche Bank's warm, shallow waters support some very valuable marine species. These include grouper, snapper, spiny lobster, and octopus. From May to September, the Carey (hawksbill) and white (green) turtles, in danger of extinction, nest on Celestún's beaches; during this time, hikers along the shore frequently find their unmistakable flipper prints in the sand, leading from the water, across the sand, to the first depression encountered, and then back to the sea again. Besides the Carey and white, three other species of marine turtle are native to the Yucatán's beaches: the Caguama (loggerhead), parrot (Ridley), and laud (leatherback) turtles.

Along the beach about 25 miles (40 km) south of Playa del Carmen, at this book's featured snorkeling location on Yucatán's Caribbean coast, immediately north of popular Xel-Ha park, there is a sea-turtle nursery at Xcacel (eesh-ca-SEL), funded by private donations and T-shirt sales. From May to October, anyone looking for a good reason to tarry in this paradise might consider checking into Chemuyil Campground near Xcacel, and then volunteering to patrol turtle-nesting spots along the beach. For more information, write to the Central Investigation of Quintana Roo, Sea Turtle Program, Zona Industrial, Km 2, Carretera, Chetumal-Bacalar, A.P. 424, 77000 Chetumal, Quintana Roo, Mexico.

People

In ancient times the southern Yucatán Peninsula was very densely populated by the Maya. Hundreds of ruins, many still undiscovered and unlooted, are found there. From the air, extensive networks of ancient stone walls between former farms still are visible. Though the northern Yucatán was heavily populated by the Maya when the Spanish arrived, the south already was depopulated. Therefore, one of the most interesting questions in all archaeology is, "What happened to all those Maya in the southern Yucatán and northern Guatemala?"

The southern Yucatán now is repopulating fast. This is because, with the extra rainfall, the land is richest in the south, and the government is bringing in hoards of settlers from the overpopulated Mexican Plateau. These settlers are organized into *ejidos* (see Attitudes for the Backcountry, Chapter 1, The Joy of Traveling Through Mexico), and are clearing away southern forests at an awful rate, even inside so-called biosphere reserves.

The Native American language throughout the Yucatán is Yucatec, one of the Maya languages. Hikers at Cobá will hear Yucatec by taking a dusk walk down the road past the little village across the lake from the ruin's entrance. So should visitors to Punta Laguna. Most Yucatec speakers have forsaken their traditional costumes for *campesino* clothing.

18 ▪ CELESTUN NATIONAL PARK

Distance: about 1 mile or more
Difficulty: easy
Terrain: dirt road, beach
Elevation: sea level
Map: ITMP Map No. 205: Yucatán Peninsula, 1:1,000,000

Celestún National Park lies on the Gulf Coast of the northwestern Yucatán Peninsula, at the end of Highway 281, around the town of Celestún, about 60 miles (95 km) west of Mérida.

Hiking possibilities along the shore and among the lagoons north of the town of Celestún are so great that this "open-ended" hike encourages hikers to define their own routes. A suggested strategy is to walk north among the lagoons, then later in the day when it is hotter, walk back along the windy, sandy beach. The lagoons are famous for bird populations that overwinter here; in addition, salt is collected here by the locals, using techniques that must be similar to those used by the ancient Maya. Much of Celestún's fame lies in the possibility for visitors to hire boats and visit large colonies of over-wintering American flamingos.

This hike's potential open-endedness is apparent from a quick glance at the map. The Gulf beach, the one-lane sand road (beginning at Calle 12), and the lagoons stretch "endlessly" to the north. Do not rely on the map to disclose the lagoons' exact location, size, and shape. With ever-changing tidal levels and occasional storms that change things around, it is easy to get disoriented among them . . . their exact configuration remains elusive. Of course,

Hike 18 Celestún National Park

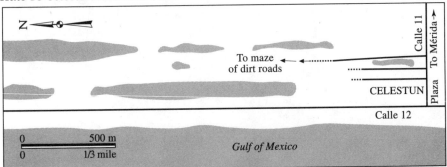

one feature of the open-ended hike is that anyone becoming confounded needs only to head west, and before long the sand road and beach will be reached. And both the road and beach, when followed southward, inevitably lead to Celestún's shaded *palapas* and cool *refrescos*.

Calle 12 is paved for about the first quarter mile before it becomes the sand road paralleling the beach. To find the sand road that is farther inland and leads north into a maze of dirt roads among the lagoons, start at Celestún's main plaza and walk along the main road, Calle 11, heading east toward Mérida. After about 6 minutes, take the third broad sand street to the left—the one after the Pemex station. For the first few minutes, the street limps past an awful dump of decaying fish heads and plastic bottles and bags, but eventually things lighten up.

Walking north along beach or sand roads, one begins feeling that "civilization is left behind" in about a half hour—about 1 mile. The duration and distance of this hike is completely up to each hiker.

The maze of one-lane dirt roads is much less traveled by hikers than by men engaged in collecting salt in shallow lagoons. Salt precipitates as the lagoons' waters evaporate. Often men are seen standing knee deep in the lagoons shoveling rock salt into sleds carved from plastic barrels. The salt is

Celestún's beach is a good place to look for sea shells.

A salty lagoon at Celestún; note the salt mound in the background and the crystals along the shore in the foreground.

dragged ashore and heaped into waist-high mounds, which dry out before being shoveled into trucks and taken to market. At first the mounds are pinkish, but as they dry out they become white. Some salt crystals exceed an inch across; cubical table-salt crystals materialize only at the refining factory. Celestún's salt must be have been collected for many centuries. Speculation is that the great Maya center now referred to as Chichén Itzá became a regional power largely because it monopolized northern Yucatán's salt trade.

Of course it is normal to want pictures of the salt collectors, but the collectors may not like to have their pictures taken. These men cannot be earning much money, yet they have told me that sharp salt crystals cut their bare feet, and that the saline water burns their wounds. The men usually laugh and kid about it, but imagine how they must feel when foreigners stand around snapping their pictures.

The most conspicuous and abundant tree north of Celestún certainly is the coconut palm, which must be one of the most useful trees in the world. Besides producing sweet coconuts, their trunks can be used for construction, their fronds can be used for thatched roofs, and sap from their trunk and flower clusters can be made into an alcoholic drink called *tuba*.

Just inland from the beach, classic coastal strand vegetation appears just as described in Vegetation Zones, Chapter 2, Mexico's Natural Environment. It is a pleasure to walk among these plants, seeing their many adaptations to the constant brisk wind laden with salt spray, the scalding midday heat and heavy sunlight, and sandy soil that hardly holds water and nutrients. Many of these plants protect themselves with tough leaves encased in waxy cuticles, and others survive such high concentrations of salt that their leaves actually taste salty.

One common bush here is the sea grape, a shrub with five- to six-inch-wide, thick, circular, red-veined leaves. Temperate-zone plant-lovers are always surprised that sea grapes are members of the buckwheat family, because northern members of this family, such as smartweed, are herbs.

Though stilted red mangrove (also described in Chapter 2) is not found along the beach north of Celestún, look for it around the mouth of Estero de Celestún during the flamingo-watching boat trip described in Getting There, below. In the lagoon area, watch for black mangrove, the one that issues vertical pneumatophores above water for absorbing air. Other mangroves to look for are the button-mangrove, with alternate leaves, and white mangrove, with opposite leaves. It is interesting how all these mangroves, spread through three different plant families, have leathery, evergreen, smooth-margined, unlobed, elliptic leaves, even though their flowers are quite different. This is a neat example of convergent evolution. One of Celestún's star plants is an endemic, xerophytic (surviving in very dry habitats) orchid called cyrtopodium.

More than 230 bird species have been spotted in Celestún National Park; 58 percent of these are resident. This is an extraordinary number, considering that Celestún's diversity of habitats is fairly limited—no oak–pine forests, no cloud forests, no rain forests or cactus deserts. Besides number of species, Celestún is home to impressive sheer numbers of individual birds; the reserve is considered the fourth most important bird overwintering site in the Gulf of Mexico.

Celestún's shorebirds are similar to those of coastal Florida and Texas. There are white and brown pelicans, magnificent frigatebirds, herring and laughing gulls, and royal, black, and least terns. Among the most conspicuous lagoon birds are little blue herons, American and reddish egrets, and, with perpetually bobbing tails, spotted sandpipers. Usually among the scattered homes, coconut groves, and vacant lots of Celestún's outskirts, it is easy to spot ruddy ground-doves, vermilion flycatchers, tropical kingbirds, tropical mockingbirds, melodious blackbirds, and bronzed cowbirds, the latter with surprising red eyes.

The scrub outside of town is home to several unusual species, such as the tiny, bronze-green hummer called the Mexican sheartail, the endemic Yucatán wren (which looks like a cactus wren), a gnatcatcher with a solid black cap called the white-lored gnatcatcher, and the yellow-faced grassquit, with its insectlike, buzzy call, *tsi-tsi-tsi-tsi-tsi*.

Seeing American flamingos at Celestún usually requires taking a ride in a motorboat. These flamingo tours constitute a kind of acid test for peoples' sensitivities to the needs of other creatures. Once boats are approaching the stately pink birds, there is every compulsion to draw closer and closer for a better snapshot. And often the boatmen are only too happy to oblige, because they know that the happier their clients are, the more likely they are to get a nice tip.

This sign on the beach north of Celestún reads: SEA-TURTLE HATCHING AREA. NO CAMPFIRES, NO DRIVING IN THIS AREA.

Of course if any wild creature is harassed frequently enough, its natural routines are upset, and who knows how that will affect their survival rate? With all the development along the Gulf Coast, clearly the flamingos have little opportunity to fly someplace else. Before stepping into a "flamingo boat," practice the sentence, "*Ojalá que no nos acerquemos a los flamencos hasta que les molestamos.*" ("I hope we do not draw so close to the flamingos that we bother them.")

From May to September the Carey (hawksbill) and white (green) sea turtles, both facing extinction, nest on the refuge's beaches. Along the beach a few miles north of town, a sign prohibits beach fires and driving (usually tire marks range everywhere) because this is a turtle nesting area. Hikers staying within 5 yards of the water need not worry about stepping on buried eggs. Turtles are not the only reptiles in the area; boa constrictors and crocodiles sometimes haunt the mangroves and the river's mouth.

In isolated corners of the reserve, not only are white-tailed deer and rac-

coons sometimes seen but also, in mud along lagoons and at the Estero de Celestún's mouth, prints of ocelots and jaguars. The estuary's opening itself is an important nursery and growing ground for lobsters, shrimps, and a variety of marine fish.

Getting There

Most long-distance bus riders arrive in Mérida at the ADO terminal at Calle 69 x 68 y 70—where north–south-running Calle 69 intersects east–west-running Calle 68 and 70. (Mérida's street-numbering system is systematically maddening for the uninitiated without a compass; remember that odd-numbered streets run north–south and the numbers increase going south, and even-numbered streets run east–west and the numbers increase going west.) The twenty blocks from the ADO terminal to the second-class terminal, from which the buses to Celestún leave, can make a good hike. To reach the second-class terminal from the ADO terminal, stand before the ADO station with your back to it, turn right, proceed about eighteen blocks, then go left about two blocks. It is hard to keep count of the blocks because the sprawling *mercado* must be skirted or passed through midway. But that is fun in itself. About every 2 hours throughout the day, the bus line called Autobuses del Occidente leaves for Celestún from Mérida's second-class terminal at Calle 67 x 50.

Many accommodation choices are available in Mérida, and a few rustic ones in Celestún. During the week, no problems should be encountered finding space in Celestún, but on weekends there may be competition from folks from Mérida. Beach camping is possible, though tents should never be left unguarded, and camps should not be established in sea-turtle egg-laying zones.

Providing motorboat service to flamingo overwintering grounds across the river is big business in Celestún; boatmen hungry for passengers greet potential clients crossing the bridge into Celestún by calling *"¿Flamencos? ¿Flamencos?"* The standard price per boatload is around $25 US; most visitors find others to go with them, to split the fee.

19 ▪ PUNTA LAGUNA

Distance: 0.6 mile (1 km)
Difficulty: easy
Terrain: trail
Elevation: near sea level
Map: ITMP Map No. 205: Yucatán Peninsula, 1:1,000,000

Punta Laguna lies in the state of Quintana Roo, on a road that connects Tulúm with Highway 180—the main route between Mérida and Cancún; Punta Laguna lies midway between Nuevo Xcan and Cobá (see map for hike 21).

The hike's two main attractions are the good possibilities of spotting some spider monkeys, and of meeting some friendly natives speaking Yucatec. The

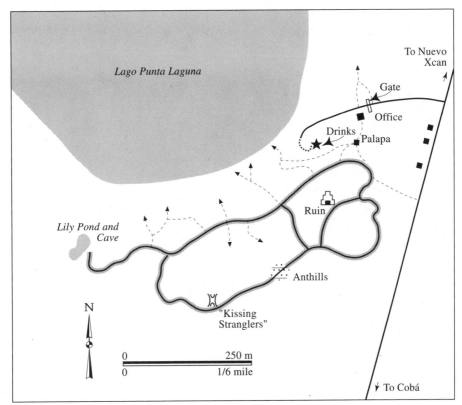

To Nuevo
Xcan

Lago Punta Laguna

Gate

Office

Drinks

Palapa

Ruin

*Lily Pond and
Cave*

Anthills

N

"Kissing
Stranglers"

0   250 m

0   1/6 mile

To Cobá

Hike 19 Punta Laguna

hike is along a footpath through dense forest similar to that at Cobá (see hike 20 later in this chapter); a small Maya ruin rises along one of the trails. An entrance fee of about $1.75 US is asked. Usually a Spanish-speaking Yucatec Indian guide is supplied.

A native Yucatec-speaking Maya, Don Serafio Canul, created the reserve, with help of Mexico's main environmental group, PRONATURA. Don Serafio and PRONATURA must struggle constantly to maintain this reserve. Surrounding Yucatec farmers want to slash-and-burn the reserve's forests to make way for cornfields, and more than a few would be happy to capture the spider monkeys for the lucrative wild-animal trade. Don Serafio, who vigorously opposes these pressures, has had his life threatened more than once. When visitors inject money into Punta Laguna's local economy, the monkeys stand a greater chance of survival, and Don Serafio's shaky position with his skeptical neighbors markedly improves.

From the highway, Punta Laguna does not present itself as much more than a dispersed cluster of seven or eight thatch-roofed huts; a gravel road leads west-northwest, and a sign points down the road to the monkey sanctuary. Follow the road 100 yards to the gate, which probably will be open, and look for someone in the welcome hut to the left. If the hut is locked up, continue down the road for 3 or 4 minutes, to the cold-beer-and-*refresco palapa*

Yucatec-speaking Serafio Canul and his mother greet visitors at the Punta Laguna Monkey Reserve.

overlooking Lago Punta Laguna.

With luck, either at the entrance or the *palapa*, Don Serafio will be encountered. Spanish-speaking hikers accompanied by Don Serafio or one of his sons will learn volumes. Non-Spanish-speakers can use the map in this book and, after signing in and paying the entrance fee, take off without a guide. The forest plot is too small to get dangerously lost in. Apparently the reserve's trail system changes from time to time, so do not be surprised if the map in this book is a little outdated. Don Serafio assures me that the trail between the welcome hut and the lily pond, and the return segment passing by the ruins, are permanent features.

Ask Don Serafio if the little temple still stands next to the *cenote*, or well-like cistern, down the footpath leading north from the welcome hut and, if so, whether you can see it. Recalling that the ancient Maya considered the gods' netherworld as being beneath waters, and that the *cenote* at Chichén Itzá was sacred, when one approaches this functional, *cenote*-side temple, the ancient Mayas' other-worldliness seems palpably, uncannily at hand.

Biota here is very similar to that described for hike 20, Cobá, 12.5 miles (20 km) to the south. The main difference is Punta Laguna's free-ranging spider monkeys. Though not tame, these monkeys are accustomed to people standing and gawking at them, so sometimes great snapshots can be taken as they swing through the treetops, grunting and shaking limbs.

Getting There

Most buses passing by Punta Laguna are first-classers and do not stop there. However, four or five second-classers a day do stop, so no one will become terribly stranded here. The main secret to using second-class buses in this area is that they run mainly between Valladolid—via Nuevo Xcan, Punta Laguna, Cobá, and Tulúm—and Playa del Carmen. The secondary road between Chemax and Cobá, present on many maps, has never existed.

Thatch-roofed huts in the Yucatán have changed little since ancient Mayan times.

No lodging is available in Punta Laguna, but a nice tent spot below the drinking *palapa* overlooks Lago Punta Laguna. Pitching a tent here costs about $2 US for the site, and $2 for each person. If this site is unavailable or other lodgings are desired, one can continue on to Cobá (see hike 20) or return to Highway 180 and find accommodations at the numerous towns along the highway, or at the cities of Valladolid or Mérida.

20 ▪ COBA

Distance: 2 miles (3 km)
Difficulty: easy
Terrain: trail
Elevation: near sea level
Map: ITMP Map No. 205: Yucatán Peninsula, 1:1,000,000

Cobá is a Maya ruin in the state of Quintana Roo midway between Nuevo Xcan, which lies on Highway 180 between Valladolid and Cancún, and Tulúm, Mayadom's most tourist-frequented ruin, which lies on the Caribbean coast

Hike 20 Coba

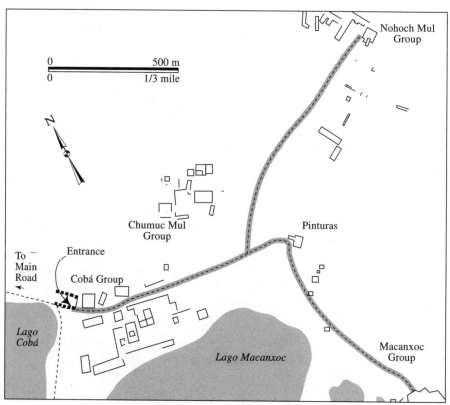

on Highway 307. Cobá is a good bit inland, about 75 miles (125 km) south-west of Cancún.

Cobá's ruins are dispersed in clusters in the forest, interconnected by wide, well-maintained paths; visiting each group requires hiking on level ground. It is hard to imagine a more convenient and pleasant way of gaining access to the plants and animals of this part of the Yucatán. Being close to sea level, Cobá's forest usually becomes steamy after 10:00 A.M.

Most of Cobá's forest trees stand only 30 to 45 feet tall, as opposed to around 175 feet in a virgin Panamanian rain forest. Its trees also grow very close together, and the forest shows only irregular or no stratification. Cobá lies in a transition zone between thorn forest to the north and tropical deciduous forest (which does show stratification) farther south; most trailside trees are "weed species" invading areas where the forest has been disturbed. Nonetheless, because the trails burrow through the forest affording wonderful close-up views, Cobá provides a marvelous forest experience.

Though all of Cobá's major trails can be hiked in a couple of hours, there are so many ruins to visit and subsidiary footpaths needing to be explored that a whole day can easily be spent here—if one can stand the heat.

Just inside the park's entrance, the big trees with gray, splotchy bark and feathery-looking, bipinnately compound leaves are guanacastes, which grow into big-trunked trees with spreading canopies, and are often seen at road intersections. Guanacastes are tropical America's shade tree par excellence. The pale trunk-splotches are lichens; close scrutiny of the splotches' margins reveals threadlike fungal mycelia expanding across the smooth trunk. Most of Cobá's smooth-trunked trees bear lichen-blotches.

Also at the entrance, just inside the gate and to the left, notice the handsome tree with locustlike leaves. During the northern winter, abundant dangling clusters of shrimp-colored, winged fruits adorn this tree, accounting for its name of pinkwing, or *camarón*, which means "shrimp." Pinkwing resides in the quassia family, to which tree-of-heaven, or ailanthus, also belongs.

The first group of ruins encountered is the Cobá group. Next, on the left, is the Chumuc Mul Group. At a y in the main trail, the left goes to the Nohoch Mul Group and the right to Pinturas and the Macanxoc Group. At Pinturas, about 30 feet directly in front of the stairs leading up the temple, notice the tree with its trunk bulging about six feet up, covered with low, conical spines, and with digitately compound (like fingers on a hand) leaves. This is a small kapok tree, or ceiba; they become enormous. A member of the bombax family, around May the kapok's cigarlike fruits split to release great gobs of tan-colored, cottony floss; this is kapok. Before synthetic fibers, kapok was collected and sold as insulation and stuffing.

On the trail to the Macanxoc Group of ruins, opposite the short stele standing halfway to the ruins, be sure to admire the wonderful strangler fig. The ancient Maya prepared long-lasting paper from the pounded inner bark of strangler figs.

At the Nohoch Mul Group, about 30 feet directly west of the stele with a thatched roof over it, notice the fine cecropia, the umbrella-shaped tree with a segmented, slender, cylindrical stem and deeply palmately lobed leaves. Remember the cecropia-stem-and-ant story in the tropical evergreen forest and tropical rain forest section of Vegetation Zones, Chapter 2, Mexico's Natural Environment.

During the northern winter, probably the most common and easy-to-identify tree along Cobá's trails is a small species with elmlike leaves and abundant, spherical, marble-size, very knobby, green or black fruits. This is prickelnut. A member of the cacao or chocolate family, prickelnut is typical of regener-

This fragile spider lily grows beside Lago Cobá.

At Cobá, Spanish moss dangles from trees along the wide stairs leading up to the **iglesia.**

ating forests. This species probably appreciates Hurricane Gilbert coming through the area in 1988, uprooting many trees in the area and creating holes in the forest that prickelnuts could invade. Another easily identifiable tree common on the side of some rubble mounds, with smooth, reddish bark peeling off in papery flakes, is the gumbo-limbo or naked Indian tree.

Notice the knee-high palms on Cobá's shady forest floor; this is as high as these dwarf palms grow. Farther south, especially in Guatemala's Petén region, men trek into the most isolated forest corners to harvest dwarf palm called *shate*. Each year tons of *shate* frond are shipped north as "parlor palm" for inclusion in floral arrangements.

Cobá is nearly as good as Palenque for spotting birds typical of neotropical forests. All three of Mexico's toucan species can be seen here: the keel-billed toucan, the collared araçari, and the emerald toucanet. Loud croakings heard at Cobá probably do not belong to frogs at all, but rather to keel-billed toucans.

Frequently, noisy flocks of Aztec parakeets are heard winging overhead. Looking like North America's pileated woodpecker, the lineated woodpecker sometimes barnstorms through the forest; the big ivory-billed woodcreeper looks like a northern brown creeper with a hormone problem. There are barred antshrikes and masked tityra, and at least three species of wren—the spot-breasted, the white-bellied, and a Yucatán race of North America's Carolina wren; here it is called the white-browed wren. The blue jay with a black head commonly seen slinking in the underbrush in small, noisy, nosy flocks is a Yucatán race of the black-and-blue jay, formerly considered a distinct species, the Yucatán jay. During late winter and early spring, often the most frequently heard bird is nothing less than North America's abundant summer resident, the red-eyed vireo.

Bushel-basket–size termite nests are commonly observed perched ten feet high on tree limbs. Lines of leafcutter ants cut across many of Cobá's trails, each ant carrying above its head a green leaf-tatter. These tatters will be composted underground, a fungus will infest them, and the ants will eat tiny, cauliflowerlike buds produced by the fungus. Ants streaming in currents dozens of ants wide, not carrying leaf tatters and all rushing in the same direction, are army ants. If a grasshopper or scorpion blunders into their way, stand back and see how coldly efficiently the blunderer is snipped to pieces and carted away.

Getting There

Numerous buses pass the short entrance road to Cobá because it is on the road between Mérida and the Cobá–Tulúm–Playa del Carmen area; however, many of these buses are first-classers that do not stop. One way to bus from Mérida and Cancún to Cobá is to buy first-class tickets to Valladolid, and then take second-class passage to Cobá.

At Cobá, at rather unpredictable hours, second-class buses enter the ruin area, rumble to the end of the road at the lake's edge, turn around, and stop at the restaurants atop the hill. Maybe four buses a day do this. On my 1993 visit, the 11:30 A.M. bus to Mérida did not appear until 6:00 P.M.

By the way, for years most maps, even excellent AAA and Rand McNally editions, have shown a road between Chemax on Highway 180 and Cobá. Such a highway would constitute a wonderful shortcut, but it has never existed except in the minds of cartographers who keep copying the same mistake from one another (see map for hike 21).

Lodging at Cobá ranges from very fancy and expensive to very rustic and inexpensive. One can camp in the spacious parking lot before the ruins' ticket office, though during rains tents have their cellars flooded.

The souvenir shop next to the ticket office sells a small selection of books worth looking at. *Incidents of Travel in Central America, Chiapas, and Yucatán*, by John Stephens, originally published in 1841, usually is on sale, and surely is one of the world's most engrossing travel-books. *Yucatán Before and After the Conquest*, by Friar Diego de Landa, Yucatán's fanatical, Indian-abusing bishop during the mid-1500s, gives fascinating, Christian-biased, eyewitness accounts of what the Maya were like before and during the Spanish conquest. Regrettably, no book here helps identify Cobá's plants and animals. The costly, thin books *Tropical Blossoms of the Caribbean* and *Tropical Trees found in the Caribbean, South America, Central America, Florida and Mexico* are fairly useless at Cobá because they cover too large an area in too few pages. The pricey little *Descriptive Guide Book to Cobá* is out of date, its map is misleading, and little interesting information is provided.

However, in the thatch-roofed restaurants across from the ruin's entrance, consider asking for traditional Yucatec meals. For example, Don Francisco May Hau (Hau is pronounced "how") is a Yucatec Indian from the village of Cobá across the lake and operates the unnamed establishment next to Restaurant El Fasán. Don Francisco speaks passable English and he and his cook, Chef Abelardo Chimal May, when given a few hours' advance notice, will prepare *pozol*, one of the basic traditional foodstuffs of indigenous Mesoamericans. It is a simple but nutritious mixture of corn and water, flavored in various ways. Their *bistek en adobo* is a considerably more substantial plate. Here beefsteak is prepared with the juice of a sour variety of orange and *recado*, which is a sauteed concoction of onion, garlic, sweet pepper, tomato, potato, and fresh oregano. *Pollo en escabeche* is barbecued chicken served in a bowl, smothered in the above *recado*.

21 ▪ SNORKELING AT PLAYA DEL CARMEN

Distance: a few feet to several hundred yards or more
Difficulty: easy to moderate
Terrain: ocean
Elevation: sea level
Map: ITMP No. 205: Yucatá Peninsula, 1:1,000,000

Playa del Carmen lies on the Yucatán's Caribbean coast, across the strait from touristy Cozumel Island. In the state of Quintana Roo, Playa del Carmen is on Highway 307 between Cancún and Chetumal, about 50 miles (80 km) south of Cancún.

Here snorkelers can explore a coral reef not as well developed as that along Cozumel's shores but, because there are fewer *turistas*, it is possibly more of an enjoyable experience. Visitors not carrying their own equipment (see Snorkeling and Diving, Chapter 1, The Joy of Traveling through Mexico)

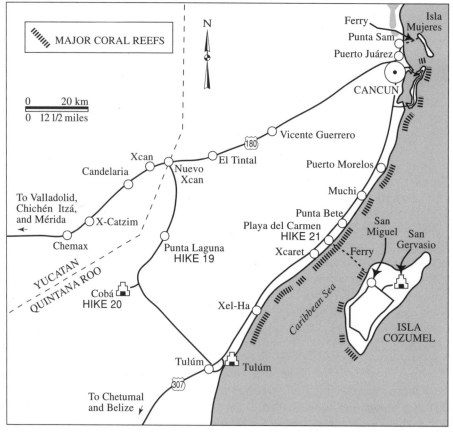

Hike 19 Punta Laguna / Hike 20 Cobá / Hike 21 Snorkeling at Playa del Carmen

can rent what they need at numerous shops along the beach.

One way to find good snorkeling spots is to hike, bike, or drive along the coast looking for dark spots in the turquoise water. Beautiful coral and marine life can be found almost everywhere along the Caribbean coast from Cancún to the Belize border. At Playa del Carmen, a good approach is to ask advice at a dive shop. Once a spot is chosen, one simply paddles out and, exercising the precautions mentioned in Chapter 1, looks around. The reefs are located at varying distances from shore, and one can explore as close to or as far from shore as desired. Less experienced snorkelers may enjoy (for a small fee) the enclosed waters at Xel-Ha Natural Park, about 30 miles (50 km) south of Playa del Carmen, where freshwater and seawater mingle in a shallow lagoon.

Coral reefs are composed of millions of close-packed polyps—small animals related to the sea anemone, usually less than an inch in diameter. As the polyps regenerate themselves through budding, they secrete calcium carbonate, or limestone. Over the millennia, the colonies grow into massive, stone-hard structures that are both a bane to naval navigators and the foundation of the reef ecosystem.

Each coral type assumes a characteristic shape. Among the most memorable are boulder-sized brain corals, actually resembling gigantic human brains. Staghorn and elkhorn corals look like fragile antlers. Many species of coral lack the rock-building capacity; in Mexico probably the most common of this type are the gorgonians, or sea fans, which come in many colors, including a vibrant purple, and resemble large, lacy fans swaying in the current. The swaying motion is their strategy for catching plankton being carried in by the tide.

A hugh diversity of fish and other life forms make their home among the coral. Several varieties of sponge, some resembling bowls or barrels, reach three feet high. Brightly colored parrotfish nibble on the coral itself, extracting algae and, in the process, grinding the reef slowly into fine sand. Tiny damselfish appear in a rainbow of colors, and stately angelfish glide by like psychedelic billboards. Grunts travel in large groups, their movements choreographed by unseen forces. If one dives amidst them, they magically part to allow one's passage, then instantly regroup behind the snorkeler.

Night dives reveal an entirely different reef environment. At night, many rock-dwelling crustaceans emerge from their hiding places while their predators sleep, and hard corals feed, waving their tentacles like fields of wheat in the wind. With flashlights extinguished, it is mesmerizing to see the phosphorescent glow generated by plankton excited by air bubbles and the snorkeler's presence. Try lying on your back beneath a coral ledge and exhaling; glowing, green bubbles will rise along the rock face, outlining the reef's eerie, beautiful shapes. Truly spectacular! In dive shops, ask for *un buseo nocturno*—a night dive.

Getting There

Many buses travel between Cancún and Chetumal, and most pull into Playa del Carmen. In Mérida, Autobuses del Occidente, at Calle 67 x 50, provides services to Playa del Carmen three or four times a day.

Lodging at Playa del Carmen is bounteous and of every color. Hammock renters and tenters have it made. Disembarking from the bus, walk down to the beach, turn left, and almost immediately a place appears called Campamento "La Ruina." A rented hammock costs about $1 US per night; pegging a small tent goes for about $2. Bathrooms and showers here are not bad.

APPENDIX A
SCIENTIFIC NAMES

By no means is the following a comprehensive list of Mexico's plants and animals; it just provides scientific names for the common names of plants and animals mentioned in this book. Thus when the scientific name for lantana is given as *Lantana involucrata*, it should be understood that only the lantana referred to in the text—one seen along Highway 70—is being referred to. The "spp." means that more than one species goes by the given common name.

Plants

acacia, boat-thorn   *Acacia cymbispina*
acacia, bullhorn   *Acacia spadicigera*
acacia, catclaw   *Acacia greggii*
acacia, flat-thorn   *Acacia gladiata*
acacia, hat-thorn   *Acacia hindsii*
acacia, sweet   *Acacia farnesiana*
acacia, twisted   *Acacia tortuosa*
agave (Zapotitlán, species 1)
     Agave macroacantha
agave (Zapotitlán, species 2)
     Agave potatorum
agave (Zapotitlán, species 3)
     Agave verchaffeltii
agave (Zapotitlán, species 4)
     Agave marmorata
agave (Zapotitlán, species 5)
     Agave triangularis
agave (Zapotitlán, species 6)
     Agave stricta
agave, desert   *Agave deserti*
agave, Shaw's   *Agave shawii*
aile   *Alnus firmifolia*
albizia   *Albizia* spp.
alder, wax   *Alnus jorullensis*
algarrobo   *Acacia pennatula*
algerita, Texas   *Mahonia trifoliolata*
allthorn   *Koeberlinia spinosa*
anacahuita   *Cordia boissieri*
anaqua   *Ehretia tehuacana*
anona   *Annona cherimola*
anthurium   *Anthurium* spp.
arrayán   Psidium sartorianum
ash   *Fraxinus uhdei*
Australian pine   *Casuarina equisetifolia*

baboso   Pachycereus hollianus
baccharus (Yerba Buena)
     Baccharis trinervis
banana   *Musa sapientum*
barretta   *Helietta parvifolia*
beak-rush   *Rhynchospora* spp.
begonia   *Begonia* spp.
begonia (Yerba Buena)   *Begonia
     nelumbifolia*
biznaga   Ferocactus flavovirens
biznaga ganchuda   Ferocactus recurvus
biznaga lechuda   Mammillaria carnea
blackbead, catclaw   *Pithecellobium
     unguis-cati*
blackgum   *Nyssa sylvatica*
bluestem   *Andropogon* spp.
bluestem (Río Balsas)   *Andropogon
     fastigiatus*
boojum   *Idria columnaris*
bougainvillea   *Bougainvillea glabra*
bracken   *Pteridium aquilinum*
brittlebush   *Encelia farinosa*
bromeliads   *Bromelia* spp.
buckeye, Mexican   *Ungnadia speciosa*
buckthorn   *Rhamnus serrata*
bulrush   *Scirpus* spp.
bunchgrass, high elevation   *Epicampes*
     and *Festuca*
bur bush   *Franseria chenopodifolia*
bur-sage, white   *Franseria dumosa*
cacao   *Theobroma cacao*
candelero   Senecio praecox
cactus, barrel   *Echinocactus* spp.
cactus, cholla   *Opuntia* spp.

cactus, comb *Pachycereus pecten-aboriginum*

cactus, galloping *Machaerocereus gummosus*

cactus, nopal *Opuntia* spp.

cactus, organpipe *Lemaireocereus* spp.

cactus, organpipe (Río Balsas) *Cephalocereus mezcalaensis*

cactus, prickly pear *Opuntia* spp.

cactus, saguaro *Cereus giganteus*

caesalpinia *Caesalpinia* spp.

calliandra *Calliandra* spp.

camarón (tree) *Alvaradoa amorphoides*

candelilla *Euphorbia antisyphillitica*

canelilla Croton pulcher

cantdulán Quercus brachystachys

capulincillo Pernettia ciliata

cardón *Pachycereus pringlei*

cattail *Typha latifolia*

cecropia *Cecropia* spp.

cedro Cedrela mexicana

ceiba (the usual big one) *Ceiba pentandra*

ceiba (Sinaloa) *Ceiba acuminata*

cenizo *Leucophyllum frutescens*

cereus, night-blooming *Hylocereus undatus*

cestrum *Cestrum guatemalensis gracile*

chamise *Adenostoma fasciculatum*

charcoal shrub *Baccharis conferta*

cherimoya *Annona cherimola*

cherry, black *Prunus serotina*

chestnut, Guiana *Pachira aquatica*

chicozapote *Achras zapote*

chili pepper *Capsicum annuum*

chinchweed *Pectis prostrata*

chiquinív Quercus acatanangensis

cholla, Christmas *Opuntia leptocaulis*

cholla, thistle *Opuntia tunicata*

cholla, tree *Opuntia imbricata*

chote Parmentiera spp.

Christmas-berry *Heteromeles arbutifolia*

cirio *Idria columnaris*

clover, prairie *Dalea brachystachys*

coconut palm *Cocos nucifera*

cocuite Gliricidia sepium

coffee *Coffea arabica*

copal (Sinaloa) *Bursera laxiflora*

coralbean *Erythrina chiapensis*

cordoncillo Piper spp.

corn *Zea mays*

cow okra *Parmentiera* spp.

coyotillo *Karwinskia humboldtiana*

Coryphantha Coryphantha pallida

creosote bush *Larrea tridentata*

crucillo Condalia lycioides

currant *Ribes brandegei*

cutgrass *Leersia* spp.

cyperus *Cyperus* spp.

cypress, Arizona *Cupressus arizonica*

cypress, Bentham's *Cupressus benthami*

cypress, Lindley's *Cupressus lindleyi*

cypress, Mexican *Cupressus lusitanica*

cyrtopodium *Cyrtopodium punctatum*

dahlia *Dahlia coccinea*

datilillo *Yucca valida*

dayflower *Commelina* spp.

devil's head *Echinocactus texensis*

dogwood *Cornus disciflora*

elder, Mexican *Sambucus mexicana*

elephant tree *Bursera microphylla*

encina negra Quercus devia

eryngium *Eryngium monocephalum*

espino (Hwy 70) *Acacia micrantha*

espino (Sonora Desert) *Acacia cymbispina*

eucalyptus *Eucalyptus globulus*

evening primrose *Oenothera* spp.

fan palm, California *Washingtonia filifera*

fan palm, Mexican *Sabal mexicana*

fern, tree *Cyatheaceae* family

fescue *Festuca rosei*

fig, strangler *Ficus* spp.

fir, sacred *Abies religiosa*

fishpoison tree *Piscidia* spp.

flax *Linum schiedeanum*

foxtail *Setaria geniculata*

fuchsia *Fuchsia microphylla quercetorum*

gallina Agave stricta

gallitos Pedilanthus aphyllus

garrambullo Myrtillocactus geometrizans

garrya, willow-leaved *Garya salicifolia*
gavia Acacia amentacea
geranium (Hwy 70, 1st species)
    Geranium kerberi
geranium (Hwy 70, 2nd species)
    Geranium seemanii
gourd tree *Crescentia alata*
grama, blue *Bouteloua gracilis*
granada Punica granatum
granadilla Passiflora edulis
grape, sea *Coccolobis uvifera*
grass, grama *Bouteloua trifida*
grass, lemon *Cymbopogon* spp.
grass, salt marsh *Spartina patens*
gromwell *Lithospermum calycosum*
ground pine *Lycopodium* spp.
guajilote Bombax palmeri
guanacaste *Enterlobium cyclocarpum*
guava *Psidium* spp.
Guiana chestnut *Pachira aquatica*
gumbo-limbo *Bursera simaruba*
guayacán Guaiacum spp.
hackberry, desert *Celtis pallida*
hackberry (Hwy 70, 2nd species) *Celtis caudata*
hairgrass *Deschampsia pringlei*
hawthorn (Hwy 70, 1st species)
    Crataegus parryana
hawthorn (Hwy 70, 2nd species)
    Crataegus rosei
hawthorn, Mexican *Crataegus mexicana*
heno (Xoconostle) *Tillandsia recurvata*
heno (Zapotitlán) *Tillandsia atroviridipetala*
hibiscus *Hibiscus bifurcatus pilosus*
hickory, Mexican *Carya mexicana*
hierba santa Piper auritum
hilo Eupatorium glabratum
hog plum *Spondias mombin*
hophornbeam *Ostrya guatemalensis*
hornbeam *Carpinus caroliniana*
horse crippler *Echinocactus texensis*
huajillo (an acacia) *Acacia berlandieri*
huajillo (not acacia) *Pithecolobium brevifolium*
huisache *Acacia farnesiana*
injerto Arceuthobium cryptopodum

ironwood *Olneya tesota*
izote Yucca filifera
Jerusalem thorn *Parkinsonia aculeata*
jobo Spondias mombin
jojoba *Simmondsia chinensis*
juniper, alligator *Juniperus deppeana*
juniper, drooping *Juniperus flaccida*
kapok *Ceiba pentandra*
lance pod *Lonchocarpus longistylus*
lantana *Lantana involucrata*
leadtree *Leucaena* spp.
leatherplant (Zapotitlán) *Jatropha cuneata*
leatherplant (Xoconostle) *Jatropha dioica*
lechuguilla *Agave lecheguilla*
lemon *Citrus lemon*
lomboy *Jatropha cinerea*
lotebush *Condalia lycioides*
lovegrass *Eragrostis* spp.
lupine (Los Azufres) *Lupinus pringlei*
lysiloma *Lysiloma* spp.
madrone (Baja) *Arbutus peninsularis*
madrone (chaparral) *Arbutus texana*
madrone (Hwy 70 & Huitepec) *Arbutus xalapensis*
magic mushroom *Psilocibe cubensis*
maguey *Agave atrovirens*
mahogany *Swietenia macrophylla*
mala mujer Cnidoscolus urens
mamey *Calocarpum sapota*
mammillaria *Mammillaria* spp.
mango *Mangifera indica*
mangrove, black *Avicennia titida*
mangrove, button *Conocarpus erectus*
mangrove, red *Rhizophora mangle*
mangrove, white *Laguncularia racemosa*
manteco Cercidium praecox
manzanita *Arctostaphylos* spp.
Mexican star *Milla biflora*
mezcal de tequila Agave tequilana
mesquite *Prosopis juliflora*
montanoa *Montanoa tehucana*
mistletoe *Phoradendron* spp.
Mormon tea *Ephedra* spp.
morning-glory *Ipomoea* spp.

morning-glory tree (oblong leaves)
  Ipomoea murucoides
morning-glory tree (heartshaped)
  Ipomoea arborescens
mouse killer   *Gliricidia sepium*
muhlygrass   *Muhlenbergia* spp.
muhly, mountain   *Muhlenbergia montana*
muhly (other high-elevation)
  Muhlenberia macroura
mushroom, magic   *Psilocibe cubensis*
naked Indian   *Bursera simaruba*
needlgrass   *Stipa ichu*
nama   *Nama dichotomum*
nolina   *Nolina* spp.
nopal   *Opuntia ficus-indica*
nopal cardón   Opuntia streptacantha
nopal crinato   Opuntia pilifera
oak, Emory   *Quercus emoryi*
oak, Mexican   *Quercus mexicana*
oak, thick-leaf   *Quercus crassifolia*
oak, wrinkle-leaf   *Quercus rugosa*
oats, sea   *Uniola paniculata*
ocotillo   *Fouquieria formosa*
ocote colorado   Pinus oocarpa
ocote blanco   Pinus tenuifolia
orange   *Citrus sinensis*
órgano (Río Balsas)   *Cephalocereus*
  mezcalaensis
órgano (Xoconostle)   *Pachycereus*
  marginatus
órgano (Zapotitlán)   *Cephalocereus*
  hoppenstedtii
oxalis   *Oxalis* spp.
pachycereus   *Pachycereus chrysomallus*
palm, coconut   *Cocos nucifera*
palm, cohune   *Orbignya cohune*
palm, corozo   *Scheelia* spp.
palm, Mexican fan   *Sabal mexicana*
palm, parlor   *Chamaedorea* spp.
palmetto, Texas   *Sabal texana*
palmita   *Nolina longifolia*
palo amarillo   Esenbeckia flava
palo blanco   *Lysiloma candida*
palo de arbol   Quercus tristis
palo dulce   *Eysenhardtia polystachya*
palo escopeta   Albizia occidentalis
paloverde, blue   *Cercidium floridum*

paloverde, foothill   *Cercidium*
  microphyllum
paloverde, Mexican   *Parkinsonia aculeata*
papaya   *Carica papaya*
paspalum   *Paspalum* spp.
passion flower   *Passiflora* spp.
passion fruit   *Passiflora edulis*
paurotis   *Paurotis wrightii*
pecan   *Carya pecan*
peppertree   *Schinus molle*
pichomel   Agave marmorata
pickle tree   *Byrsonima crassifolia*
pine, Australian   *Casuarina equisetifolia*
pine, Aztec   *Pinus teocote*
pine, Chiapas   *Pinus chiapensis*
pine, false white   *Pinus pseudostrobus*
pine, ground   *Lycopodium* spp.
pine, jelecote   *Pinus patula*
pine, Mexican white   *Pinus ayacahuite*
pine, Michoacán   *Pinus michoacana*
pine, Montezuma   *Pinus montezumae*
pine, ponderosa   *Pinus ponderosa*
pine, sugar   *Pinus lambertiana*
pine, timberline Montezuma   *Pinus*
  hartwegii
pine, yellow   *Pinus ponderosa arizonica*
pinkwing   *Alvaradoa amorphoides*
piñón   Pinus cembroides
plantain, wild (Agua Azul)   *Heliconia*
  latispatha
plantain, wild (marshes)   *Heliconia bihai*
plum, icaco coco   *Chrysobalanus icaco*
pomegranate   *Punica granatum*
ponytail, Mexican   *Beaucarnea gracilis*
portulaca   *Portulaca parvula*
pricklenut   *Guazuma ulmifolia*
primrose, beach evening   *Oenothera*
  drummondi
railroad vine   *Ipomoea pes-caprae*
ramon   *Brosimum alicastrum*
redbud, Eastern   *Cercis canadensis*
rhipsalis   *Rhipsalis* spp.
roble (Hwy 70, species 1)
  Quercus rugulosa
roble (Hwy 70, species 2)
  Quercus hartwegii

roble (Hwy 70, species 3)
  Quercus diversifolia
roble (Hwy 70, species 4)
  Quercus crassifolia
roble (Hwy 70, species 5)
  Quercus castanea
roble (Hwy 70, species 6)
  Quercus polymorpha
roble (Hwy 70, species 7)
  Quercus furfuracea
rouge plant   *Rivina humilis*
royal poinciana   *Delonix regia*
rush   *Juncus* spp.
saguaro   *Cereus giganteus*
salvia (Hwy 70)   *Salvia melissodora*
salvia, lantana-leaf   *Salvia lantanaefolia*
sangre de drago   *Jatropha dioica*
sea grape   *Coccolobis uvifera*
sedge   *Carex* spp.
sedum   *Sedum* spp.
senna, four-leaf   *Cassia oxyphylla*
shate   *Chamaedorea* spp.
sida, New Mexico   *Sida neomexicana*
smokethorn   *Dalea spinosa*
sotol   *Dasylirion* spp.
sotol (Zapotitlán)   *Dasylirion lucidum*
Spanish moss   *Tillandsia usneoides*
springbells   *Cybistax donnell-smithii*
sweetgum   *Liquidambar styraciflua*
sycamore, American   *Platanus occidentalis*
tepeguaje   *Lysiloma divaricata*
tequila   *Agave tequilana*
teteche   *Neobuxbaumia tetetzo*
three-awn grass   *Aristida* spp.
tomato   *Lycopersicon esculentum*
tree fern   Cyatheaceae family
trumpet tree   *Tabebuia palmeri*
tuna cardona   *Opuntia streptacantha*
tzaquioco   *Quercus candicans*
uña de gato   *Mimosa monancistra*
verbesina   *Verbesina perymenioides*
viburnum   *Viburnum hartwegii*
violet   *Viola* spp.
walnut (hairy-leafed)   *Juglans mollis*
willow, black   *Salix nigra*
yellow trumpet   *Tecoma stans*

yucca (NE Mexico mesquite zone)   *Yucca treculeana*
yucca (Zapotitlán)   *Yucca periculosa*
yucca, Potosí   *Yucca potosina*
yucca, soaptree   *Yucca elata*
zinnia, redstar   *Zinnia multiflora*

Animals
agouti   *Dasyprocta punctata*
albacore   *Thunnus albacares*
angelfish   *Holacanthus* or *Pomacanthus*
ani, groove-bill   *Crotophaga sulcirostris*
ant, army   *Eciton* spp.
ant, leafcutter   *Atta* spp.
anteater, collared   *Tamandua tetradactyla*
antelope, pronghorn   *Antilocapra americana*
antshrike, barred   *Thamnophilus doliatus*
ant-tanager, red-crowned   *Habia rubica*
ant-tanager, red-throated   *Habia gutturalis*
antwren, dot-winged   *Microrhopias quixensis*
araçari, collared   *Pteroglossus torquatus*
armadillo   *Dasypus novemcinctus*
badger   *Taxidea taxus*
bananaquit   *Coereba flaveloa*
barba amarilla   Bothrops atrox
barracuda, California   *Sphyraena argentea*
bat, Mexican freetail   *Tadarida mexicana*
bear, black   *Ursus americanus*
beaver   *Castor canadensis*
blackbird, melodious   *Dives dives*
bluebird, Eastern   *Sialia sialis*
bluefish   *Kyphosus cinerascens*
boa constrictor   *Constrictor constrictor*
bobcat   *Lynx rufus*
bobwhite, black-throated   *Colinus nigrogularis*
bobwhite, Northern   *Colinus virginianus*
bonito   *Sarda* spp.
brush-finch, rufous-capped   *Atlapetes pileatus*
bunting, orange-breasted   *Passerina leclancherii*
butterfly, heliconian   *Heliconius* spp.
butterfly, monarch   *Danaus plexippus*
butterfly, morpho   *Morpho* spp.

caiman, spectacled   *Caiman sclerops*
caracara, Guadalupe   *Polyborus lutosus*
caracara, crested   *Polyborus plancus*
cat, ringtail (North, Central)   *Bassariscus astutus*
cat, ringtail (Southeast, Yuc)   *Bassariscus sumichrasti*
chachalaca, plain   *Ortalis vetula*
chigger (arthropod)   order Acarina
chipmunk, Merriam   *Eutamias merriami*
coati   *Nasau nasau*
cochineal insect   *Coccus cacti*
constrictor, boa   *Constrictor constrictor*
coral, brain   *Diploria* spp.
coral, elkhorn   *Acropora* spp.
coral, staghorn   *Acropora* spp.
cormorant, neotropic   *Phalacrocorax olivaceous*
cottontail, desert   *Sylvilagus auduboni*
cottontail, Mexican   *Sylvilagus cunicularius*
cottontail, tropical-forest   *Sylvilagus brasiliensis*
cow   *Bos* spp.
cowbird, bronzed   *Molothrus aeneus*
coyote   *Canis latrans*
creeper, brown   *Certhis familiaris*
crocodile, American   *Crocodylus acutus*
damselfish   *Abudefduf* spp.
deer, mule   *Odocoileus hemionus*
deer, white-tailed   *Odocoileus virginianus*
dog   *Canis familiaris*
dorado   *Coryphaena hippurus*
dove, common ground   *Columbina passerina*
dove, mourning   *Zenaida macroura*
dove, ruddy ground   *Columbina talpacoti*
dove, scaled   *Columbina squammata*
dove, white-winged   *Zenaida asiatica*
egret, American   *Egretta alba*
egret, reddish   *Egretta rufescens*
egret, snowy   *Egretta thula*
elaenia, Caribbean   *Elaenia martinica*
elaenia, yellow-bellied   *Elaenia flavogaster*
emerald, white-bellied   *Amazilia candida*

euphonia, yellow-throated   *Euphonia hirundinacea*
fer-de-lance   *Bothrops atrox*
finch, rufous-capped brush   *Atlapetes pileatus*
flamingo, American   *Phoenicopterus ruber*
flicker   *Colaptes auratus*
flounder   *Paralichthys* spp.
flower-piercer, slaty   *Diglossa baritula*
flycatcher, ash-throated   *Myiarchus cinerascens*
flycatcher, fork-tailed   *Muscivora tyrannus*
flycatcher, gray silky   *Ptilogonys cinereus*
flycatcher, Northern tody   *Todirostrum cinereum*
flycatcher, tufted   *Mitrephanes phaeocercus*
flycatcher, vermilion   *Pyrocephalus rubinus*
fox, gray   *Urocyon cinereoargenteus*
fox, kit   *Vulpes macrotis*
frigatebird, magnificent   *Fregata magnificens*
gecko, banded   *Coleonyx variegatus*
gnatcatcher, white-lored   *Polioptila albiloris*
goldfinch, dark-backed   *Carduelis psaltria*
grassquit, blue-black   *Volatinia jacarina*
grassquit, yellow-faced   *Tiaris olivacea*
grebe, least   *Podiceps dominicus*
grebe, pied-billed   *Podilymbus podiceps*
ground-dove, common   *Columbina passerina*
ground-dove, ruddy   *Columbina talpacoti*
grouper   *Epinephelus* spp.
grunt   *Haemulon* spp.
gull, Heermann's   *Larus heermanni*
gull, herring   *Larus argentatus*
gull, laughing   *Larus atricilla*
hawk, red-tailed   *Buteo jamaicensis*
heron, green   *Butorides virescens*
heron, little blue   *Florida caerulea*
honeycreeper, red-legged   *Cyanerpes cyaneus*
hookworm   *Necator americanus*
hookworm   *Ancylostoma duodenale*
horse   *Equus* spp.

hummingbird, beautiful   *Calothorax pulcher*

hummingbird, black-fronted   *Hylocharis xantusii*

hummingbird, cinnamon   *Amazilia rutila*

hummingbird, garnet-throated   *Lamprolaima rhami*

hummingbird, rufous-tailed   *Amazilia tzacatl*

hummingbird, sparkling-tailed   *Tilmatura dupontii*

ibis, wood   *Mycteria americana*

iguana, desert   *Dipsosaurus dorsalis*

jacana, Northern   *Jacana spinosa*

jackrabbit, blacktail   *Lepus californicus*

jackrabbit, white-sided   *Lepus callotis*

jaguar   *Felis onca*

jaguarundi   *Felis yagouroundi*

jay, black-and-blue   *Cissilopha sanblasiana*

jay, black-throated   *Cyanolyca pumilo*

jay, gray-breasted   *Aphelocoma ultramarina*

jay, magpie   *Calocitta formosa*

jay, scrub   *Aphelocoma coerulescens*

jay, Steller's   *Cyanocitta stelleri*

kestrel, American   *Falco sparverius*

kingbird, Cassin's   *Tyrannus vociferans*

kingbird, gray   *Tyrannus dominicensis*

kingbird, tropical   *Tyrannus melancholicus*

kingfisher, green   *Chloroceryle americana*

kingfisher, ringed   *Ceryle torquata*

kinglet, ruby-crowned   *Regulus calendula*

kinkajou   *Potos flavus*

lion, mountain   *Felis concolor*

lizard, banded rock   *Petrosaurus mearnsi*

lizard, coast horned   *Phrynosoma coronatum*

lizard, desert horned   *Phrynosoma platyrhinos*

lizard, desert spiny   *Sceloporus magister*

lizard, leopard   *Gambelia wislizenii*

lizard, mesquite   *Sceloporus grammicus*

lizard, side-blotched   *Uta stansburiana*

lizard, small-scaled tree   *Urosaurus microscutatus*

lizard, zebra-tailed   *Callisaurus draconoides*

lobster, spiny   *Panulirus argus*

malaria organism   *Plasmodium* spp.

man   *Homo sapiens*

margay   *Felis wiedii*

meadowlark, Eastern   *Sturnella magna*

metalmark, blue   *Lasaia sula*

mockingbird   *Mimus polyglottos*

mockingbird, blue-and-white   *Melanotis hypoleucus*

monkey, howler   *Alouatta palliata*

monkey, spider   *Ateles geoffroyi*

morpho (butterfly)   *Morpho* spp.

mosquito, malaria   *Anopheles* spp.

motmot, blue-crowned   *Momotus momota*

motmot, blue-throated   *Aspatha gularis*

motmot, russet-crowned   *Momotus mexicanus*

motmot, tody   *Hylomanes momotula*

motmot, turquoise-browed   *Eumomota superciliosa*

mouse, cactus   *Peromyscus eremicus*

mullet   *Mugil cephalus*

nightingale-thrush, ruddy-capped   *Catharus frantzii*

nuthatch, white-breasted   *Sitta carolinensis*

ocelot   *Felis pardalis*

octopus   *Octopus vulgaris*

oppossum   *Didelphis virginia*

oriole, spot-breasted   *Icterus graduacauda*

otter, river   *Lutra canadensis*

paca   *Cuniculus paca*

parakeet, Aztec   *Aratinga nana*

parakeet, orange-fronted   *Aratinga canicularis*

parrot, white-fronted   *Amazona albifrons*

parrot, lilac-crowned   *Amazona finschi*

parrotfish   *Sparisoma* spp.

peccary, collared   *Pecari tajacu*

peccary, white-lipped   *Tayassu pecari*

pelican, brown   *Pelecanus occidentalis*

pelican, white   *Pelecanus erythrorhynchos*

peppershrike, rufous-browed   *Cyclarhis gujanensis*

pewee, Eastern wood   *Contopus virens*

phainopepla   *Phainopepla nitens*

phoebe, Say's   *Sayornis phoebe*

pigeon, white-headed   *Columba flavirostris*

pinworm   *Enterobius vermicularis*

plover, collared   *Charadrius collaris*

porcupine, prehensile-tailed   *Coendu mexicanus*

puma   *Felis concolor*

quail, banded   *Philortyx fasciatus*

quail, elegant   *Lophortyx douglasii*

quail, spotted wood   *Odontophorus guttatus*

quetzal, resplendent   *Pharomachrus mocinno*

rabbit, brush   *Sylvilagus bachmani*

rabbit, cottontail   *Sylvilagus floridanus*

rabbit, volcano   *Romerolagus diazi*

raccoon   *Procyon lotor*

rattlesnake, red diamond   *Crotalus ruber*

rattlesnake, speckled   *Crotalus mitchelli*

rattlesnake, Western   *Crotalus viridis*

redstart, American   *Setophaga ruticilla*

redstart, slate-throated   *Myioborus miniatus*

roadrunner, greater   *Geococcyx californianus*

robin, American   *Turdus migratorius*

roundworm   *Ascaris lumbricoides*

sabrewing, wedge-tailed   *Campylopterus curvipennis*

salamander, arboreal   *Aneides lugubris*

salamander, garden slender   *Batrachoseps major*

salamander, Mexican flat-toed   *Bolitoglossa platydactyla*

saltator, black-headed   *Saltator atriceps*

sardine, Pacific   *Sardinops caerulea*

sandpiper, spotted   *Tringa macularia*

seafan   order Gorgonaria

sea lion, California   *Zalophus californianus*

sea lion, Steller's   *Eumetopias jubata*

seal, elephant   *Mirounga angustirostris*

seal, Guadalupe fur   *Arctocephalus townsendi*

seal, harbor   *Phoca richardii*

seedeater, ruddy-breasted   *Sporophila minuta*

seedeater, white-collared   *Sporophila torqueola*

sheartail, Mexican   *Doricha eliza*

sheartail, slender   *Doricha enicura*

sheep, bighorn   *Ovis canadensis*

shrimp   order Decapoda

shrike, loggerhead   *Lanius ludovicianus*

sidewinder   *Crotalus cerastes*

silky-flycatcher, gray   *Ptilogonys cinereus*

siskin, black-headed   *Carduelis notatus*

skink, Western   *Eumeces skiltonianus*

skunk, hog-nosed (all but Gulf)   *Conepatus mesoleucus*

skunk, hog-nosed (Northern Gulf)   *Conepatus leuconotus*

skunk, hog-nosed (Southern Gulf & Yucatán)   *Conepatus semistriatus*

skunk, spotted (Baja & Northwest)   *Spilogale gracilis*

skunk, spotted (Northern Gulf)   *Spilogale indianola*

skunk, spotted (Central, South & West)   *Spilogale augustifrons*

skunk, striped   *Mephitis macroura*

snake, coachwip   *Masticophis flagellum*

snake, pine-gopher   *Pituophis melanoleucus*

snake, Western hognose   *Heterodon nasicus*

snake, Western patch-nosed   *Salvadora hexalepis*

snapper   *Lutianus* spp.

solitaire, brown-backed   *Myadestes obscurus*

sparrow, black-throated   *Amphispiza bilineata*

sparrow, Botteri's   *Aimophila botterii*

sparrow, bridled   *Aimophila mystacalis*

sparrow, chipping   *Spizella passerina*

sparrow, clay-colored   *Spizella pallida*

sparrow, striped   *Oriturus superciliosus*

spoonbill, roseate   *Ajaia ajaja*

squirrel, Abert   *Sciurus aberti*

squirrel, Deppe   *Sciurus deppei*

squirrel, fox (Los Azufres)   *Sciurus oculatus*

squirrel, gray (central Chiapas) *Sciurus griseoflavus*

squirrel, gray (Los Azufres) *Sciurus poliopus*

squirrel, gray (Gulf, Northern Chiapas) *Sciurus aureogaster*

squirrel, gray (Pacific Chiapas) *Sciurus socialis*

squirrel, gray (Yucatán) *Sciurus yucatanensis*

squirrel, roundtail ground *Citellus tereticaudus*

squirrel, whitetail antelope *Ammospermophilus leucurus*

swallow, mangrove *Tachycineta albilinea*

swordfish *Xiphias gladius*

tanager, blue-gray *Thraupis episcopus*

tanager, crimson-collared *Ramphocelus sanguinolenta*

tanager, red-crowned ant *Habia rubica*

tanager, red-throated ant *Habia gutturalis*

tanager, rosy thrush *Rhodinocichla rosea*

tanager, scarlet-rumped *Ramphocelus passerinii*

tanager, strip-headed *Spindalis zena*

tanager, yellow-winged *Thraupis abbas*

tepescuintle *Cuniculus paca*

termite order Isoptera

tern, black *Chlidonias niger*

tern, elegant *Thalasseus elegans*

tern, least *Sterna albifrons*

tern, royal *Sterna maximus*

thrasher, Cozumel *Toxostoma guttatum*

thrasher, curve-billed *Toxostoma curvirostre*

thrush, ruddy-capped nightingale- *Catharus frantzii*

tick (arthropod) order Acarina

tinamou, great *Tinamus major*

tinamou, little *Crypturellus soui*

titmouse, bridled *Parus wollweberi*

tityra, masked *Tityra semifasciata*

toad, red-spotted *Bufo punctatus*

toad, Southwestern *Bufo microscaphus*

toad, Western *Bufo boreas nelsoni*

toucan, keel-billed *Ramphastos sulfuratus*

toucanet, emerald *Aulacorhynchus prasinus*

towhee, brown *Pipilo fuscus*

towhee, collared *Pipilo ocai*

towhee, rufous-sided *Pipilo erythrophthalmus*

treefrog, California *Hyla cadaverina*

treefrog, Pacific *Hyla regilla*

trogon, citreoline *Trogon citreolus*

trogon, mountain *Trogon mexicanus*

trogon, violaceous *Trogon violaceus*

tuna, white *Thunnus alalunga*

turtle, Caguama *Caretta caretta*

turtle, carey *Eretmochelys imbricata*

turtle, green *Chelonia mydas*

turtle, hawksbill *Eretmochelys imbricata*

turtle, laud *Dermochelys coriacea*

turtle, leatherback *Dermochelys coriacea*

turtle, loggerhead *Caretta caretta*

turtle, parrot *Lepidochelys kempii*

turtle, Ridley *Lepidochelys kempii*

turtle, white *Chelonia mydas*

vaquita *Phocoena sinus*

verdin *Auriparus flaviceps*

violet-ear, green *Colibri thalassinus*

vireo, Cozumel *Vireo bairdi*

vireo, Hutton's *Vireo huttoni*

vireo, red-eyed *Vireo olivaceus*

vulture, black *Coragyps atratus*

vulture, lesser yellow-headed *Cathartes burrovianus*

vulture, turkey *Cathartes aura*

warbler, black-and-white *Mniotila varia*

warbler, black-throated green *Dendroica virens*

warbler, crescent-chested *Vermivora superciliosa*

warbler, hooded *Wilsonia citrina*

warbler, olive *Peucedramus taeniatus*

warbler, red *Ergaticus ruber*

warbler, rufous-capped *Basileuterus rufifrons*

warbler, Townsend's *Dendroica townsendi*

warbler, Wilson's *Wilsonia pusilla*

warbler, yellow *Dendroica petechia*

warbler, yellow-throated   *Dendroica dominica*

weasel   *Mustela frenata*

whale, blue   *Sibbaldus musculus*

whale, gray   *Eschrichtius glaucus*

whale, humpback   *Megaptera novaeangliae*

whale, sperm   *Physeter catadon*

whippoorwill   *Caprimulgus vociferus*

whiptail, Western   *Cnemidophorus tigris*

wolf   *Canis lupus*

woodcreeper, barred   *Dendrocolaptes certhia*

woodcreeper, ivory-billed   *Xiphorhynchus flavigaster*

woodcreeper, tawny-winged   *Dendrocincla anabatina*

woodpecker, acorn   *Melanerpes formicivorus*

woodpecker, bronze-winged   *Piculus aeruginosus*

woodpecker, golden-fronted   *Melanerpes aurifrons*

woodpecker, gray-breasted   *Centurus hypopolius*

woodpecker, ladder-backed   *Dendrocopos scalaris*

woodpecker, lineated   *Dryocopus lineatus*

woodpecker, pale-billed   *Campephilus guatemalensis*

wren, Bewick's   *Thryomanes bewickii*

wren, cactus   *Campylorhynchus brunneicapillus*

wren, canyon   *Salpinctes mexicanus*

wren, Carolina   *Thryothorus ludovicianus*

wren, gray-barred   *Campylorhynchus megalopterus*

wren, happy   *Thryothorus felix*

wren, house   *Troglodytes aedon*

wren, plain   *Thryothorus modestus*

wren, rock   *Salpinctes obsoletus*

wren, spot-breasted   *Thryothorus maculipectus*

wren, spotted   *Campylorhynchus gularis*

wren, white-bellied   *Uropsila leucogastra*

wren, white-breasted wood-   *Henicorhina leucosticta*

wren, white-browed   *Thryothorus ludovicianus*

wren, Yucatan   *Campylorhynchus yucatanicus*

yellowthroat   *Geothlypis poliocephala*

KEY TO THORN-FOREST BEAN-FAMILY TREES AND SHRUBS

A Leaves twice-compound, or usually absent .... see B

  B Spines or thorns present.. see C

    C Stamens more than 10 per flower .... see D

      D Stamen filaments not connected to one another .... acacias

      DD Stamens with filaments united.. blackbeads

    CC Stamens 10 or fewer... see E

      E Flowers tiny, in cylindrical spikes; tree trunk and major branches not green or bluish, 2 short spines at base of each leaf petiole, leaves usually present .... mesquites

      EE Flowers not tiny or grouped in cylindrical spikes; leaves and spines various, trunks sometimes green .... see F

        F Leaves usually present; trunk and branches not conspicuously green or blue .... caesalpinias

        FF Leaves present only after rains; trunk and branches conspicuously green or blue .... see G

          G Leaves, when present, like "eel's skeleton with flat, green ribs"; fruit with conspicuous contractions between seeds; thorns often forked .... Jerusalem thorn

          GG Leaves not as above; fruit only slightly constricted between seeds; spines slender, at base of leaf petiole, never forked .... palo verdes

  BB Spines and thorns absent .... see H

    H Becoming very large tree; flowers small, in spherical heads; fruits curved into thickly curved "ear-shaped" disks ± 3–4 inches across .... guanacaste

    HH Not as above .... see I

      I Stamens more than 10 per flower.. see J

        J Long, pink-tipped stamens extending far beyond flower, giving flower-cluster a powder-puff appearance; flower-cluster often only half-spherical .... calliandras

        JJ Stamens shorter, inflorescence more perfectly spherical .... lysilomas

      II Stamens 10 or fewer per flower .... see K

        K Individual flowers tiny, in spherical heads .... leadtrees

        KK Individual flowers showy, not in spherical heads .... caesalpinias

AA Leaves once divided or simple .... see L

  L Leaves undivided (simple) .... smoketree

  LL Leaves once-divided .... see M

    M No spines or thorns; flowers usually yellow; slender bush or small tree up to ± 6 feet; flowers only weakly pea-blossom shaped .... sennas

    MM Not as above .... see N

      N Flower cluster branched twice or more (paniculate); fruit pod conspicuously 4-winged .... fishpoison tree

      NN Flower stalks attaching directly to flower cluster's central stem (racemose); pods without wings .... ironwood

BIBLIOGRAPHY

NATURAL HISTORY

In English

Simple-to-use, comprehensive, and easily accessible field guides are available in English enabling the identification of Mexico's birds, and that makes bird watching in Mexico a pure delight. Unfortunately, no such field guides exist for the rest of Mexico's living things. Sometimes slim volumes with promising titles like *The Trees of Mexico* are spotted, but when these are used in the field it quickly becomes apparent that the vast majority of species are simply ignored. Even if a species is featured in the slim guide, one can never be certain that similar species with different names and virtues do not exist. What to do? What little literature is available must be sought out and used efficiently.

People not knowing a stigma from a stipule probably will find some of the works mentioned below too technical. On the other hand, few vacation activities are more pleasant than carrying a ponderous flora and a botany text, and learning both local flora and basic botany while exploring the Mexican landscape. Technical botanical works usually employ "keys" that "key out" the organisms being talked about. To see what a key looks like, check out the one identifying thorn-forest tree and shrub members of the bean family in appendix B.

Many of northern Mexico's ecosystems extend into the United States, so the many excellent field guides for North America are useful in northern Mexico. On the Mamulique Pass hike in Chapter 4, The Gulf Coast, for instance, *Trees of North America* can be used to identify look-alike, thorny, feathery-leafed members of the bean family such as mesquite, huajillo, catclaw blackbead, catclaw acacia, twisted acacia, and blue paloverde, because all of these also exist in Texas. Several oaks and pines follow the Rockies from the United States deep into upland Mexico.

In fact, any of the very many books describing the plants and animals of the Sonoran Desert of southern Arizona and southeastern California are very useful in most of Baja California and the Mexican state of Sonora. Similarly, descriptions of the Chihuahuan desert ecosystem of western Texas and south-central New Mexico are useful in the desert parts of the Mexican states of Chihuahua and Coahuila.

Anyone able to handle very technical biological papers can get a lot of mileage out of university science libraries. One way to find such publications is to slog through those awful *Biological Abstracts*. Another is to simply go into the library stacks where the above journals are stored, and look in each year's cumulative index. In university libraries there are also mountains of technical literature dealing with Mexican anthropological, ethnological, and archaeological topics.

Anderson, W. R., ed. *Flora Novo-Galiciana, Volume 17, Gymosperms and Pteridophytes.* Ann Arbor: University of Michigan Herbarium, 1992. Covers ferns and pines of western Mexico.

Bailey, L. H. *Manual of Cultivated Plants.* New York: Macmillan Publishing Co., 1951. Anyone with a particular affinity for cultivated plants should know about this masterpiece. Using it, cultivated species such as guava, night-blooming cereus, royal poinciana, bougainvillea, and hundreds of other Mexican favorites can be "keyed out," using rather technical characters. Unfortunately, it provides few drawings.

Behler, J. L., and King, F. W. *The Audubon Society Field Guide to North American Reptiles and Amphibians.* New York: Alfred A. Knopf, 1979.

Benson, Lyman. *The Cacti of Arizona.* Tucson: University of Arizona Press, 1969.

Breedlove, D. *Introduction to The Flora of Chiapas.* Cambridge: Cambridge University Press, 1981.

Brockman, C. F. *Trees of North America.* New York: Western Publishing Co., 1979. A mall-bookstore staple.

Conrad, Jim. *On the Road to Tetlama.* New York: Walker Publishing Co., 1991. Based on the author's experiences in Colonia el Sacrificio on the Tetlama hike in Chapter 4, The Gulf Coast, among the Nahuatl speakers in the mountains.

———. *Yerba Buena: Word-Snapshots from a Missionary Clinic in Southern Mexico's Indian Territory.* Poland Spring, Maine: Southern Missionary Society, 1994. (Available from publisher at RFD 1, Box 4035, Poland Spring, ME 04274, for $9.95 plus $2.00 handling.)

Correll, Donovan Stewart, and Johnston, M.C. *Manual of the Vascular Plants of Texas.* Renner, Texas: Texas Research Foundation, 1970. Travelers not ranging far from the U.S. border will find this book handy.

Coyle, Jeanette, and Roberts, Norman C. *A Field Guide to the Common and Interesting Plants of Baja California.* New York: Natural History Publishing Co., 1976.

Edwards, Ernest P. *Regional and Habitat Guide for Finding Birds in Mexico.* Sweetbriar, Va.: Ernest P. Edwards, 1968. A general guide. (Available from the author at Box AQ, Sweet Briar, VA 24595; in 1993 priced at $5.50 plus $2.00 handling charge.)

Golden Nature Guide. *Exotic Plants.* New York: Western Publishing Co., 1971. For botanical semi-illiterates, this book illustrates maybe twenty species native to Mexico.

Graham, Alan, ed. *Vegetation and Vegetational History of Northern Latin America.* Amsterdam, London, and New York: Elsevier Scientific Publishing Co., 1973.

Jackson, D. D., and Wood, Peter. *The Sierra Madre.* New York: Time-Life Books, 1975.

Johnson, W. W. *Baja California.* New York: Time-Life Books, 1972. This is a picture-filled coffee-table book.

Krutch, Joseph Wood. *The Forgotten Peninsula: A Naturalist in Baja California.* New York: William Sloane Associates, 1961.

Larson, Peggy. *The Deserts of the Southwest.* San Francisco: Sierra Club Books, 1977.

———. *A Sierra Club Naturalist's Guide.* San Francisco: Sierra Club Books, 1977. In Mexico's northern deserts, this book can be a wonderful companion. Most of the Sonoran and Chihuahuan deserts, which she thoroughly describes, exist more in Mexico than the United States.

Leopold, A. Starker. *Wildlife of Mexico: The Game Birds and Mammals*. Berkeley: University of California Press, 1959. This book provides line drawings, detailed descriptions, and excellent Mexico-based distribution maps for nearly all Mexican animals that are hunted—from great tinamous (birds) to collared anteaters and bighorn sheep. If this wonderful book cannot be found in the United States (it is a bit rare), look in good Mexican bookstores for the Spanish translation, *Fauna Silvestre de Mexico*.

Mabry, T. J., et al, ed. *Creosote Bush: Biology and Chemistry of Larrea in New World Deserts* (U.S./IBP Synthesis Series; 6). Stroudsburg, Penn.: Dowden, Hutchinson & Ross, Inc., 1977.

Mackintosh, Graham. *Into a Desert Place*. Idyllwild, Calif.: Graham Mackintosh, 1987. This riveting book describes Mackintosh's hike along Baja's entire coastline, from Ensenada to San Felipe, from April 1983 to March 1985. He recounts surviving off the sea and desert, including his use of three different kinds of water distilleries. (Available for $24.95 from the author at P.O. Box 1196, Idyllwild, CA 92549.)

Pesman, M. Walter. *Meet Flora Mexicana*. Globe, Ariz.: Dale Stuart King, 1962. In many good local libraries throughout the United States and Canada (but seldom in bookstores), there is a fair chance of finding this book, which profiles more than 200 of Mexico's most common and conspicuous plants. The line drawings are helpful, and plentiful background notes describe each species. "The Mayans used to make a fermented drink from the bark, used in religious ceremonies (*balche*)," Pesman relates about the southern Mexican tree called lance pod, which grows near the entrance to the monkey reserve at Punta Laguna. It is too bad this book profiles only 200 or so species.

Peterson, Roger Tory, and Chalif, Edward L. *A Field Guide to Mexican Birds*. Boston: Houghton Mifflin Company, 1973.

Pough, F. H. *A Field Guide to Rocks and Minerals*. Peterson Field Guide Series. Boston: Houghton Mifflin Co., 1960. Usually can be found at mall bookstores.

Ramamoorthy, T. P., et al, ed. *The Biological Diversity of Mexico: Origins and Distribution*. New York: Oxford University Press, 1993.

Rhodes, F. H. T., et al. *Fossils*. New York: Western Publishing Co., 1962.

Shreve, Forrest, and Wiggins, Ira L. *Vegetation and Flora of the Sonoran Desert*. 2 vols. Stanford, Calif.: Stanford University Press, 1946.

Simpson, B. B. *Mesquite: Its Biology in Two Desert Ecosystems*. Stroudsburg, Penn.: Dowden, Hutchinson and Ross, 1977.

Standley, P. C. *Flora of Yucatan*. Botanical Series, Vol. III. Chicago: Field Museum of Natural History, 1930.

———. *Trees and Shrubs of Mexico*. Washington, D.C.: Smithsonian Institution Press, 1967 and 1969. Two-volume reprint of 1,721-page technical work appearing from 1920 to 1926 (see journal section below). Travelers able to handle technical botany should look for this book. Though woefully outdated, both works have long been standard references for field workers in Mexico. Standley had a broad definition for "trees and shrubs"; in this book he includes such groups as yuccas, cacti, and agaves.

University of East Anglia Mexico. *Expedition 1987 Final Report*. England: University of East Anglia, 1987.

Vines, Robert A. *Trees, Shrubs and Woody Vines of the Southwest*. Austin: University of Texas Press, 1960. Travelers not ranging far from the U.S. border will find this book handy.

Weniger, Del. *Cacti of Texas and Neighboring States*. Austin: University of Texas Press, 1984.

Wiggins, I. L. *Flora of Baja California*. Stanford, Calif.: Stanford University Press, 1980. This 1,025-page book includes 970 drawings.

Williams, L. O. *The Orchidaceae of Mexico*. Honduras: Agrícola Panamericana, 1965.

Yañez-Arancibia, A., and Day, J. W., Jr. *Ecology of Coastal Ecosystems on the Southern Gulf of Mexico: The Region of Laguna de Términos*. Ed. by Universidad Nacional Autónoma de México, Organization of American States, and Louisiana State University, 1988.

In Spanish

Anyone lucky enough to both read Spanish *and* possess botanical savvy should scour larger bookstores in Mexico's main cities for Oscar Sánchez Sánchez's *La Flora del Valle de Mexico*. Non-Spanish–speaking travelers with a little biological savvy should not automatically eschew all Spanish publications. Most technical Spanish is based on the same Latin and Greek roots as technical English. Thus *"Estigma bífido, los filamentos unidos en tubo"* almost translates itself to "Stigmas bifed, filaments united into a tube." Of course this similarity is useless to anyone not knowing what bifed stigmas and tube-like filaments are.

Cabrera, Ángel L., and Willink, Abraham. *Biogeografía de America Latina*. Washington, D.C.: The General Secretariat of the Organization of American States, 1973.

García, Jorge Meyrán. *Guía Botánica de Cactáceas y Otras Suculentas del Valle de Tehuacán*. Mexico, D.F.: Sociedad Mexicana de Cactología A.C. (Spanish and English sections), 1973.

Martinez, M. *Plantas útiles de la Flora Mexicana*. 3d ed. Mexico City: Ediciones Botas, 1959.

Pennington, T. D., and Sarukhan, J. *Arboles Tropicales de México*. México D.F. and Rome: Instituto Nacional de Investigaciones Forestales and Organización de las Naciones Unidas para la Agricultura y la Alimentación, 1968. Excellent but technical, this is the most complete guide in existence to tropical Mexican trees.

Rzedowsky, J. *Vegetación de México*. México: Editorial Limusa, 1978.

Sánchez, Oscar Sánchez. *La Flora del Valle de México*. México D.F.: Editorial Herrero, S.A., 1979. This is a fairly complete field guide to the flowering plants and pines of the Valley of Mexico—a rather small area around Mexico City. With hundreds of line drawings, it is useful in high, dry areas of the Mexican Plateau far beyond the Mexican Valley, but not in the lowlands.

Sociedad Botánica de México. *Guía de la Excursión, Primer Congreso Mexicano de Botánica, 24 a 26 de Octubre de 1960*. México D.F.: Sociedad Botánica de México, 1960.

Tamayo, Jorge L. *Geografía General de México*. 2 vol. Mexico, D.F.: Talleres Gráficos de la Nación, 1949.

SCIENTIFIC ARTICLES

Annals of the Missouri Botanical Garden. Journal in which studies of Mexican plants often are published.

Beard, J. S. "Climax vegetation in tropical America." *Ecology* 25 (1944):127-158.

Copeia. This journal sometimes includes works on Mexican animals.

Dobzhansky, T. "Evolution in the tropics." *American Scientist* 38 (1950):209-221.

Dressler, Robert L. "Tropical Orchids near the Texas Border." *American Orchid Society Bulletin,* December 1961.

Duellman, W. E. "A Biogeographic Account of the Herpetofauna of Michoacán, Mexico." *Univ. Kansas, Publ., Mus. Nat. Hist.* 15 (1965):627-709.

————. "The Central American Herpetofauna: An Ecological Perspective." *Copeia* 4 (1966):700-719.

Goldman, E. A., and Moore, R. T. "The Biotic Provinces of Mexico." *Journal of Mammalogy* 26 (1946):347-360.

Hall, E. R., and Dalquest, W. W. "The Mammals of Veracruz." *Univ. Kansas Publ., Mus. Nat. Hist.* 14 (1963):165-362.

Leopold, A. Starker. "Vegetation Zones of Mexico." *Ecology* 31 (1950).

Parrish, Judith Totman. "Global palaeogeography and palaeoclimate of the Late Cretaceous and Early Tertiary." *The Origins of Angiosperms and their Biological Consequences,* edited by E. M. Friis et al. Cambridge: Cambridge University Press, 1987.

Pindell, J., and Dewey, J. F. "Permo-Triassic reconstruction of western Pangaea and the evolution of the Gulf of Mexico/Caribbean region." *Tectonics,* 1 (1982):1179-1211.

Rhodora. Journal in which studies of Mexican plants often are published.

Rzedowsky, J., and de Rzedowski, Graciela C. "Notas sobre la flora y la vegetación del Estado de San Luis Potosí." *Acta Científica Potosina* 1 (1957):7-68.

Smith, C. E., Jr. "Flora of the Tehuacán Valley." *Fieldiana Botany* 4 (1965):107-143.

Standley, P. C. "Trees and Shrubs of Mexico." *Contr. U.S. Natl. Herb.* 23:1920-26.

————. "Flora of Yucatán." *Publ. Field Columbian Mus., Bot. Ser.,* 3 (1930).

Williams, L. L. "Arboles y arbustos del Istmo de Tehuantepec, Mexico." *Lilloa,* 4 (1939):137-171.

ARCHAEOLOGY AND ANTHROPOLOGY

Alcorn, Janis. *Huastec Mayan Ethnobotany.* Austin: University of Texas Press, 1984.

Berlin, B., et al. *Principles of Tzeltal Plant Classification: An Introduction to the Botanical Ethnography of a Mayan-Speaking Community of Highland Chiapas.* New York: Academic Press, 1974.

Davis, Mary, and Pack, Greta. *Mexican Jewelry.* Austin: University of Texas Press, 1963.

Hunn, Eugene S. *Tzeltal Folk Zoology: The Classification of Discontinuities in Nature.* New York: Academic Press, 1977.

Hunter, C. Bruce. *A Guide to Ancient Maya Ruins.* Rev. ed. Norman, Okla.: University of Oklahoma Press, 1986.

Laughlin, R. M. *The Great Tzotzil Dictionary of San Lorenzo Zinacantan.* Washington, D.C.: Smithsonian Contributions to Anthropology #19, 1975.

Nash, M., ed. *Handbook of Middle American Indians.* Vol. 6. Austin: University of Texas Press, 1960. This volume covers social anthropology.

Paredes, Américo. *Folklore and Culture on the Texas-Mexican Border*. Austin: University of Texas Press, 1993.

Pennington, Campbell W. *The Tarahumar of Mexico: Their Environment and Material Culture*. Salt Lake City: University of Utah Press, 1963.

Sayer, Chloë. *Costumes of Mexico*. Austin: University of Texas Press, 1985.

————. *The Skeleton at the Feast: The Day of the Dead in Mexico*. Austin: University of Texas Press, 1991.

Schele, Linda. *Maya Glyphs: The Verbs*. Austin: University of Texas Press, 1982.

Suarez, Jorge A. *The Mesoamerican Indian Languages*. Cambridge: Cambridge University Press, 1983.

Vogt, E. Z. *Handbook of Middle American Indians*. Vol. 7. Austin: University of Texas Press, 1960. This volume is on ethnology.

————. *Zinacantan: A Maya Community in the Highlands of Chiapas*. Cambridge, Mass.: Belknap Press, 1969.

Wasserstrom, R. *Class and Society in Central Chiapas*. Berkeley: University of California Press, 1983.

GENERAL TRAVEL GUIDES

Box, Ben, ed. *Mexico & Central American Handbook*. Bath, England: Trade & Travel Publications, updated yearly.

Burleson, Bob, and Riskind, David. *Backcountry Mexico: A Traveler's Guide and Phrase Book*. Austin: University of Texas Press, 1986.

Conrad, Jim. *The Maya Road*. Bucks, England: Bradt Publications, 1992.

Harvard Student Agency, Inc. *Let's Go Mexico*. New York: St. Martin's Press, updated yearly.

Secor, R. J. *Mexico's Volcanoes: A Climbing Guide*. Seattle: The Mountaineers, 1981.

Weisbroth, Ericka, and Ellman, Eric. *Bicycling Mexico*. Edison, N.J.: Hunter Publishing, 1990.

West, Robert. *Sonora: Its Geographical Personality*. Austin: University of Texas Press, 1993.

INDEX

ABOUT THE AUTHOR

Jim Conrad grew up in Kentucky and received a B. Sc. in biology and an M. Sc. in botany from Kentucky universities. A quarter of a century ago he made his first trip to Mexico and immediately fell in love with the country's people, plants, and animals. Since then he has returned nearly every year, each time finding something new there, and something new within himself reacting to Mexico.

Jim has written over 200 magazine articles, and, including this one, five books on Mexico. For most of his career he has worked as a freelance writer and botanical expeditioneer, visiting about 40 countries in the process. At the moment he lives and works in Belize, developing ecotourism programs.

THE MOUNTAINEERS, founded in 1906, is a nonprofit outdoor activity and conservation club, whose mission is "to explore, study, preserve, and enjoy the natural beauty of the outdoors. . . ." Based in Seattle, Washington, the club is now the third-largest such organization in the United States, with 14,000 members and four branches throughout Washington State.

The Mountaineers sponsors both classes and year-round outdoor activities in the Pacific Northwest, which include hiking, mountain climbing, ski-touring, snowshoeing, bicycling, camping, kayaking and canoeing, nature study, sailing, and adventure travel. The club's conservation division supports environmental causes through educational activities, sponsoring legislation, and presenting informational programs. All club activities are led by skilled, experienced volunteers, who are dedicated to promoting safe and responsible enjoyment and preservation of the outdoors.

The Mountaineers Books, an active, nonprofit publishing program of the club, produces guidebooks, instructional texts, historical works, natural history guides, and works on environmental conservation. All books produced by The Mountaineers are aimed at fulfilling the club's mission.

If you would like to participate in these organized outdoor activities or the club's programs, consider a membership in The Mountaineers. For information and an application, write or call The Mountaineers, Club Headquarters, 300 Third Avenue West, Seattle, Washington 98119; (206) 284-6310. Send or call for our catalog of more than 300 outdoor titles:

The Mountaineers Books
1011 SW Klickitat Way, Suite 107
Seattle, WA 98134
1-800-553-4453